THE SACRAMENTS

OTHER BOOKS BY G. C. BERKOUWER

Studies in Dogmatics

The Sacraments

BY

G. C. BERKOUWER

PROFESSOR OF SYSTEMATIC THEOLOGY
FREE UNIVERSITY OF AMSTERDAM

WILLIAM B. EERDMANS PUBLISHING COMPANY
GRAND RAPIDS, MICHIGAN

Translated by Hugo Bekker
from
the Dutch edition, *De Sacramenten,*
published by J. H. Kok N.V., Kampen, The Netherlands

PHOTOLITHOPRINTED BY GRAND RAPIDS BOOK MANUFACTURERS, INC.
GRAND RAPIDS, MICHIGAN
1969

CONTENTS

31923

ABBREVIATIONS

Conf.	— Nederlandse Geloofsbelijdenis (Belgic Confession)
Denz.	— *Enchiridion Symbolorum, Definitionum et Declarationum de Rebus Fidei et Morum,* H. Denzinger, C. Bannwart *et. al.*
DTC	— *Dictionnaire de Théologie Catholique*
EvT	— *Evangelische Theologie* (Munich)
Geref. Dog.	— Bavinck, *Gereformeerde Dogmatiek*
GTT	— *Gereformeerd theologisch tijdschrift* (Heusden; Kampen)
H.C.	— Heidelberg Catechism
Inst.	— Calvin, *Institutes of the Christian Religion*
K.D.	— Karl Barth, *Kirchliche Dogmatik*
NedTT	— *Nederlands theologisch tijdschrift* (Wageningen)
S.T.	— Thomas Aquinas, *Summa Theologica*
TLZ	— *Theologische Literaturzeitung* (Leipzig)
TS	— *Theologische studiën* (Utrecht)
TWNT	— G. Kittel (ed.), *Theologisches Wörterbuch zum Neuen Testament* (eight vols., I-V in English trans.)
VT	— *Vox theologica;* Interacademicaal theologisch tijdschrift (Assen)

INTRODUCTION

THERE IS a question of method that should precede our reflection on the doctrine of the sacraments. This question pertains to the division of this study, which first treats "the sacraments" and then baptism and the Lord's Supper. Many have objected to this order as being scholastic, since it allegedly begins by defining a general essence of the sacraments and then fills this essence with concrete content through the doctrines of baptism and the Lord's Supper. Futhermore, it is said, Scripture itself, on which dogmatics must be based, provides no warrant for such a general concept of the sacraments in abstraction from the particular sacraments.

These objections, we think, are based on a misunderstanding. To be sure, it is possible to construct a general concept of the sacraments with the aid of Scripture into which the sacraments proper are then made to fit. But this approach is not at all necessary and will not be followed here. As a matter of fact, we shall later have occasion to criticize such a methodology on the ground that it does not lead to the concrete sacraments. We do not seek to analyze the essence of "the sacraments" prior to a consideration of the individual sacraments, for the nature of the sacraments turns precisely upon the concrete givenness of baptism and the Lord's Supper in the historical revelation in Jesus Christ. And the sacraments can be understood only in the light of that historical revelation.

Accordingly, we have chosen to begin with "the sacraments," not for speculative reasons, but only for the sake of clarity. We are not interested in some sort of natural theology or sacramentology that would precede the doctrines of baptism and the Lord's Supper. Neither do we separate the general doctrine of the sacraments from the specific doctrines as if these were mutually independent. Rather, in the study of "the sacraments" we shall discuss a number of questions that were raised long ago in the history of the Church, namely, questions regarding the number of sacraments, the relation between Word and sacrament, and the working of the sacraments. In the discussion of such questions

9

we cannot for a moment ignore the concrete sacraments. One can cite a parallel in the Heidelberg Catechism, where the question: "What are the sacraments?" is already preceded by the thesis that the Holy Spirit strengthens our belief by the use of the sacraments; and the answer to this question places the sacramental reality in immediate relation to their institution by God and to the promise of the gospel.[1]

In the first part of our study, then, we do not intend to minimize these relations; on the contrary, we wish to honor them fully. Neither an a priori, philosophical clarification of the sacraments, nor a phenomenological analysis, can give the foundation for the doctrine of the sacraments, for these are based in the historical contingency of revelation. The history of the Church proves the danger of any other approach. Moreover, the general doctrine of the sacraments must have its foundation in Scripture, and we must remember from the very outset that Jesus Christ is the "truth" of the sacraments.[2]

It may be granted that the general doctrine of the sacraments sometimes appears to be arid and dull. Concepts must be defined, and distinctions made; but a closer look reveals that none of this analysis is done for its own sake. Rather, we must remember that these concepts and distinctions occur in the concrete context of the signs and seals of God and of his covenant in Jesus Christ, who is the focal point and the profound context of the sacraments. Thus, a general doctrine of the sacraments is not necessarily a scholastic and dull affair.

The scholastic element of the medieval doctrine of the sacraments did not lie in its attention to the sacraments in general. At that time, too, people were aware of the connections in which the sacrament was placed. This is clear, for instance, in Peter Lombard, when he defines the sacrament as a sign of the grace of God, and in Thomas Aquinas, when he begins his discussion of the sacraments by saying that he is going to speak of "the sacra-

---

1. Q. 66. We find it thus where Calvin (*Inst.*, IV, XIV) connects the treatment of "the sacraments" with the message of Scripture regarding the salvation of God, when, e.g., he speaks of the relation between Word and sacrament (IV, XIV, 5), sacrament and grace (7), the strengthening of faith (9), the efficacy of the sacraments (14), the sign and the signified matter (15), Christ and the sacraments (16), etc.
2. Cf. Heppe, *Dogmatik der evangelischen Kirche*, 1861, pp. 426ff. *Synopsis puriores Theol. Disp.*, XLIII (*de sacramentis in genere*). In our time: H. Bavinck, *Geref. Dog.*, IV, 441ff.; G. C. van Niftrik, *Kleine Dogmatiek*, 4th ed., 1953.

ments of the holy Church, which receive their efficacy from the word become flesh."[3] To that purpose, says Thomas, we should first consider the sacraments in general, then each sacrament in particular. He, too, cares nothing for an abstract concept of sacraments as such; his concern lies with the sacraments of the Church. Thus, he respectively discusses the necessity, the effect, the sign, and the cause of the sacraments, and also their number. We shall not discuss here what the typically scholastic element in the medieval doctrine of the sacraments was; we only wish to point out that it is possible to speak of "the sacraments" without constructing an "essence" of the sacrament apart from the revelation of Jesus Christ. That has never been the intention of the Reformed doctrine of the sacraments.[4]

Dogmatic reflection can be safeguarded from mere theorizing about the sacraments of the Church only when it enables us better to hear the gospel of divine grace. Such reflection will not deviate from Scripture. It will not attempt to nationalize the sacraments or to discourage their faithful use; it will not only reflect on what God in the sacraments has given to his Church. The sacraments are too important to be obscured by speculations, for they are occasions for the strengthening of belief and the certainty of salvation. Dogmatic reflections should avoid pretentiousness, and must not seek to overshadow the power of the Spirit who makes use of the sacrament. From beginning to end, dogmatic theology is normatively determined by the Word of God, and it will serve the Church only if it refuses to give a separate "gnosis" regarding the sacraments. Its only task is to point to Scripture itself, and thus to honor the divine institution of the sacraments.

3. Lombard, *Sentences,* iv, Dist. 1, 2; Aquinas, *S.T.*, III, Q. 60-65.
4. Cf. T. Preiss, "Die Kindertaufe und das N. T.," *TLZ*, LXXIII (1948), 653; W. F. Dankbaar, *De sacramentsleer van Calvijn,* 1941, pp. 15ff.

CHAPTER ONE

CONTEMPORARY ISSUES

THE DOCTRINE of the sacraments is today by no means a settled issue. Many questions are being raised that were supposedly answered long ago, especially in the confessions and the corresponding practice of the Church. But now the ferment that pervades practically the whole of dogmatics has also affected the doctrine of the sacraments, not merely at the level of theory but also existentially. We need not be surprised at this, for in the catholic confession of the Church the sacraments are said to deal with the acts of God and men, of which the mystery of divine revelation in Jesus Christ stands at the focal point. Futhermore, the sacraments are immediately related to the certainty of salvation and man's firm foundation in belief. Since the sacraments, according to the Reformed confession, are signs and seals of God's promise (and according to Rome also signs of grace), reflection on the sacraments touches upon the reality of faith. That is why any change in the doctrine of the sacraments affects the practice of the Church directly, for the question arises immediately whether the earlier confession of the Church needs correction because of this change.

It is clear, moreover, that controversies about the sacraments will influence strongly the ecumenical prospects of the Church. Just as profound discord in the time of the Reformation arose in part from a dispute about the sacraments, so today varying insights regarding the sacraments affect interchurch relations. In a world divided, the Church is confronted with the question of its own unity — a unity whose realization depends upon such crucial issues as the recognition of baptism in other churches and interchurch communion in the Lord's Supper.

Even within Roman Catholic reflection about the sacraments various tensions can be observed. We think especially of the so-called "doctrine of the mysteries" of Odo Casel and others, which involves the essence of the eucharist, especially the relation between the offering of the cross and that of the mass. The question is even discussed whether Casel's doctrine is condemned by the papal encyclical *Mediator Dei* of 1947.[1] This, however, does not imply that there is a tremendous crisis in the Roman Catholic doctrine of the sacraments. These tensions arise wholly within the framework of official doctrinal pronouncements regarding the essence and efficacy of the sacraments, which are questioned by nobody.[2] Compared to this calmness in the midst of uncertainty, the unrest in the Protestant world is striking.

This unrest is especially revealed in the question whether we can be content with the solutions of the sixteenth century and whether it is not necessary, because of the new exegetical investigations,[3] to start reviewing the old Reformed doctrine. The critics often add immediately that they are alarmed about the devaluation of the sacraments in the practice of the Protestant churches, which they attribute to an incorrect insight into the essence and the efficacy of the sacraments. Reflection and practice meet each other here. From many sides, efforts are being made to arrive at a new and purer appreciation of the sacraments, viewed not simply as external and relatively unimportant rites of the Church, but as elevated and sacred occasions in the presence of God. We think of the striving after liturgical renewal,[4] which goes together with a fervent demand for reality in the sacraments, for sacramental encounter with Jesus Christ, the living Lord of the sacraments, for his holy and divine presence, which is correlate to the adoration brought to him by the Church because of and in this presence.

It is pointed out that this real presence of Christ in the sacraments is not sufficiently acknowledged, and that for that reason Christ is not properly central in the believers' worship. This fault has been connected especially with the theory that the sacraments are "symbols" rather than realities. A symbol, say the

---

1. Cf. Burkhard Neunheuser, "Der positive Sinn der päpstlichen Grenzsetzung in der Enzyklia Mediator Dei," in *Vom Christlichen Mysterium, Gesamm. Aufs. zum Gedächtnis Odo Casels,* 1951.
2. Cf., among the abundance of literature: G. Söhngen, *Symbol und Wirklichkeit im Kultmysterium,* 1937; Söhngen, *Der Wesensaufbau des Mysteriums,* 1938; L. Monden, *Het misoffer als mysterie,* 1948; T. Filthaut, *Die Kontroverse über die Mysterienlehre,* 1947; W. F. Golterman, *Liturgiek,* 1951, pp. 91ff.; J. van 't Westeinde, *De moderne theologie over het misoffer,* 1953.
3. Cf. F. Delekat, "Methodenkritische und dogmatische Probleme angesichts der gegenwärtigen Exegese der N. T. Abendmahlstexte, *EvT,* 1953, Heft 9.
4. Cf. K. Dijk, *Liturgie (VT,* 1946).

critics, may have significance in its clear reference to reality, but it is not reality itself; so hence a "symbolical" concept of sacrament easily leads one to misjudge the actual mystery of the sacraments. This problem of symbol and reality (which we must discuss later at some length) has led in our day to the demand for sacramental reality.

Were the Reformers of the sixteenth century, in their opposition to the Roman Catholic doctrine of the sacraments, guilty of a one-sided reaction? Did they ignore some teachings of Scripture regarding the sacraments, and thus neglect essential elements in them? Was the Reformation not especially impoverished by its conviction that the Word of God is primary in comparison with the sacraments? Thus, it is charged, the sacraments threatened to acquire a "secondary" character. They became an "addition" to the Word, an "appendix," having value only because they underlined and accentuated the decisive significance of the Word. By this theory the sacraments should be completely equal to the Word, not secondary to it.

The point at issue is whether Word and sacraments stand side by side in the one reality of salvation. The Reformation was thought to have been correct in opposing the "materialization" of the Roman Catholic doctrine of the sacraments, but mistaken in not being sufficiently aware of the dangers of reaction; thus it contributed to the depreciation of the sacraments. And, according to this opinion, we in our time have the task of overcoming this reaction and its results. We must abandon the dubious distinction between primary and secondary, and instead find an independent structure of the sacraments that, with the Word, indicates God's salvation and immediately confronts us with that salvation. This new kind of thinking is found, for example, in the publication *Hervorming en Catholiciteit,* where the question is raised whether it is correct to see in baptism only "affirmation and sealing of a gift of grace that must already be considered present, for instance, on the basis of the concept of the Covenant (so that the sacrament of baptism would seem to be unnecessary)." And with respect to the Lord's Supper it is asked "whether this sacrament is appreciated, precisely when one learns that it is only a sign and seal of the salvation that is communicated in preaching."[5]

To be sure, the sign-character of the sacraments is not denied; but the sacrament is not exhausted in that, for its meaning is not

5. *Hervorming en Catholiciteit.* "Een verklaring," 1950, p. 9.

merely "sign, indication, and strengthening of faith" but "the
holy actuality of salvation" (*ibid.*, p. 55) . We see here very clearly
that "merely sign" is *opposed* to "actuality." Symbolical interpretation is contrasted with sacramental reality. With respect to the
reality implied in the sacrament, the author speaks of a "real
means to salvation, which extinguishes man's sin and grants new
life in Christ" (p. 57). The sacrament is more than symbol,
image, *nudum signum* without its own reality, more than a mere
pointing at another reality. Rather, it is itself a "sacred reality
of salvation," so that, for instance, baptism becomes necessary
for entering into God's Kingdom (p. 56) . "The sacrament gives
what it signifies, it carries God's rich gifts of grace" (p. 58) .

One could speak here of a turn from symbolism to realism.
If the sacrament is only a secondary symbol, an illustration, then,
according to this view, it could be dispensed with, for its function
would then be only cognitive. But, it is said, the sacrament carries
reality with it, the reality and actuality of sacramental grace.
K. H. Miskotte, for example, criticizes the Reformed doctrine of
the Lord's Supper because it created a breach in the unified confession of the pre-reformed Church, because it excluded the concept of offering from the Lord's Supper and thus sacrificed a
tremendous aspect of reality (*ibid.*, p. 74). Miskotte points out
that Christ is really present in the Lord's Supper, as offering and
as Offerer (p. 75). The distinction between Old and New Testament lies precisely in the fact that the Old Testament offer "had
a symbolical and temporal character, while the offering of the
New Covenant is realistic in character." The Lord's Supper is
reality, a "representative" presence of Christ's offering at the
cross (p. 76) .

Once again we hear the call for reality as opposed to "symbolism," which unveils the mysteries of the sacrament and thus
discourages true sacramental service. Such criticism, in other
words, is directed against the merely cognitive character of the
sacrament, the merely noetic, which is opposed to the "ontic"
(real) dimension of the sacrament. How, then, is this new emphasis to be distinguished from the Roman Catholic doctrine of the
sacraments, which emphasizes so strongly the actuality-aspect
of the sacrament and — in contrast to the merely cognitive —
points to the "ex operato opere" of the sacrament, by which
supernatural grace actually is infused into man's soul?[6] Clearly,

6. Cf. W. H. van de Pol, *Karakteristiek van het reformatorisch Christendom,*
   1952, pp. 228f., 243ff.

the call for sacramental reality evokes many questions. How must this "sacramental reality" be understood? What shall we think of the definition of "sacramental realism,"[7] and how shall we understand the reference to preaching and sacrament as "two equivalent poles"?

This question about the character of sacramental reality becomes no less urgent when we hear that the Reformation was too spiritualistically inclined, and that it did not pay enough attention to the significance of the "external" signs. The problem is clearly revealed in Van der Leeuw's *Sacramentstheologie*. Van der Leeuw is of the opinion that the Reformed Fathers deviated from the biblical view, "certainly as far as the Roman Catholics,"[8] because they made the sacrament "a mere affirmation of the promise of God" and an appendix to the Word. He says that this is very closely connected with "the fatal pedagogical explanation of the sacrament: because of our sinfulness and weakness," of which Article 33 of the Confession of Faith speaks. Van der Leeuw affirms that this is spiritualism, because it suggests that man naturally understands the material better than the immaterial, and that the Word is immaterial. In this manner, Van der Leeuw says, the sacrament becomes secondary. Although Calvin thought less rationalistically than did the Reformed Fathers, he also was guilty of spiritualism, and Van der Leeuw reproaches him for abandoning biblical thought at a decisive point.[9]

It is clear that this criticism is based upon a different view of sacrament, which must lead to important consequences for the whole doctrine of the sacraments. One may, without exaggeration, speak of a crisis here. Van der Leeuw's viewpoint becomes clearer when we find him urging that the sacrament has too frequently been discussed as a specifically Christian phenomenon, ignoring

---

7. W. Aalders, "Liturgische vernieuwing," *Kerk en Eredienst*, I, 23.
8. G. van der Leeuw, *Sacramentstheologie*, 1949, p. 246.
9. Van der Leeuw encounters the greatest difficulties with Calvin and with the defining of his own conception with respect to him. He thinks Calvin's interpretation of the sacraments to be "very complicated" and "certainly not logical in structure" (p. 81). Although he sees Calvin also standing at the edge of rationalism with spiritualistic tendencies, Calvin's thinking reveals "a very strong awareness of the real presence of Christ, of the mystery, and of the efficacy of the sacraments" (p. 81). He does not think that Calvin's position between Luther and Zwingli is very clear (p. 84), but acknowledges that Calvin is far removed from Zwingli when he maintains that the sacraments are gifts of the Spirit, and not just means, so that he (Calvin) even can say: "sacramenta conferunt gratiam." Cf. G. van der Leeuw, *Liturgiek*, p. 30.

the fact that it is connected with all sorts of human structures. This isolation of the sacrament had as its necessary result the contrast between Word and sacrament,[10] while a true sacramental theology depends upon taking a broader approach. The sacramental, says Van der Leeuw, is an extremely important and widespread phenomenon in reality. Sacraments are not arbitrary institutions, but are anchored deeply in man's nature.[11]

Even when it is impossible to think in Christian terms, the sacramental meets us. By way of his phenomenological considerations Van der Leeuw comes to the "understanding" of what "a sacrament is, also in the Christian religion, but without immediate definition from Christian belief" (op. cit., p. 219). The Christian sacrament receives its background from general sacramentality, which originates from the fact that man cannot directly arrive at the essence of things "but only by way of something else." Signs are always necessary to indicate the reality we seek. The sacramental always refers "to something else, never to that which is immediately given" (p. 220). In the sacrament we encounter a widespread phenomenon of anthropological character, which is analyzed by Van der Leeuw before he begins the properly theological part of his sacramental theology.[12]

This radical aspect of contemporary sacrament-problematics is strikingly confirmed in the writing of the Roman Catholic scholar Schillebeeckx. He, too, sees sacramental piety as a generally human, religious phenomenon.[13] The sacramental approach to God, he says, is deeply rooted in man's religious and social psychology. Man's religious disposition expresses itself in conformity with his matter-bound spirituality. In this connection, Schillebeeckx refers to Jung's psychological types as forms of symbol-creating activity, presupposing that there exists a structural similarity between the pagan mystery and the Christian sacrament, which can be clarified through a study of man's anthropological structure, although a direct genetic dependency is not necessarily involved. According to Schillebeeckx, general sacramentality is a providential herald of the Christian sacrament, a tutor to Christ.[14] The created human structure causes us to expect a priori many kinds of relations, while the Christian

---

10. *Liturgiek,* p. 51.
11. G. van der Leeuw, *Sacramentstheologie,* p. 219.
12. Cf. G. van der Leeuw, *De primitieve mens en het religie,* 1937.
13. Schillebeeckx, *De sacramentele heilseconomie,* pp. 50ff.
14. Cf. G. van der Leeuw, *Sacramentstheologie,* p. 219.

sacrament may be seen as a culmination of the "natural sacrament."[15]

On the one hand, Schillebeeckx rejects the theory of genetic dependence as held by Reitzenstein; on the other hand, he opposes the one-sided supranaturalism that denies all basic relation between pagan mystery and Christian sacrament. There is, according to him, a real *basis-symbolique* (p. 61) in which the significance of the Christian sacrament is brought to light. The transcendental character of the Christian sacraments is not at all affected by that.

The views of Van der Leeuw and Schillebeeckx are obviously related, especially in their assumption that the Christian sacrament should be understood against the background of general sacramentality as anthropological structure. For both, the actual problem is the transition from general sacramentality to the specifically Christian concept of sacrament. If sacraments as such are anchored in the nature of man, how then is it still possible to find a way that leads to the Christian sacraments or to what Schillebeeckx calls the "transcendence" of the sacraments? Can the Christian sacraments without further ado be subsumed under general sacramentality, or does some specific feature radically distinguish them? It is clear that the phenomenological approach leads to at least one urgent problem, namely, that of pansacramentalism.

Van der Leeuw could not but see this problem, especially since pansacramentalism speaks so emphatically of nature's "sacramental faculty." He notes at one point "the truth of pansacramentalism," which, as he sees it, does not become unacceptable until it is coupled with pantheism.[16] But the problem of pansacramentalism does not lie wholly in its possible association with pantheism, but rather in its very reference to an anthropologically anchored general sacramentality. How can this thesis be reconciled with the transcendence of the Christian sacraments? This question is especially consequential for Van der Leeuw, who cannot appeal, as does the Roman Catholic Schillebeeckx, to a principle of transcendence secured in the official Church doctrine of the institution of the seven sacraments by Christ.

We need not be surprised that Van der Leeuw has difficulties

---

15. Schillebeeckx, *op. cit.*, p. 58.
16. G. van der Leeuw, *Sacramentstheologie*, p. 227. Cf. p. 228 concerning the "possibility of pansacramentalism."

with the sacramentalia (p. 253). This is because his phenomenology and his sacramental theology are logically connected. He
speaks of the "tremendous" significance of the general-phenome-
nological point of view for the understanding of baptism (p. 172),
and he asserts that a general sacramentality will continue to
exist alongside of the Christian concept of sacrament (p. 227).
The Reformation, he charges, formed an inadequate concept of
the sacramentalia because, it considered only the two Christian
sacraments. Hence the Reformation solved the problem of delimitation too simplistically. Van der Leeuw declares that he does
not wish to argue about the institution of the sacraments. Now
that the "humanistic" appeal to the historical institution of the
Lord "has been shown to be invalid," there is, he thinks, greater
need than ever to revise sacramental theology.[17] "The appeal to
the institution of the sacraments by Christ, making the sacramentalia only ecclesiastical institutions, is doubtful and hardly a
point of principle" (p. 52). To be sure, Van der Leeuw speaks
in connection with the focal point of worship, of the serving of
the Lord's Supper, which the Lord himself has given to us (p.
32); and in the Lord's Supper he sees the basic form of all
worship; but he wants nothing to do with a sharp distinction
between sacrament and sacramentalia (p. 42). He says of the
problem proper: "This is not a matter of authority, but of belief, which in the sacramental act makes use of our act" (p. 41).
A strange dilemma — which gives a striking illustration of his
sacramental theology.

Whereas the Reformation, according to Van der Leeuw, was
occupied with the transcendence of the sacraments, that is to
say, with the question regarding their institution, in which the
polemics with Rome reached its high point, Van der Leeuw
prefers to pose the theological question; he wishes to begin by
considering the subject of the sacraments rather than their number.[18] This dichotomy is not altogether fair, however, since the
Reformation concerned itself with the institution of the sacraments precisely in order to be able to speak responsibly of the
significance of the sacraments as divine signs and seals. Van der
Leeuw's dilemma —"not numbers, but the subject"— fails to
recognize that the Reformation was interested in the number
for the sake of the subject, being convinced that the broadening

17. *Liturgiek,* pp. 44, 46.
18. *Sacramentstheologie,* p. 253.

of the Christian sacraments beyond a certain number threatened belief and the certainty of salvation.[19]

Van der Leeuw's devaluation of the "number question" clearly leads to a broadening of the concept of sacrament, though he ultimately ends up with the Christian sacraments by suddenly appealing to what the Lord himself has given us. On the one hand, he argues from the basis of general sacramentality, which for him is the same as anthropology; on the other hand, he feels that he cannot simply transport non-Christian sacamentality inside the boundaries of Christian faith, for in that case the Christian would have only general features and traits. One might expect, then, that Van der Leeuw would be less harsh in his judgment of the Reformed interest in the institution of the sacraments. But not so: he thinks that the Reformers made a grave error when they returned from seven sacraments to two by appealing to the principle of divine institution.[20] By so doing they isolated the sacraments from their background in general sacramentality, which in turn is based upon anthropological structure.

It should be added that Van der Leeuw traces general sacramentality to a foundation in creation, to an *analogia entis* between creation and re-creation. "... Sacramental theology is impossible if the category of creation is not wholly and fully recognized as the point of departure for all theology."[21] Moreover, the incarnation has significance for sacramental theology because it shows us that "the divine has entered completely-historical, concrete reality" (p. 225). The Word become flesh is the foundation for the Christian faith, and Van der Leeuw warns against docetism *(ibid.)*, which fails to appreciate that Christ has taken on our nature and, in doing so, has sanctified that nature in such a manner that it can function in God's revelation. Created reality can be correctly understood only in the light of the incarnation, and the incarnation also makes it possible to understand that in the sacrament created life becomes the medium of God's act.[22] The incarnation brings our earthly

---

19. Cf. Polman, *Onze Nederlandse Geloofsbelijdenis*, IV (1953), 150, 115. Polman speaks of the soteriological and theological point of view and of the defense against all speculation (p. 115).
20. *Liturgiek*, p. 31.
21. *Sacramentstheologie*, p. 225.
22. *Liturgiek*, p. 237.

reality into communion with God, "whether it be a word that is spoken or bread that is eaten."[23]

Thus, for Van der Leeuw, the incarnation delimits the concept of sacrament. The *analogia entis* and the intelligibility of nature establish the connection between sacramental theology and the phenomenology of religion, but the incarnation serves to focus and crystallize these insights.[24] Sacramental theology as incarnation-theology not only opens the prospect on the broadness of the sacramental, but also on its delimitation, for the sacrament must be related to Christ.[25] This is closely connected with the revelation of the mystery that came to light in Christ. In the sacraments we meet the One revealed as *Kurios* (p. 235); the sacraments are "appearances" of the Christ-mystery (p. 256). The number of these appearances is not very important. There is actually only one sacrament, namely, "the incarnate, crucified, and resurrected Christ" (p. 256). He opens up to us a sacramental world "of which the boundaries can never be distinctly drawn" (p. 257). There is a sacramental center and a periphery, sacraments, deduced sacraments, and sacramentalia. But all sacramental acts can be traced to these three: the Lord's Supper, Word, and baptism (p. 257; although elsewhere on p. 333 Van der Leeuw speaks of the Lord's Supper, baptism, preaching of the Word, and marriage), while there are also other sacramental acts, such as confirmation, which are only meaningful if connected to the ones mentioned, although the sacramental significance of confirmation "is certainly not less than any of the other four." Van der Leeuw says at the end with respect to the Roman Catholic doctrine of the sacraments: "From the seven sacraments determined upon we can posit nearly everything." All this shows how greatly Van der Leeuw broadens the concept of sacrament on the basis of his phenomenological background. His sacramental theology results from a struggle to make two lines converge: the one of general sacramentality, and the other of the specifically Christian concept of sacrament. This insoluble duality in his sacramental thinking is the basic problem of his entire theology.

* * *

Van der Leeuw says emphatically that he owes much to Paul

---

23. *Sacramentstheologie*, p. 225.
24. Cf. H. van Oyen, "Op weg naar een nieuwe sacramentstheologie," *Kerk en Eredienst*, 1946, pp. 258ff.
25. G. van der Leeuw, *Sacramentstheologie*, p. 224.

Tillich, for whom the sacraments are also to be viewed in the light of general sacramentality.[26] Tillich, also, begins his search with general sacramentality and "Naturmächtigkeit" ("power of nature"), proceeding thence to the specifically Christian sacrament.[27] The essential problem of this method stems from the fact that broadening of the concept of sacrament opposes concretization. Although the Reformers are criticized for their concern with the number of sacraments, these critics must ultimately fall back on the same biblical considerations when they seek to delimit the Christian sacraments. A broad sacramental sphere, connected only with the generally-human of creation, loses as much in depth and concreteness as it gains in universality. Therefore, to focus upon the institution of the sacraments is not to indulge in mere mechanics, as it may appear at first sight. Deeper reflection shows that this study bears upon a decisive question, namely, concerning the qualification of the earthly elements to be signs in the acts of God. Precisely because of the re-evaluation of the sacraments in sacramentalism, the question about their institution has again become acute. Only in this way can we be sure that in the sacraments we encounter not merely fragments of earthly reality, but rather, signs in which the living God himself acts, taking up the earthly element as a testimony to his trustworthy promise.

* * *

In pointing out the unavoidable problematics of sacramental theology based on phenomenology, we do not intend to deny all connections between sacrament and "signs" in the general sense of the word. Surely, the institution of the sacrament is closely linked with the fact that signs exist everywhere in the world. When in the crowning ceremonies in England the new kings are presented with certain symbols of royal dignity, these serve to evoke in men's minds the less tangible reality of royal government. Signs in general can of course become objects of scientific investigation, and it is clear that God in his revelation does not pass by this general area of reality, but rather, he incorporates it in the means of his revelation. That was generally acknowledged long before phenomenology drew our emphatic attention to it. Bavinck, for example, has pointed out

26. *Ibid.*, p. 227.
27. Cf. *The Protestant Era*, 1951, p. xxxviii, pp. 105ff. "Of course the power of nature alone does not create a Christian sacrament. Nature must be brought into the unity of the history of salvation" (p. 125).

that God employed existing customs. "As God conformed with existing customs in other nations when He instituted the temple and the priesthood, the offering and the altar, the laws and the ordinances for Israel, so He did with respect to circumcision as well."[28] The same can be said with respect to baptism, which was not entirely new with the Christian religion.[29]

But such considerations do not suffice for a biblical doctrine of the sacraments; they only provide the background for this doctrine. Not every sign is a sacrament, and for that reason it is impossible to base the Christian sacrament on a phenomenological analysis. In normal life signs refer to specific realities in many sorts of ways. Roman Catholic as well as Protestant authors often distinguish between natural and so-called artificial signs, that is to say, between signs that arise from the nature of things, such as smoke from fire and footprints in snow, and artificial signs such as a uniform and a flag, which are meaningful not in themselves but by mutual agreement.[30] Scripture is full of signs that point to the acts of God. It is noteworthy, however, that their meaning is not gained by human insight into obvious analogies, but by divine revelation. Detached from this revelation the elements lose their sign-character, so that those who do not understand or recognize God's revelation pay the signs no heed,[31] while those who have heard this revelation understand the meaning and the power of the signs, simple as they may be.

The rainbow, for example, can be seen as a physical phenomenon, which as such is meaningful in physics; but God's Word has qualified this rainbow, this natural phenomenon, to be a sign of the Covenant.[32] And Gideon asked for a sign: "that it is Thou with whom I speak," and God's sign was in Gideon's life the reference to victory. We are not dealing here with a

---

28. *Geref. Dog.*, IV, 474.
29. *Ibid.*
30. Cf. I Sam. 6:12 and I Sam. 14:8-10. Cf. C. J. Goslinga, *Korte Verklaring, 1 Samuel, ad loc.*
31. For the relation between faith and sign, consider the desire of the Pharisees for a sign from heaven. This sign falls beyond the sphere of faith. They want to tempt Christ (Mark 8:12). They do not see the God-given signs. No sign is given to this generation (8:12). Cf. Matt. 12:39: no sign but the one of ... Jonah.
32. Compare the sign that David receives before the fight with the Philistines (II Sam. 5:24).

self-evident *analogia entis,* an independent revelation of God that can be seen in nature by anyone who is not entirely blind, but with a divine choice of revelation, a selection that he employs in guiding his people. That is why divine selection and qualification are of decisive significance for the power and the nature of the sign in God's acting.

The Roman Catholic and Protestant doctrines of the sacraments are one in this, that they wish to honor the biblical insight that the earthly element receives its sacramental character only and exclusively from the act and the speaking of God, which does not change the character of the earthly element but which does make it a sacrament. Rome as well as the Reformation has emphasized that the sacraments are neither "natural" nor humanly constructed "artificial" signs, but rather they exist because of a divine "signifying." It is precisely that divine revelatory act which invests the simplest sign with power, and places tremendous responsibility upon him who receives the sign. Herein lies the only, but sufficient, defense against sacramentalism, which cannot help losing this power of the signs because of its broadening of the sacraments and its emphasis upon the sacramental *"Fähigkeit"* (faculty) of nature in general.

It is clear then, that Word and sacrament cannot simplistically be juxtaposed as equals. That does not imply a devaluation of the sacraments, but simply means that we fully maintain their truth and power. We are interested in their institution because this determines their essence. It is the crisis of sacramentalism in our time that it introduces a vagueness that ultimately must lead to serious devaluation of the sacraments. Insofar as sacramentalism reacts against an actual devaluation of the sacraments in Protestant churches, we may not simply reject it. To lack interest in the sacraments and regard them as external and empty signs is to render poor service to the Reformation.

Neither should sacramentalism be opposed in the name of a "spiritualism" that fails to appreciate the real use of earthly elements in the divine acts. These earthly signs are full of power and meaning. That is why the controversy about the sacraments in the time of the Reformation is still full of significance. For then the Reformers had to contend not only with realism in the doctrine of the sacraments, but also with spiritualism, which Calvin, among others, rejected emphatically. Calvin did not search for a synthesis between realism and spiritualism,[33] but he did fully honor the significance of the signs in the hand of God. Turning in faith toward these divine acts, he was able to transcend false dilemmas and to appreciate the sacraments in the light of Scripture. For that reason it will be no vain exercise for us to refer repeatedly to the classical Reformed doctrine of the sacraments. Only if we reject false dilemmas can we find an alternative to the contemporary call for "sacramental reality." Then, hopefully, it will be possible to delve deeper, to discern the sovereign manner in which God stoops down to us, taking up simple earthly elements and using them for the affirmation and strengthening of our faith.

33. In the sense of which Van Royen writes: "The Protestant interpretations of the sacraments sway between realism and symbolism." J. P. van Royen, "Liturgie," in *VT*, 1946, special issue on liturgy, p. 74. Cf. O. C. Quick, *The Christian Sacraments*, 1946.

CHAPTER TWO

THE NUMBER OF SACRAMENTS

IN DISCUSSING the institution of the sacraments, we must
first point out that the questions about the essence and
the number of sacraments cannot be answered by starting with
the meaning of the word "sacrament." This word appears nowhere in Scripture, nor is there any mention of the sacraments
in general. The word *sacramentum* does appear in the Vulgate
in Ephesians 5:32 as translation of the Greek *mysterion,* but
this cannot help to determine the essence of sacrament. It is
clear that Paul does not speak in Ephesians 5 of what we now
call sacrament. The word *mysterion* is used in various contexts
in the New Testament, and it certainly does not have the meaning of our "sacraments."[1] The Roman Catholics, Schillebeeckx,
for instance, agree with this. Schillebeeckx declares that Paul
never calls baptism itself or any other sacrament a mystery,[2]
although he believes that all the givens are there to call also
the sacramental cultus a "mystery."

The word "sacrament" has come into use in ecclesiastical
and theological language to indicate specifically religious events.
Its increasing use has to do with its root meaning, which indicates the assigning of something to the deity *(sacrare),* for example in the Roman legions or in other connections.[3] The word
was used to indicate certain rites of the Church that had particular bearing on the mysteries of faith, so that the term could
come about *"mysterium sacramenti."*[4] The distinction between
"sacramentum" and *"mysterium"* became flexible, which ex-

1. Cf. my *The Work of Christ,* 1965, pp. 88ff.
2. Schillebeeckx, *De Sacramentele Heilseconomie,* p. 46. Cf. *DTC,* XIV, 468.
3. Schillebeeckx, *loc. cit.;* Bavinck, *Geref. Dog.,* IV, 443.
4. Cf. H. de Lubac, *Corpus Mysticum. L'Eucharistie et l'église au moyen age,*
   1949, pp. 344-350. "In the language of liturgy, exegesis, and theology, the
   words 'sacramentum' and 'mysterium' are often used one for the other"
   (p. 55). Cf. *TWNT,* IV, 833f.

plains why the Church had a very broad concept of the sacraments for a long time.[5] The word "sacrament" became a definite
part of the ecclesiastical vocabulary, but its meaning was often
changed.[6]

In the medieval era the concept of sacrament was gradually
sharpened, especially in the distinction between sacraments and
sacramentalia. These sacramentalia surround the sacraments of
the Church; they were added deliberately, but "have as their
only purpose to give the sacraments greater worthiness... they
are not a component part of the visible sign."[7] According to
Rome they were not instituted by Christ, but by the Church.
Therefore they may be replaced or discarded without affecting
the authority of Christ.

The above distinction resulted in a problem that occupied
Church and theology continually: to what extent can one speak
of specific sacraments among the multiplicity of sacramental acts
that are somehow linked with the mystery of salvation in the New
Testament sense? Clearly, the problem of selection began to play
an important role, and this led to a consideration of the institution of the sacraments. Even though the appeal to tradition
played a great role in the scholastic development of the doctrine
of the sacraments, the selective principle was ultimately sought
in the divine institution of the sacraments. This development
moved increasingly toward the sacred seven that in later ecclesiastical doctrine became circumscribed by an inviolable
boundary.[8]

We can disregard the Roman Catholic explanation of the
fact that the sharp fixation of the concept of sacrament and of
the seven sacraments occurred rather late[9] — not before the
twelfth century — because since then the Church has spoken
with great emphasis of the seven as of revelational truth supported by divine authority. The councils of Lyon[10] and Flor-

---

5. "Before the fourth century, the word 'mysterion' retains its classical
   meaning of 'sacred thing'" (*DTC*, XIV, 486).
6. For newer terminology, see W. F. Golterman. "Teken, symbool of chiffre?"
   NedTT, III (1948-49), 435ff.
7. J. Braun, *Handlexicon der kath. Dogm.*, 1926, p. 251.
8. Oswald, *Die dogmatische Lehre von den heil. Sakramenten der Kath.
   Kirche*, I, 119.
9. Cf. Bartmann, *Dogm.*, II, 241ff.; Pohle, *Dogm.*, III, 25ff.; Diekamp, *Dogm.*,
   1946, IV.
10. Denz. 465.

ence[11] definitively declared in favor of the seven sacraments, while Trent affirms even more sharply that there are no more and no less than seven.[12] These seven are beyond all question because they have been proclaimed by the doctrinal authority of the Church.[13]

That does not mean, however, that the Roman Catholic Church pretends to offer scriptural proofs for the institution of its seven sacraments. The decision lies, rather, with the tradition and authority of the Church. Bartmann acknowledges that "nowhere in Scripture is there mention of seven sacraments,"[14] although he maintains that they "all have their individual foundation in the New Testament." If the light of tradition is not allowed to shine upon Scripture, the proof for a certain sacrament can be rather defective, but when Scripture is read in the light of tradition there can be no uncertainty.[15]

Furthermore, the identity of these seven sacraments is thought all the more inviolable because it is very easy to discern profound significance in them. Not only do they remind us of the sacred number seven in Scripture and of the connection between three and four, as the link between the divine and the human, but they also yield a "systematics" of the sacraments, an "organic pragmatics" which is especially revealed in the beautiful parallel between the seven sacraments and man's natural course of life. Man's natural life from beginning to end is, so to speak, enveloped in and blessed by the seven means of grace, by sevenfold, efficacious, supernatural grace.

We meet this parallel already in Thomas Aquinas, who points to a certain similarity between "spiritual" and "natural" life, and then applies it to the sacraments.[16] Baptism corresponds to birth, confirmation to the growth of the body, the eucharist to nourishment, penitence to healing, while extreme unction is also mentioned in this connection because it destroys the last remains of sin and prepares man for final glory. Added to these five sacraments is the point of view of perfection with respect to society: consecration of the priest, and marriage. We find these efforts to indicate a direct connection between natural and super-

11. Denz. 695.
12. Denz. 844.
13. Cf. Thomas, *S.T.*, III, Q. 64, Art. 2. Cf. Denz. 875, 894, 826, 971.
14. Oswald, *op. cit.*, I, 117.
15. Cf. P. Schoonenberg, *Geloofsinhoud en Geloofsbeleving*, 1951, p. 175.
16. *S.T.*, III, 65, 1. Cf. Schmaus, *Kath. Dogmatik*, IV, 1, 86ff.

natural sacramental life already in the pronouncement of the council of Florence, in which the parallel becomes clearly visible.[17]

Roman Catholics like to point to the beauty of these connections, adding that this evidence is so strong that even Goethe was enthralled by it.[18] It is understandable that this parallel should play such an important role, since it conforms to the fundamental view of Rome on the relation between natural and supernatural life, the latter of which is, through the sacraments, poured into man's soul. The essence of the sacraments is correlated with their number, indicating that the totality of man's life from birth to death is flooded with sacramental, supernatural light.

The origin of this stream of grace lies in the redemption of Christ. "The sacraments are the seven mouths into which the stream of the divine life of grace, which has its spring in the cross of Christ, empties itself in the wilderness of human existence."[19] The great transformation and healing that originates in the *passio magna* "is via the efficaciousness of the sacraments applied to concrete man and to the individual phases and situations of his life." The light of the redeeming cross diverges in seven rays "like the seven colored rays from the one white lightbeam."[20] All of life is in the grip of grace, of sacramental grace. All of man is involved and he is thus elevated to supernatural life. Supernatural grace stands as an unfathomable mystery of condescension spanned over birth, growth, and death as the protecting blessing of God's salvation.

It is necessary, when reflecting on the number of the sacraments, to avoid romanticism and to keep under restaint our natural love of system and harmony. We are not building a thing of beauty, but trying to discover the facts regarding the institution of the sacraments. There is beauty, to be sure, in the sacraments, but the beauty lies in the majesty with which God goes his way in history, making earthly elements to become sacraments by his word. Hence a mere appeal to the harmony of the

17. Denz. 695.
18. Goethe, *Dichtung und Wahrheit* (I, Bk. 7). Cf. Eugene Bizer, *Das Christusgeheimnis der Sakramente*, 1950, pp. 14f.
19. Bizer, *op. cit.*, p. 16. Cf. P. Haneveer, "Het sacramenteel merkteken en de sacramentele genade in de afzonderlijke sacramenten," *Studia Catholica*, Jan. 1953, pp. 20-38.
20. Bizer, *op. cit.*, p. 17.

seven sacraments carries little weight with anyone who focuses upon the institution of the sacraments. The Reformation repeatedly urged that the Roman Catholic doctrine had insufficient foundation in Scripture, and it criticized the sacred number of seven because of this insufficiency.

This Reformed view has often been sharply rejected as positivistic;[21] supposedly it is a purely formal appeal, which ignores the essence of the sacraments. But this objection fails to appreciate the religious background of the Reformed defense. Not a formalistic principle of knowledge, but questions of belief and certainty were at stake. Just because the sacraments are signs and seals of the divine promises, the Reformers held it to be of great importance whether the sacraments really were fixed and selected in special divine acts.[22]

This approach to the problem of the sacraments is manifest in the Reformed confessions. We read there of the institution of the sacraments with a definite purpose,[23] the instituted washing with water (H.C., Q. 69, 71), God's speaking (Q. 73), the command of Christ (Q. 75; cf. Q. 74, 77, 81), the ordained sacraments (Conf., Art. 33), the command to baptize (Art. 34), the ordaining and instituting of the Lord's Supper (Art. 35). These accents reveal a great concern to avoid arbitrariness with respect to sacramental reality; as Calvin says, "the judgment of the institution of a sacrament can only be made by God." In the sacrament the consciences of the believers are comforted; this makes the *certainty* of divine goodwill a central issue, concerning which "no man or angel can be a witness." God himself is "the only One who witnesses to us regarding himself through his Word and with lawful authority" (*Inst.*, IV, XIX, 2). If the sacrament is a seal of God's promise and Covenant, only God's power can form it to that purpose (*ibid.*).

It can be said that both Rome and the Reformation rejected all pansacramentalism, and that they both sought a boundary that is founded in the revelation of God himself. It is all the more striking, therefore, that while they both spoke of the institution of the sacraments by Christ, they did not come to the same conclusions. Moreover, the disagreement concerns more than the

---

21. Tillich speaks of "ritualistic" and "nominalistic" in connection with the Protestant interpretation of the sacraments, which emphasizes the divine command (P. Tillich, *Religiöse Verwirklichung*, 1930, p. 144).
22. Cf. Calvin, *Inst.*, XIV, XIV, 19 regarding the will of God.
23. H.C., Q. 66; cf. Q. 68.

number; it is not simply the case that the two parties had a common concept of sacrament while the Reformation accepted only two sacraments and Rome seven. Even the two "common" sacraments of baptism and the Lord's Supper differ profoundly. Nevertheless, both sides appealed to divine institution, which explains why the contention about those other five sacraments was so fierce.

Upon closer investigation, we find that this dispute involves more than just an appeal to a few Scripture references or to tradition. The very nature of the sacraments is at stake. In order to see that, it is necessary to note some problems directly related to the large number of sacraments recognized by Roman Catholics. Consider, first, the sacrament of penance. The forgiveness of sin by the priest is based upon those words in Scripture that speak of the forgiveness of sins, for instance, John 20:22ff., where Christ says to his disciples: "Whose soever sins ye forgive, they are forgiven unto them; whose soever sins ye retain, they are retained." This word, says Rome, makes it very clear that Christ transferred to his apostles the general power to forgive sins, which was already implied in the command to bind and unbind in Matthew 16 where Christ is supposed to have promised the power to forgive, which he then fulfilled in John 20. It is emphatically said that this is the foundation for the sacrament of penance, because here Christ reckons with sins that are committed in the Church *after* baptism. These postbaptismal sins are the reason for the institution of a new sacrament other than baptism. The controversy concerning the sacrament of penance was therefore focused upon how postbaptismal sins are forgiven. Because of the general structure of Roman Catholic sacramentology (infusion of supernatural grace), Rome needed a new sacramental act. For supernatural grace, given in the sacrament of baptism, can be lost again through mortal sin; this necessitates a new infusion of supernatural grace into man, and that, Rome concludes, happens in the sacrament of penance.

It is clear that this concept of infused and again-to-be-infused grace decisively influences the exegesis of the instituting words. The infusion of supernatural grace as the essence of the sacrament forms the basis for the sacrament of penance. And it is precisely this supposition that the Reformation criticized so sharply. The Reformation turned against the addition of the sacrament of penance as a new sacrament of forgiveness. To be sure, Rome maintains that the sacrament of baptism is also connected with the forgiveness of sins as the first infusion of grace, but insists that baptism is not sufficient for later sins. Hence Rome reproached the Reformation for accepting only baptism as a sacrament of forgiveness while disregarding the following sacrament of penance. Rome was consistent when it accused the Reformation of seeking forgiveness for new sins in the practice of *regressus ad baptismum,* a perpetual harking back to baptism. Such a "return" was impossible for Rome because of the nature and the effect of baptism. A new sacrament was necessary in order to restore the damage that could no longer be repaired by the past sacrament of baptism. The grace that was lost had to be infused anew. With this new act (contrasted with the Reformed concept of the permanence of baptism) Christ's words about the power to forgive were connected. Thus, the sacrament of penance became a judicial act of the Church which once again brought restoration.

* * *

We meet the same background in the sacrament of confirmation. This is not a sacrament for the dead but for the living,[24] because the recipient is already in a state of grace; this grace is not infused anew in the sacrament of confirmation, but increased. In confirmation, the baptismal grace that has already been received is increased and strengthened.[25] It is not just a human ceremony of encouragement, but a true and real sacrament,[26] a sacramental, supernatural reality, the announcement of the promised Spirit, which is given by the apostles "as something that differs from the grace of baptism."[27]

Confirmation has its own efficacy of grace, the strengthening and confirmation by a more complete communication of the Spirit.[28] Supernatural life as it is given in baptism is only a beginning, and this beginning must grow through struggle within the context of the Church. It is the growth to adulthood to which the supernatural grace of confirmation leads the baptized person,

---

24. The sacraments of the living assume the state of grace, while the sacraments of the dead do not.
25. A. Janssens, *Doopsel en vormsel* (*Serie Kath. Kerk,* XII, 85).
26. Denz. 871; Cf. 697 and the encyclical against the Modernists (2055).
27. Janssens, *op. cit.,* p. 88.
28. *Ibid.,* p. 110.

the coming to the *perfecta acta*.[29] The supernatural also plays an important role in confirmation, since for every special effect of grace a different sacrament was instituted.[30] To be sure, says Bartmann, there are no formal scriptural references for the institution of this sacrament by Christ;[31] but the rite of laying-on of hands, together with the gift of the Spirit, cannot possibly originate in human authority, but can only be based on the institution of a new sacrament that is symbolized by this laying-on of hands as sign of the communication of the Spirit. "The power of the Holy Spirit streams symbolically from the hand of the ordained priest onto the recipient."[32]

A similar trend of thought, which again illustrates the significance of the number seven, we find in the last sacrament, extreme unction. According to Trent, it was instituted by Christ and propagated by James.[33] According to Bartmann, the institution remains "unclear"[34] but at any rate it is presupposed in the New Testament. In the distress of life a new sacrament is necessary, which, like confirmation, infuses new strength "when at the end of this life man is in need of strength and help to be able to endure the presence of the Divine Judge."[35] So, the supernatural strengthening from baptism to confirmation, and from confirmation to extreme unction, comes by an ever new sacramental infusion of grace. Already in baptism a person receives a certain "similarity to Christ," which gains "new colors" from later sacraments; extreme unction, accordingly, may be called the completion of baptism and penance.[36]

In the *ordo* or priestly consecration, which is not at all a human invention but a sacrament instituted by Christ (Denz. 963) supernatural grace is also infused, namely, visible and external priesthood (964), which implies the power of consecration and forgiveness. Through this *ordo* is given the Holy Spirit and

---

29. "... in baptismum regeneratur ad vitam; post baptismum confirmatur ad pubnam; in baptismo abluimur; post baptismum roboramur" (Thomas, *S.T.*, III, 72, 1).
30. *Ibid.*
31. Bartmann, *Dogm.*, II, 277.
32. Schmaus, *op. cit.*, IV, 1, p. 179.
33. Denz. 926; cf. 908.
34. Bartmann, *op. cit.*, II, 427.
35. *Ad Catholici Sacerdotii*, 1935 (*Ecclesia docens*), p. 15; cf. on extreme unction, e.g., Matth. Rath, "De extrema unctione et de ordine," *Inst. Theol.*, 1912.
36. Schmaus, *op. cit.*, IV, 1, p. 37; cf. p. 564.

a priestly character (964) . This sacrament, too, brings with it a certain "similarity to Christ," and it enables the recipient "to symbolize Christ in a special manner."[37] The communion and likeness to Christ is "further developed and provided with new traits."[38]

Finally, in the sacrament of marriage the recipients are also infused with grace. The *Decretum pro Armenis* (1439) calls marriage a sign of the relation between Christ and his Church with reference to Ephesians 5:32,[39] while Trent declares firmly that he who does not acknowledge marriage to be a true sacrament, and thinks that it is not in need of grace, is condemned.[40] But why is marriage a sacrament? That is to say, why does it go together with infusion of grace? According to Steur, the sacramental character of marriage cannot be deduced from the Pauline word *mysterion* translated by Hieronymus *sacramentum,* for the term "sacrament" did not then have technical significance.[41]

Marriage is a sacrament, an external rite that works supernatural grace *ex opere operato.*[42] If it is a true sacrament, it must be a "cause" of grace.[43] According to Steur, Ephesians 5:32 — the great mystery — refers to the supernatural efficacy of the marriage of those who are baptized,[44] even though the explanation of "great" does not necessarily warrant that. But there is no doubt about the sacramental character of marriage. "The marriage of Christians has supernatural efficacy.' Through that, the marriage is Christian, a true sacrament of the new law."[45] We see clearly that the concept of sacrament (supernatural grace; *ex opere operato*) influences the determination of the number of sacraments, as Steur explains: "The fact that the bond of marriage possesses causality with respect to grace is simply a consequence of the doctrine of the sacraments, which couples the efficacy of grace with the sign."[46] What is difficult to deduce from

---

37. Schmaus, *op. cit.,* IV, 1, p. 575.
38. *Ibid.,* p. 598.
39. Denz. 702.
40. Denz. 971; see also 1640, 1765, 1583, 2051 (against the rejection of marriage as a sacrament).
41. Steur, *Dogm. Tractaat over het Sacr. v.h. huwelijk,* 1947, p. 14; Schmaus, *op. cit.,* p. 621.
42. Steur, *op. cit.,* p. 29.
43. *Ibid.,* p. 31.
44. *Ibid.,* p. 36.
45. *Ibid.,* p. 37.
46. *Ibid.,* p. 140.

Ephesians 5:32, is easily inferred from the doctrine of the sacraments, which is concentrated in the sacramental communication of grace.

It is noteworthy that in Ephesians 5 Paul appeals to Genesis, while according to Rome only New Testament Christian marriage may be called a sacrament. Catholic theology tries to escape this paradox by saying that already in Genesis "the sacramentality of marriage is prefigured in a rather profound manner."[47] Christ supposedly took up marriage into the sacramental order,[48] so that it, too, confers a new "similarity to Christ"[49] and an increase of sanctifying grace, especially of communal grace.[50] To be sure, Paul stresses the sign in Ephesians 5; but that sign implies the efficacy of grace, so marriage is also a *causa gratiae*.

This brief review of the five special sacraments makes it clear that Roman Catholic theology fixes the number of sacraments on the basis of its view that they constitute a series of supernatural acts that infuse supernatural grace into all of life from beginning to end, rather than upon an indubitable foundation of biblical exegesis. The idea of renewal, and especially of the increase of grace, plays an important role. The sacraments are "radiations (*Ausstrahlungen*) into the here and now of history from the redemptive work that was finished at Golgotha."[51] The fulness of Christ thus becomes revealed in the Church via the priests. Baptism is the beginning of this revelation of fulness. No matter how important this sacrament is, however, one cannot fall back on it as a trustworthy witness of God's grace. For Rome is not concerned primarily with this element of witness, but rather with the infused grace, with "the total efficacy of the mystical Christ,"[52] which radiates from the eucharist: the sacrament of sacraments.[53]

In the eucharist Christ himself is present, and from him all sacraments as supernatural efficacies of grace receive value. The background of the Roman Catholic doctrine of the sacraments lies in this doctrine of the eucharistic Christ; he is the supernatural reality in whom we participate through the sacraments.

47. Schmaus, *op. cit.*, p. 619.
48. *Ibid.*, p. 621.
49. *Ibid.*, p. 643.
50. Steur, *op. cit.*, p. 143.
51. Bizer, *op. cit.*, p. 43.
52. *Ibid.*, p. 114.
53. *Ibid.*, p. 116.

At the time of the Reformation, contention about the essence and efficacy of the sacraments also came to involve the number of sacraments. It is striking that Calvin's polemics on this subject focuses on the alleged necessity of repeated infusions of grace — *ex opere operato* — in all the sacraments. For example, Calvin opposes confirmation by speaking of baptism as follows: "Have not we then been buried in baptism with Christ, made partakers in his death, that we may also be sharers in his resurrection [Rom. 6:4-5]? Moreover, this fellowship with Christ's death and life Paul explains to be the mortifying of our flesh and the quickening of the Spirit, because 'our old man has been crucified' [Rom. 6:6, Vg.] in order that 'we may walk in newness of life' [Rom. 6:5, Vg.]. What is it to be equipped for battle, but this?" (*Inst.*, IV, XIX, 8). We see here clearly Calvin's line of argument against confirmation. He believes that it represents a serious devaluation and misappreciation of the significance of baptism, and against Rome he quotes a resolution taken by the council of Miletus: "Whoever says that baptism is given only for forgiveness of sins, and not as a help for grace to come, let him be anathema."

The devil is at work, says Calvin, in this impoverishment of baptism, "In order stealthily to draw the unwary from baptism. ... Who now can doubt that this is a doctrine of Satan, which, cutting off from baptism the promises proper to baptism, conveys and transfers them elsewhere?" (IV, XIX, 8). Calvin calls confirmation a manifest insult against baptism because it "obscures, indeed abolishes, its function" (*ibid.*). The significance of this contention, which touches directly upon the number of sacraments, cannot be overestimated. According to Calvin, Rome views baptism as an incidental event, which to be sure infuses supernatural grace but which cannot function decisively in the struggles of life, whereas Paul in Romans 6 indicates precisely the efficacy and development of the new life against the background of baptism. It is usually said that Rome esteems baptism more highly than did the Reformation, because it sees in baptism the cause of regeneration; but in the time of the Reformation itself we see the actual situation more profoundly, with Calvin reproaching Rome for seriously underestimating baptism in its doctrine of the sacraments as a whole, and of penance in particular.[54]

For Calvin speaks of penance as well as confirmation in this

---

54. *Inst.*, IV, XIX, 17. Cf. Bavinck, *Geref. Dog.*, IV, 471.

connection. Not only does he urge that penance cannot be based on a special promise, but he also rejects the concept of "the second plank after shipwreck" with these words: "As if baptism were wiped out by sin, and is not rather to be recalled to the memory of the sinner whenever he thinks of forgiveness of sins, so that from it he may gather himself together, take courage, and confirm his faith that he will obtain the forgiveness of sins, which has been promised him in baptism!" (IV, XIX, 17). Is not baptism the sacrament of penance, Calvin asks, since the New Testament speaks of the baptism of repentance for the remission of sins? We touch here upon the core of the conflict over the number of sacraments. Rome was not convinced by Calvin's argument and it continued to see baptism as an infusion of supernatural grace that could be lost and that therefore could not have the universal and enduring significance that it had with Calvin. When determining the number of sacraments, Rome could not help thinking in this category of "supernaturalness." Grace was seen as the grace of infusion, as *gratia infusa,* whereby all attention was directed toward the sacramental transformation of man to a supernatural life. It was a matter of possession of grace that could be lost again. And where grace was preserved, the issue was the augmentation of that treasure of grace.

But Rome paid too dearly for the beauty and harmony of its doctrine: for she reduced the significance of baptism while still praising it as the cause of regeneration. The profound contrast can be indicated most clearly in this connection by reminding ourselves of the Reformed pronouncement regarding baptism, in which Calvin's conviction received its pregnant expression: "But baptism is not only useful as long as the water is on us and we receive the water, but also for the whole span of our lives" (Conf., Art. 34).

All this indicates sufficiently clearly that the question about the number of sacraments is not just a question about number, but about the nature of the sacraments. The Roman Catholic number (seven sacraments) is connected indissolubly with the concept of the infusion of supernatural grace, which belongs to the essence of the sacrament. Hence, also, the number (seven) came to be fixed only through a process of doctrinal development, not immediately. As this development continued, the need was felt to see all of life encompassed in the grip of supernatural grace. The sacraments of penance and confirmation, especially, find their deepest origin in this.[55]

It is therefore quite understandable that Protestant polemics was aimed primarily against the continued necessity for renewed infusion of grace. Bavinck speaks in this connection of the uncertainty with this number seven, which suggests that sanctifying grace can always be lost again.[56] He focuses upon the concept of renewal: there is "no separate grace needed in confirmation, penance, and extreme unction, for through Word, baptism, and the Lord's Supper man receives all the grace he needs in life and death, for time and eternity."

Over against this multiplicity of sacraments stands the austerity of the Reformed doctrine of the sacraments. At first there had been some uncertainty in the "counting" of the sacraments, among the Lutherans[57] as well as among the Reformed; but to both it became increasingly evident that they should return to the clear institution of Christ: baptism and the Lord's Supper. Rome charged that this meant a tremendous impoverishment and reduction, and placed over against it the enrichment of all of human life, stage by stage, through supernatural grace. The Reformers countered, however, that in their austerity they were manifesting a new appreciation of the sacraments of God. The problem of the number of sacraments cannot be solved by appealing to harmony and beauty, but only from the scriptural account of their institution in the context of Christ's historical work of redemption. Rome's solution, on the other hand, rested upon an antithesis between "nature" and "supernature," an antithesis that makes a true solution impossible.

The Roman Catholic concept of grace must be drastically changed if the continuous connection of the sacraments with grace as God's goodwill is to be re-established. Rome also knows, of course, that God's grace is *favor Dei*, but she came increasingly to stress the infusion of supernatural grace. That is why the sacrament of penance was founded on the insufficiency of baptism,

55. Cf. the remark of Elderenbosch on this arbitrariness. "The comparison that confirmation is related to baptism as the growth of life to birth is not satisfactory; growth continues also after the seventh year, but confirmation is administered only once." P. Elderenbosch, *De oplegging der handen*, 1953, p. 93.
56. Bavinck, *Geref. Dog.*, IV, 473.
57. Luther and Melanchthon sometimes still called absolution a sacrament (cf. *Geref. Dog.*, IV, 469).

and why it became necessary again and again to receive new "grace." And that is also the basis of some very important decisions in the controversy about the number of sacraments. These decisions affected not only the five added sacraments, but also and simultaneously those two others which Rome and the Reformation had in common. The conflict over the number of sacraments was a conflict over the nature of grace.

* * *

The whole controversy can finally be summarized by saying that for Rome, with its multiplicity of sacraments, the sacrament becomes more and more a "mystery."[58] Roman Catholic sacramentology culminates in its vision of this mystery, and precisely here we see how seriously the New Testament idea of mystery has become obscured. To be sure, Rome emphasized fully that the mysteries of the sacraments became "possible" and real only through the one historical mystery of salvation; but the manner in which these mysteries receive a place poses a serious threat to the unique significance of the one great *mysterion*. That is why, later on, we shall have to discuss fully the relation between the offering of the cross and the mass. Once again we have the problem of reduplication, or representation, or repetition. Because the sacraments are interpreted as ever renewed infusions of grace, they acquire their character as mystery. The Reformation in contrast emphasizes the involvement of the sacrament with *the* "mystery." In ,that acknowledgment lies the only defense against the autonomatizing of the sacrament as a mystery.

When the sacrament is raised to autonomy, it cannot help becoming a mystery. Even though it is called an application and effect of the great *mysterion*, it displays its full efficacy only as it is carried into history, into the history of all times. That is why the controversy repeatedly focused upon the interpretation of the relation between *mysterion* and sacrament. It certainly is no accident, for example, that when the Reformers raised the important question regarding the essence of penance they placed the sacrament of penance in antithetical opposition to the preaching of the gospel.[59] No matter how much Rome praises and

---

58. Cf. F. Delekat, "Methodenkritische und dogmatische Probleme angesichts der gegenwärtigen Exegese der N.T. Abendmahlsworte," *EvT*, 1953, p. 407.
59. Denz. 913.

appreciates the preaching of the gospel,[60] the shadow of the autonomous mystery as *causa gratiae* falls over the function and meaning of the Word and of the preaching of God's Word. Grossouw admits that since the Reformation the efficacy of the preached Word of God has retreated somewhat to the background in the Catholic mind, and he judges this to be one of the fatal results of reaction and polemic.[61] But it is clear that this is not the whole explanation; the place of the Word and of preaching was crowded to the background not merely because of reaction but because of the Roman Catholic understanding of the sacraments.

It was the idea of "mystery" that pushed the Word back. The sacramental reality surrounding the mystery of the eucharist automatically threatened the primary significance of the divine communication to man. For partaking believers, the involvement of the mystery with the communication of the gospel became vague when they were immediately confronted in the sacraments with the reality of salvation; and in theology it also became quite evident that the sacrament threatened the preaching of the New Testament mystery, which more and more lost its relation to the Word. That is why the relation between Word and sacrament for Roman Catholic theology is fundamentally different from the one for Reformed theology.[62]

To be sure, in our time there are many discussions by Roman Catholics about the nature of the mystery in the present, the sacramental mystery; but in these discussions it becomes evident that, although various interpretations of the sacramental mystery have been advanced, there are serious objections to Casel's interpretation of the "presence of the mysteries,"[63] and there is adherence to a real mystery added alongside the mystery of the New Testament. This added mystery is an effect of the sacraments proper, for the sacraments effect what they signify, in the

---

60. See also the encyclical *Humani generis redemptionem* by Benedictus XV (June 15, 1917) regarding the preaching of the Word of God.

61. W. K. M. Grossouw, *Antwoord op het herderlijk schrijven*, 1959, p. 55.

62. Especially Grossouw has tried to explain that according to Rome Word and sacrament are not opposed to each other, but that they are closely linked. See his articles about "Woord en Sacrament" in *Het Schild*, XXVII, Nos. 2-5.

63. See especially G. Söhngen, *Der Wesensaufbau des Mysteriums*, 1938, pp. 10f., 13, 29 ("Die einmalige Tatsächlichkeit des Mysteriums in der Geschichte").

full sense of the word.[64] And as long as this reduplication re-mains, one will discover that the relation between Word and sacrament is immediately affected by it, and that in the disturb-ance of this relationship the shadows fall over the reconciling power of the suffering and dying of Christ. That is why the con-troversy about the relation between Word and sacrament will not only deal with the five special Roman Catholic sacraments, but will also involve the whole doctrine of the sacraments — including baptism and the Lord's Supper — and that, conversely, the latter issue will automatically lead to the one about the relation between Word and sacrament and to the no less impor-tant question about the efficacy and effect of the sacraments.

64. Söhngen says that the discussion within the Church regarding the doctrine of the mystery "is not a polemic against the doctrine of the mystery, but a difference of opinion about the comprehensibility of the mystery" (*op. cit.,* p. 37).

CHAPTER THREE

WORD AND SACRAMENT

A S WE TURN to the problem of the relation between Word and sacrament, we find ourselves at the very center of the whole doctrine of the sacraments, for here we encounter the question about the "primary" and "secondary" words often used to indicate that the Reformed doctrine of the sacraments is dangerously one-sided because too often it has called the sacraments secondary while regarding the Word as primary. Rather, it is said, we should recognize the equality of Word and sacrament.

It is true that the words "primary" and "secondary" can lead one to underestimate the sacraments. If the sacraments are secondary in the sense of being less important, one may infer that possibly they could even be dispensed with altogether without resulting in serious damage. This is clearly not the case, nor is this what the churches of the Reformation meant when they called the sacraments "secondary." It is necessary, therefore, to reflect on the relation between Word and sacrament if we do not want to call the sacraments secondary in a degrading sense.

It cannot be denied that the Reformers did not simply place Word and sacrament side by side as equals. They always emphasized that the relation was of a special sort, which they described in many ways. The Heidelberg Catechism teaches, for instance, that the sacraments are visible signs and seals that render the promise of the gospel more understandable. This pronouncement begins with the promise, and adds the sacraments to it for the specific purpose of shedding light upon that promise.[1] It is striking that the Catechism always associates Word and sacrament closely, and never sets one against the other. Question 67 speaks of what Word and sacrament have in common, namely, that they

---

1. Cf. Q. 67. Cf. also the admonition and the confirmation through baptism (Q. 69) and through the Lord's Supper (Q. 75).

direct our belief to Christ's offering at the cross. But though they have something in common, they are nevertheless different. Question 65 says that the Holy Spirit effects belief in our hearts through the preaching of the gospel, and that he strengthens this belief through the use of the sacraments. There is a certain relation between Word and sacrament. In Article 33 of the Confession of Faith the sacraments are spoken of as seals of the promise, which God has added to the Word of the gospel.[2] Such a description we find often in the early Reformed confessions, along with a reference to what the Word and the sacraments have in common.[3] Regarding the sacrament of baptism we are told that it serves us "as a witness" that God will forever be our God, being a gracious Father unto us.[4] God gives us something to understand in baptism. Baptism signifies something, it points at something. In Article 35 the Lord's Supper is mentioned in connection with the nourishment and support of those whom he has already incorporated in his Church. It is also said of the Lord's Supper that God has ordained it to support the spiritual and heavenly life, with the living bread that is represented in the Lord's Supper: the earthly and visible bread is a sacrament of his body, and the wine is a sacrament of his blood.

The "pointing" character of the sacraments is thus accentuated in many ways. It is because they point to something other than themselves that the sacraments are so profoundly significant. The question arises now whether this does not precisely indicate the exact parity of the sacraments and the Word. Does not this "pointing" character imply their absolute equality? This is a central problem in the relation between Word and sacrament.

When the confessions begin to specify what the Word and the sacraments have in common, they mention that they both are instruments used by the Holy Spirit, that they both must be accepted in faith, and that they do not cease to be that to which God ordained them, even if man in unbelief rejects Word and sacrament.[5] Evidently, however, this does not lead to the conclusion that the Word and the sacraments are absolute equivalents. The Hungarian Confession affirms that the Word can be without the sacraments, while the sacraments cannot be without

---

2. J. N. Bakhuizen van den Brink, *De Ned. Belijdenisschriften*, 1940, p. 125.
3. Cf. Ungarisches Bekenntnis (1562) in Müller, *Bekenntnisschriften*, p. 415.
4. *Ibid.*, p. 413.
5. *Ibid.*, p. 414.

the Word.[6] The intention thereby is not to devalue the sacraments, but rather to show that they are divine additions, confirming and sealing the word of promise, which they presuppose. It is sheer rationalism to conclude from this relation that the sacrament is not really very significant because it is not a new revelation of God and because it is added to the Word; such reasoning fails altogether to do justice to the divine institution of the sacrament. The Genevan Catechism speaks on the one hand of the sacraments as *secunda organa,* but on the other hand, the question whether the sacraments are dispensable is answered with a definite No. There is even mention of a disdain for Christ, and of the extinguishing of the Holy Spirit in him who disdains these *secunda organa.*[7]

The Reformed confessions evidently presuppose that the sacraments can be "additions" to the Word and yet receive all the honor due them. Indeed, if we detach the words "primary" and "secondary" from their popular connotation of "important" and "relatively unimportant," one can say that the Reformed doctrine of the sacraments *has* wanted to maintain the "primary" character of the Word, and, in doing so, has confessed the secondary, additional character of the sacrament.

Some serious objections have been raised against this position in our time, on the ground that Word and sacrament are parts of the created order in precisely the same sense and on the same level. The Word is audible in preaching, and it is visible in the sacraments, just as the tradition of the Church has always indicated in the formulas *verbum audibile* and *verbum visibile.* It would seem to follow that the one "word" (the visible) may not be made subservient to the other (audible) word of preaching.[8] Van der Leeuw, especially, has said emphatically that the Word may not be placed above the "sensory" sacrament, because man's speaking is as much a product of creation as bread, wine, and water.[9] They all possess the same possibilities in the service of God,[10] and there is therefore no reason to call baptism and the Lord's Supper sacraments but not the Word. There is also no reason to elevate the "Word" to the side of God and to speak

6. *Ibid.,* p. 416.
7. *Ibid.,* p. 147.
8. *Kerk en Eerdedienst,* I, 254.
9. G. van der Leeuw, *Liturgiek,* p. 51.
10. *Ibid.*

mystically about it.[11] Thus, word and sacrament are placed side by side because they are both creaturely indicators of something else.

It is clear that this kind of "commonness" is altogether different from what the Reformed confessions had in mind. If we accept Van der Leeuw's view, we cannot go on to distinguish the sacraments from the Word in the Reformed way, since this distinction is directly based upon the formula, quoted by Van der Leeuw, that the Word is added *to the element.*[12] In this formula the presupposed word of promise is already implied — a word that simultaneously selects and qualifies the sacraments themselves, as we have indicated when we treated the number of sacraments. Moreover, Van der Leeuw himself cites all sorts of sacramental acts that are coupled "with a word that confers upon them their decisive character."[13] Thus by implication he acknowledges the distinction between Word and sacrament, because this added sacrament can acquire decisive significance only by virtue of the Word and the institution by God. If there is no explanatory and designating Word, there is only a multiplicity of earthly elements which in themselves are meaningless. One may, of course, attempt to find analogies and to select certain created elements as indicating signs, but all such signs will lack divine authority.

When the Second Helvetic Confession speaks of the relation between Word and sacrament, it emphasizes strongly what the elements *become* through the Word.[14] That "becoming" is the key to the specific relation between Word and sacrament. Evidently the Word and the sacraments may not be placed side by side, for the signs become sacraments only by virtue of the Word of God. The Reformed confessions also say that the elements are "consecrated" by the Word. That does not mean that the elements are changed or transubstantiated, but rather, this term (which Rome also employs for the "consecration") is used to indicate the very important fact that the elements become seals

---

11. *Sacramentstheologie,* p. 183.
12. Quoted from Augustine: "accedit verbum ad elementum et fit sacramentum, etiam ipsum tamquam visibile verbum" (Augustine, *In Joh. tract.* 80, 3). Cf. Van der Leeuw, *Sacramentstheologie,* p. 183.
13. Van der Leeuw, *loc. cit.*
14. "Nam verbo Dei fiunt, quae antea non fuerant, sacramenta." "Consecrantur enim verbo et sanctificata esse ostenditus ab eo, qui instituit" (Müller, *Bekenntnisschriften,* p. 209).

by virtue of divine grace, and thus receive their functions in the acts of God. As signs they become very important; they can no longer be regarded as meaningless and unimportant "symbols." This relation, which by virtue of divine revelation makes the sign something added to the word of promise, is nullified if we simply place Word and sacrament side by side.[15]

Neither, to be sure, is the preaching of the Word something purely mystical, as Van der Leeuw rightly maintains. It is not a *vox angelica,* or a *vox divina* that comes to us without human mediation. In the preaching of the Word, God makes use of the human word and speech, but in such a way that Paul can be grateful that the Thessalonians have accepted the word of preaching "not as the word of men, but, as it is in truth, the word of God" (I Thess. 2:13). No doubt God has chosen, for this purpose of revelation, from among a multiplicity of men and words; but this is not the same as taking present, created elements and stamping them with his words as part of his revelation. It is precisely the uniqueness of the preached word, that it is immediately based upon and comes out of divine revelation. Nothing above this sovereign revelation, which employs the possibilities of human language, is needed to make the preached word authoritative. There is only reason for thanksgiving when men accept this word as the Word of God. When the false prophet says, together with the true prophet: "Thus saith the Lord," all that Jeremiah can do is to go and wait for what God will do. Nothing of any other sort can qualify the true prophecy as true prophecy.

With the sacraments, however, the situation is totally different. They *are* authenticated by something else, namely, the Word. That is why the consideration which places word, bread, wine, and water on one level as "sensory" elements, and which thus places Word and sacrament side by side as equals, is fundamentally incorrect. When the Reformation made a sharp distinction between Word and sacrament, the motivation was not to elevate the preaching of the Word to mystical or spiritual or nonhuman status, in contrast to the earthly and "sensory" elements of the sacraments. Rather, the motive lay in the fact that the Word of God is conveyed uniquely by speech. This Word of God did not qualify human words uttered, as revelation after they were uttered, but through divine inspiration it called forth

15. Cf. the trenchant critique by O. Noordmans, *Liturgie,* pp. 45ff.

precisely these words. And that makes it impossible to equalize the Word and the sacrament. Van Oyen saw the weakness of this line of thinking very clearly when he wrote, concerning the remark that preaching is also sacramental, that it "indicates the typical short-circuiting of this broad sacramentalism." Those who call it an error "to appreciate the word other than as a piece of sensory production like taste, smell, or some other part of that which is created" are likewise mistaken.[16]

The Reformed have never adopted this mode of thinking; they have seen clearly the primary significance of the human word in the service of divine speaking, and their sacramental concept was conformed to that. With Augustine they have spoken in this connection of the Word that was added to the sacrament. This Word chose the elements and thus made them an affirmation of the word of promise. One may not, therefore, draw hasty conclusions from the expression "audible and visible word," as if this negated the difference in order between Word and sacrament. One should not, as Noordmans has so correctly pointed out,[17] subsume the audible and the visible "logically" under one abstract denominator. It would still be necessary to grant a peculiar, independent speech to the sacrament, and this leads almost inevitably to natural theology and even to pansacramentalism. That is why Golterman is correct when he speaks in this connection of "a disregard of the concept of sacrament," because the sacrament certainly does contain a certain act with specific material elements, which act can be linked with "the word" only by means of a very forced construction (e.g., the using of vocal cords or lips, or, in the listener, of the auditory organs).[18] The co-ordination of Word and sacrament in this sense yields no new, fruitful insight into the structure of salvation; it even makes for more difficulties, which certainly will not contribute to a profounder appreciation of the sacraments.

For now, to say it with Golterman, "the aspect of choice"

16. H. van Oyen, "Op weg naar een nieuwe sacramentstheologie," *Kerk en Eerdedienst,* I, 263.
17. Noordmans says with respect to Calvin: "When the Reformer says with Augustine that the sacrament is *verbum visibile,* he does not mean to do away with the difference between Word and Sacrament" (*Liturgie,* p. 50).
18. W. F. Golterman, *Liturgiek,* 1951, p. 80; cf. J. Koopmans in his discussion of the liturgy of Van der Leeuw: "Onder het Woord," *Verz. Opstellen,* 1949, p. 350.

is lacking.[19] The sacrament becomes opaque in its meaning, and that is why many who begin with the equality of Word and sacrament will later on begin to introduce somehow an element of "choice" and selection. On the other hand, those who acknowledge from the very beginning of their reflection that the Word of institution qualifies and selects, and that therein the efficacy and the significance of the sacramental signs are implied, will also understand what the Reformation meant by the *secunda organa*. In this *secunda* the Reformers harked back to God's revelation, which was confirmed and sealed by the signs. And because the Word of the gospel is important, so also is the sacrament. It does not come as a secondary — in the sense of unimportant — addition, but it becomes important because it is fully directed toward the richness of the Word and toward the trustworthiness of that Word. The secondary sacrament is, because of its absolute directedness toward the primary Word, absolutely important.

The question now arises about the significance of adding the sacrament to the Word. Must we accept this addition without understanding it, or is it possible to apprehend something of its meaning? The Reformed confessions have clearly answered this question. They point out that the meaning of the sacrament cannot be deduced from the insufficiency or lack of clarity of the Word, but that it has to do with our insight into the clear and powerful gospel. According to the Heidelberg Catechism, it is a matter of man's being better able to understand (Q. 66), of a promise that Christ will wash us with his blood and Spirit as certainly as we are washed outwardly with water (Q. 69), of signs and seals (Q. 66), of pledges and indications (Q. 73), while it is said with respect to the Lord's Supper that the issue therein is that we should trust and believe that we belong to this covenant of grace. In the prayer of the form for the Lord's Supper it is asked that we may be nourished with the heavenly bread, and that we shall not doubt "that Thou shalt be forever our gracious Father." But precisely because the sacraments are added to the promise of God, the question arises as to the basis for this addition. Article 33 of the Confession of Faith gives a clear answer, in which we read of the pledges of God's willingness and grace toward us, to nourish and support our belief, and added because God took into account our coarseness and

19. Golterman, *Liturgiek*, p. 85; cf. p. 84: "Sacrament depends on the choice of God."

weakness. In other words, a relation is indicated here between the addition of the sacraments and a certain condition of the believers, namely, their weakness.

Van der Leeuw, especially, has objected seriously to this connection. He calls it a "fatal, pedagogical explanation of the sacrament," and attempts to refute it by saying: "as if we would understand the material better than the immaterial"[20] — a view that he finds already in Calvin. This criticism is very unjust, however, because the Reformed doctrine of the sacraments does not rest upon a fundamental contrast between hearing and seeing, and between material and spiritual, but rather stresses our weakness, doubt, unbelief, and smallness of faith. It does not disqualify the hearing of the word and accordingly urge that we need a better means of comprehension; rather, it sees the sacrament as a unique addition, a second after the first, which together with the first directs us toward the single goal of fulness of faith.

There is a "logical" criticism of this view that supposedly proves that the sacraments are superfluous. Calvin, who gave this argument full attention, calls it "a dilemma more subtle than solid." He says: "We either know, they say, or do not know that the word of God which precedes the sacrament is the true will of God. If we know it, we learn nothing new from the sacrament, which comes after. If we do not know it, the sacrament (whose whole force rests in the word) also will not teach it." (*Inst.*, IV, XIV, 5). In response Calvin does not impugn the trustworthiness of the Word of God, but he does reject the conclusion that the sacraments are superfluous, because this conclusion runs counter to what God has actually done. And it is on that basis that he endeavors to understand the meaning of this addition. As far as Calvin is concerned, the acuteness of human reasoning is overcome by the wisdom, the will, and the mercy of God.

It is important to realize that the reasoning which Calvin opposes is not valid. If it were, then God could never use means for the strengthening of faith. For example, we would have to reject the plain teaching of Scripture in Hebrews 6:13, which speaks of God's promise to Abraham, which he has confirmed with an oath. He has made a covenant with Abraham with an oath, "that by two immutable things, in which it is impossible for God to lie, we may have a strong encouragement, who have fled for refuge to lay hold of the hope set before us" (6:18).

---

20. Van der Leeuw, *Sacramentstheologie,* p. 247.

Even though it does not mention the sacraments, this part of Scripture can teach us much about the problem that occupies us at the moment. The speaking of God in the promise is taken here as point of departure; then, by God's oath, it is placed in the light of his immutability (Heb. 6:17), and of the confirmation (6:16), and of the end of all contradiction. The trustworthiness of God is not an issue here; the author says in the same context that it is impossible for God to lie (6:18). That is why the confirmation in question is not applied to something that in itself is unstable and untrustworthy. Let us put it this way: the "addition" does not presuppose the untrustworthiness of the word of promise, but rather intends to emphasize precisely the trustworthiness of the promise. Van Oyen has pointed out that Philo and the Talmud have wondered how God can be said to swear an oath, whose every word is truthful, and they concluded that this is only for the sake of our weakness, since we sometimes forget that God is not like us human beings, who cannot do without that oath.[21] Indeed, in God's swearing an oath we meet with a confirmation of what is already in itself fixed and exalted.[22]

Calvin has said that this passage contains "a special comfort, that God, who cannot lie, and not being content with His promise, adds the oath to that promise."[23] Calvin wants to make it clear that God, for the sake of the trustworthiness of his promise, adds an oath in order to end all contradiction. Men answer, according to the epistle, by that which is greater (Heb. 6:18); but God swears by himself, in order thus to lay the foundation for complete certainty and to fill man's heart with comfort. In the oath he guarantees his promise.[24]

Here there are striking analogies with the sacrament added to the Word. The sacrament is also a "second" way, which neither denies nor devaluates the trustworthiness of the first. On the

21. H. van Oyen, *Christus de Hogepriester*, p. 109.
22. Schneider (*TWNT*, V, 183) says that the epistle to the Hebrews adheres to the exegetical givens "and does not realize that such a view of the N. T. concept of God is actually impossible." It is not at all clear, however, why the latter should be the case, for the secret of the swearing of this oath lies precisely in God's condescending goodness, in the assurance that stands over against hesitation and uncertainty (cf. p. 184).
23. Calvin, *Comm.* on Heb. 6:18: "From this we have strong encouragement in that God who cannot lie when He speaks is not content merely to promise but gives His sworn Word.
24. Otto Nichel, *Der Brief an die Hebräer*, 1949, p. 157.

contrary: the second has no other meaning than to point to the absolute trustworthiness of the first. What Van der Leeuw calls a fatal, pedagogical explanation refers to nothing less than the divine pedagogy, which *in* the "second way" is directed to the primary word of promise. The "making better understandable" does not mean, therefore, that we favor the eye above the ear, or seeing above hearing, or that man's heart is more receptive to the promise of God through seeing than through hearing. Rather, the addition of the sacrament to the word shows us with undeniable clarity that we can depend on the promise, although both the Word and the sacrament can only be understood in faith. The point is not the power of the evidence that would be rendered by the visible signs in distinction from the *verbum audibile* — for the signs that are visible have been qualified and consecrated and have become signs because of the Word — but rather that in this way God secures the certainty of his promise in our hearts. Only through the power of the Spirit are the visible signs subservient to God's salvation and to the certainty of that salvation — and not simply because they are visible. Hence their visibility does not at all render the Word itself superfluous, any more than the swearing of an oath makes God's word of promise superfluous. And since the sacraments are therefore not to be understood without the Word of God, we understand why the confessions emphasize the involvement of the added sacraments with our subjectivity, and why Calvin also speaks of our "dullness."[25]

Calvin has attempted to give expression to this relation between the Word and the sacrament added to it. He says, for example, that the sacraments are exhibited under corporeal symbols "because we are carnal," and God "testifies His benevolence and love toward us more expressly by the sacraments than He does by His word."[26] One may ask whether such expressions clearly reveal the relation between Word and sacrament, and whether this does not give the impression that the visible sacrament is after all a more expressive revelation than the Word. One can better say that the emphasis of the sacrament is precisely to be located in the twofoldedness of Word and sacrament together, with the intent that our eyes should be opened to the emphasis of the expressed word of promise. Again, the image of the pillars

25. *Inst.*, IV, XIV, 6.
26. *Ibid.*

placed under the edifice can give the impression that the visible sacrament is more meaningful than the spoken word. It must be maintained, therefore, that this relation between Word and sacrament must exclusively be seen in the light of "better understanding," because the sacrament contains not a single element that could place the trustworthiness of the Word in question. The addition of the sacrament is not a critique of the mode of God's spoken revelation, but a critique of man's insensitive, unreceptive, resisting and contradicting heart.

The significance of the sacrament lies in the divine act in which God directs our attention again to the trustworthiness of his Word, upon which man can depend without fear and with great boldness.

When Noordmans emphatically maintains the difference between Word and sacrament, and when he defends the Word against every form of sacramentalism, he remarks that we must not look for that difference in the distinction between hearing and seeing, for then the real differences fade away.[27] He does not wish to approach the difference from the point of view of creation, but rather by making a spiritual distinction between Word and sacrament. It is difficult to see, however, how creation and "spiritual understanding" can be opposed to each other, since, after all, the normal creaturely-human is fully honored in the sacrament. Besides, Noordmans himself says that Word and sacrament must be distinguished "according to the will, wisdom, and mercy of God, who places His promises in a twofold manner in the hearts of His children." This does not make it necessary or even permissible to say that we must not speak of the difference between Word and sacrament from the point of view of creation, but rather of Pentecost. For with respect to the sacrament this contrast does not even begin to become visible, since the Spirit deals with the creaturely, and since, as Noordmans himself says, this takes place along the two ways of the hearing of the Word and of the visible sacrament. When Noordmans writes that the difference must be sought in the fact "that God's mercy reveals itself in various manners," this is perfectly correct; but it does not explain why the difference between hearing and seeing is not the crucial one.

Furthermore, Noordmans himself quotes Augustine, who

---

27. Noordmans, *Liturgie,* p. 53; cf. p. 54: "It is only a difference between eye and ear, and that would be practically the same in effect."

calls the sacrament "the visible word."[28] Precisely that twofoldedness to which Noordmans correctly directs our attention, creates
the opportunity to discount the difference between the audible
and the visible word. We actually find Noordmans making this
point when he says that God by means of a special grace confirms with sign and seal that he will not let the sinner perish
(p. 62). Noordmans' criticism is probably a reaction against
the type of approach that places eye and ear (as abstract anthropological givens) side by side, and on that basis misconstrues the
relation between Word and sacrament. This appears, for example, in his criticism of the report on *Kerkopbouw,* when he
reproaches it for reducing the difference between Word and
sacrament to the difference between eye and ear (p. 56). Evidently he wants to oppose the idea that salvation enters our
existence by two different gates. But there is another way to honor
the duality of audible and visible, namely, by pointing out that
God in that second way sends us the confirmation of his salvation
as a divine accentuation of the trustworthy Word of promise. So
understood, it is no longer necessary to oppose creation to Pentecost. Man can thus keep his eye directed toward the content of
the promise, and on its trustworthiness. That is actually also
Noordmans' view when in his description of the sacraments he
incorporates the element of visibility: "For that reason God
writes these promises down for His children, so that in fear and
need they will look at it" (p. 64), an image that he uses following Augustine and Calvin: God's promises are portrayed "as
in a picture."[29]

The twofoldedness of the Word and sacrament in the Church
of Jesus Christ can only be understood in humility. This twofoldedness does not cast a shadow over the trustworthiness of God's
words; rather, it is directed *in concreto* against the obscuring of
this trustworthiness in man's heart. God does not withdraw into
impenetrable darkness in the face of this obscuring, but he
evokes trust in the midst of smallness of belief and the temptation of man's heart. That is why it is not from us as point of
departure, but from God that the sacrament becomes the way to
a song of praise for God's trustworthiness. The words of Psalm 62,
though spoken in a different context, may also be remembered

28. *Ibid.,* p. 51.
29. Cf. *Inst.,* IV, XIV, 6 and 5.

here: "God has spoken once, Twice have I heard this, That power belongeth unto God" (v. 11).

In the twofoldedness we are confronted with the unity and the simplicity of God's sure salvation. That is why in every sacrament the confession of sin is implied, for it is sin that brings forth questions in the presence of the evident clarity of the Word, and that surrounds God's trustworthiness with objections. In the sacrament we are confronted with these resistances of the human heart. The criticism from systematic theology, which acutely but invalidly concludes that the sacraments are superfluous, is not undone by another systematics, but by God's condescending goodness, which not only confirms his promise to Abraham with an oath, but which in the continuing temptation and weakness of the Church promotes in a divine manner, and then shows us *anew,* what he has already *said,* so that all contradiction may be ended and we may firmly believe that we belong to that Covenant which stands as a rock.

CHAPTER FOUR

THE EFFICACY OF THE SACRAMENTS

THE REFORMATION has frequently been reproached for reducing the sacraments to mere symbols, having only psychological effects but not actually conveying "grace." Their effect is subjective, depending on the recipient's remembering and believing, not on the sacrament as such. Since for the Reformation the way to salvation was through belief, the opponents concluded that no place was left for concretely effective sacraments.[1] Especially in view of the message of the New Testament, this was seen as a serious impoverishment of the doctrine of the sacraments. It was only to be expected, according to the critics, that the Reformers should allow the sacraments to retreat into the background, because in principle man was already fully justified by faith.[2]

It is clear that the famous dilemma between symbolism and realism, mentioned in Chapter I, plays an important role here as well. The critics have linked the symbolic view with ineffectiveness, even though they should have realized that their interpretation did not tally with the actual situation and that it was completely contradictory to what Calvin maintained so emphatically over against spiritualism, namely, the significance and especially the efficacy of the sacraments.

Sometimes, however, it is admitted that this interpretation does not do full justice to the Reformation. For instance, in 1952 the following thesis was posed at the University of Nijmegen: "It is contrary to the form for the Lord's Supper to speak, as in the Dutch Reformed Church and the Reformed Churches in Holland, of a symbolical significance of the ceremony of the

1. Cf. Bartmann, *Dogm.*, II, 212: "The Reformers had no place in their system of *sola fide* for outwardly efficacious means of grace. The sacrament can at most be an outward guarantee or proclamation of forensic justice."
2. Cf. Consensus Tigurinus, Art. II.

Lord's Supper. Several expressions (in the form) point to a definite awareness of reality."[3] This thesis attempts to remove, or at least to soften, the contrast between symbolism (Reformation) and realism (Rome). Evidently, the author of this thesis has been impressed by the fact that the form very clearly speaks of "realities." His phraseology ("a definite awareness of reality") is, however, too vague, for the form and the confession articulate a positive conviction regarding an unmistakable and very important reality.

If "symbolical" means that the sacraments are inactive *nuda signa*, without real efficacy, then the Reformed doctrine of the sacraments can certainly not be called symbolical.[4] This is especially evident in the Reformed polemic against spiritualism, which emphasizes the work of the Holy Spirit apart from "exterior," earthly, corporeal means. Spiritualism maintains that these means are "unproportioned" for the high and sacred acts of God.[5] Against this view the form, and also the confession, express a profound concern with reality, when, for example, the form for the Lord's Supper mentions the true communion with Christ, and the prayer asks that we may be "nourished and refreshed with His true body and blood, yea with Him, true God and man, the only heavenly bread. . . ." This shows clearly that "symbol" is not being opposed to "reality."

The symbol-reality antithesis obscures the significance of the sacraments in the Reformed sense. Bavinck once wrote that the peculiar characteristic of the Reformed sacramental doctrine is often not understood.[6] He does not say of whom he is thinking, but he certainly could have cited those Roman Catholic and modern Protestant views that fail to see the profound vision of reality in the Reformed doctrine of the sacraments. Without elaborately discussing the Lord's Supper at this point, we want to say that the problem of sacramental reality can be understood only by abandoning completely the above-mentioned dichotomy between symbol and reality.

The dispute regarding the reality aspect and the efficacy of the sacraments is most clearly revealed in Van de Pol's phenomenological approach to the differences between the Reforma-

3. J. A. Micklinghoff, *Openbaring en Geloofsgenade*, thesis 15.
4. Cf. H. Ordning, "Symbol und Wirklichkeit," *TLZ*, LXXIII (1948), 133.
5. Cf. H. Urner, "Die Taufe bei Caspar Schwenckfeld," *TLZ*, 1948.
6. H. Bavinck, "Calvijns leer over het avondmaal," in *Kennis en leven*, 1922. The article is from *De Vrije Kerk*, 1887.

tion and Rome. He does this in terms of the distinction between _belief_ and _reality_. With regard to the sacrament, he says
that the Reformation does not admit to a real ontic-sacramental
grace which is infused in a unique way. Insofar as the Reformation deals with reality, it is a reality that exists only for belief
and through belief. But this view, says Van de Pol, implies a
devaluation of the reality of salvation — a criticism that he has
continued to maintain in spite of objections from various quar-
ters.[7] Evidently, Van de Pol discerns a weakening of the mystic-
ontic in the "for and through belief." His criticism is important
because he recognized clearly the great significance of the _sola
fide_ in every Reformed pronouncement regarding the reality of
salvation, and it must be evaluated in the light of his own interpretation of the reality of salvation.

For the Catholic, revelation means "that a Reality of higher
order has come to manifest itself in time and in the forms of
corporeal reality in a manner which man cannot understand."[8]
There is an "incursion" of the Reality "in the ontic sense, in
the midst of our earthly reality." But Reformed Christians, says
Van de Pol, see things quite differently. "The Church is a natural communion of believers; the believers have not been en-
riched with a new, supernatural life through baptism; the
presence of Christ in the Lord's Supper is not an ontic presence as belonging to 'our' reality, it is not a real presence which
as such enters 'our' reality under visible forms so that it may
expect an act of adoration from the side of the believers; the
sacraments are not exterior signs of a supernatural communication of grace." Rather, our reality remains unchanged, according to the Reformed insight. To be sure, there is belief, the
act of belief, but this is directed toward God's Word (p. 229).
Through that Word the believer knows of a new relation toward
God, of God's love, of reconciliation and justification; but all
this does not concern an ontic reality, but something that is
preached and as such must be accepted through belief. This,
says Van de Pol, shows up the cardinal difference between Rome
and the Reformation (p. 230). For the Reformation, the reality
is _relational_ (p. 231).

7. W. H. van de Pol, _Het Christelijk dilemma_, 1948; _Geloof en werkelijkheid
in het reformatorisch Protestantisme_, 1948; _Karakteristiek van het reformatorisch Christendom_, 1952.
8. Van de Pol, _Karakteristiek_, p. 228.

Van de Pol's view can be summarized in this word. He does not deny that the Reformed Christian speaks of "reality,"[9] but this reality is always seen in connection with belief and with the sacrament as seal of the Word that is preached. Word and sacrament are both "forms of preaching,"[10] and man participates in God's salvation if he performs the act of believing (p. 245). The sacrament as well as the Word proclaims salvation; "the received reality is none other, however, than the reality which is offered in the preached Word" (p. 245). The sacrament has no new, ontic reality, but it is a "pointer" to the Word. Van de Pol says that this is also the teaching of the confessions, as, for example, when Question 66 of the Heidelberg Catechism portrays the sacraments as signs and seals through which God's promise is confirmed. "They do not effect 'grace' in the ontic sense as infused supernatural *qualitas;* they effect and strengthen belief" (p. 247).

It cannot be denied that Van de Pol has pointed to essential elements in the Reformed sacramental doctrine, such as the close connection between belief and sacrament, and the relation between sacrament and promise. At the same time it is quite clear that Van de Pol has a completely different understanding of the reality of salvation. He seeks, but does not find, in the Reformation the reality that he considers essential for the revelation of God, namely, supernatural reality, which he usually defines as reality in the mystic-ontic sense. That is why, again and again, he contrasts word and revelation of reality. Because Christ has withdrawn himself from "our" reality until his return, "there is now no place on earth where Christ, as such belonging to 'our' reality, is present and efficacious so that we could and should adore Him in the same manner as the disciples did when they saw Him" (p. 224).

Van de Pol is looking for a different sort of reality from that of which the Reformation spoke, namely, the supernatural reality of Christ's continued, saving efficacy on earth. He believes in a reality that is daily and everywhere portrayed in the Church audibly, visibly, and tangibly: the continuation of the mystery of the incarnation, sacred Reality as such, in which the believer himself is taken up without the "continual intervention of the word" (p. 227). This last word makes it clear what the real

9. *Ibid.,* p. 243; cf. *Geloof en werkelijkheid,* p. 7.
10. *Karakteristiek,* p. 244.

issue is: the directness and immediacy of reality, of mystical reality. Van de Pol's criticism of Reformed sacramental doctrine can be fully understood in terms of this immediacy of the mystical which is ontic, and of the ontic which is mystical. For the Reformation there is also a real communion with Christ, but only in the sense of a communion through faith (p. 253). This is, however, a remarkable "but," when we think of Paul's word: "that Christ may dwell in your hearts through faith" (Eph. 3:17), where it is evident that the "through faith" does not at all minimize the reality of Christ's dwelling in our hearts.

Van de Pol recognizes aspects of reality in the form for the Lord's Supper, but even though he admits that in the nourishing and refreshing a "reality ... takes place in man's heart" (pp. 254ff.), and that this reality is even strongly emphasized, there is nevertheless no divine reality that comes to us in the ontic sense through the signs.[11] The gap between God and man is not really bridged.[12] There is nothing beyond the "through faith." And this, for Van de Pol, is the crucial point. Where no supernatural reality comes to us, and no supernatural grace is infused, there can be no ontic, actual Reality. The Word is always interposed.

It has become clear, after much discussion and clarification, that the real issue does not so much involve the confusing distinction between word and revelation of reality, as the relation between nature and supernature. Precisely because of his phenomenological approach, Van de Pol cannot — in view of his own emphasis on the reality aspect in the Reformation — maintain this contrast between word and reality without beginning to judge the Reformation from the Roman Catholic point of view.[13] And hence he cannot see the "reality" in the Reforma-

---

11. It is noteworthy in this connection that Van de Pol is of the opinion that the Canons of Dordt deviate from the Reformed confessions because they condemn the errors of those who teach "that in the true conversion of man no new powers or gifts can be infused by God into man's will." This is a strange view because the impression is given that only the Canons speak of the real efficacy of the Spirit in the hearts of believers. Could he *possibly* be of the opinion that the Reformation failed to do justice to the reality of the firstfruits of the Spirit? The distinction between the Canons and the other confessions is purely imaginary. Cf. my *Faith and Sanctification,* chap. IV, "The Genesis of Sanctification."

12. Cf. Van de Pol, *Karakteristiek,* p. 267.

13. Cf. R. Weel, "Waardering van de karakteristiek van het reformatorisch Christendom," *Studia Catholica,* Jan. 1953, p. 42 (on the phenomenological character of Van de Pol's *Karakteristiek*).

tion as actual reality, because it lacks supernatural character
in the Roman Catholic sense. The continuous intervention of
the Word confessed by the Reformation as a blessing detracts
from the mystical immediacy of sacramental grace.

For the Reformation, however, the formula "through faith"
did not imply a disregard for the reality of salvation; on the
contrary, it was the recognition of it. There can be no tension
between the reality of salvation in Christ and the "through
faith" as long as faith is directed absolutely and exclusively
toward that reality. That is why the Reformation stressed the
preaching of the Word and the administration of the sacraments as signs and seals of that Word; in this way faith encounters the reality of salvation, not as man's contribution to
the process of redemption, but as a resting in the reality of an
accomplished salvation and a communion with the living Lord.
Just as Paul did not challenge the reality aspect of salvation
when he wrote that we do not live by virtue of contemplation,
but by virtue of faith, so the Reformation did not deny this
reality aspect when it joyfully confessed the "intervention" of
the Word in the way to fulness of life in God. Hence the sacraments do not strengthen faith through an independent grow-
ing-process in human subjectivity, but through communion
with Christ. This is a different "reality," however, from the
infused "supernatural" grace of Roman Catholic sacramental
doctrine.

When the Reformers stressed the intervention of the Word,
they were concerned to eliminate a confusion between *belief*
and *beholding*. That is the reason why Van de Pol's phenomenological analysis of the cardinal difference between Rome
and the Reformation involves eschatology as well. Przywara
once said, in an unguarded moment, that the reality of Christ
in "our" reality is "almost a withdrawal of the Ascension." I
think that Van de Pol would object to this bold definition,
which originates from the directness and the immediacy of
Christ's "present" reality in the Church and the eucharist, as
a continuation, so to speak, of the incarnation. It must be
remembered, however, that Przywara did say "almost." Without this "almost" he would have robbed the ascension of Jesus
Christ of its significance. With the "almost," however, we see
that the boundaries set by the very fact of Christ's ascension
have not been definitely trespassed. It is well that this is so,
for otherwise there are real difficulties with the Scriptural teach-

ing concerning the "presence" of Jesus Christ at the end of time.

The call for "reality" is understandable, but it must always be critically examined. The real touchstone lies in the manner in which this reality is represented. Only within the boundaries of the doctrine of the ascension can one fruitfully reflect on the significance and the effect of the sacraments. Van de Pol's acknowledgment that in Reformed belief there is also a concern for "reality" may then form the point of departure for a still profounder reflection on the question wherein, according to the Reformed view, the effect of the sacraments exists. And we shall see in the center of the Reformed sacramental doctrine the conviction that we shall never be able to do without the "intervention" of the Word.

Historically, the most vigorous controversies about the effect of the sacraments have centered upon the Roman Catholic view that they work *ex opere operato*. It is important to understand the exact difference between this doctrine of the *opus operantum* and the Reformed doctrine that was opposed to it. From the Reformed side, the issue did not involve the efficacy of the sacraments at all, but rather, a totally different understanding of what this efficacy is. To see this clearly, we must examine what is meant by *opus operantum*.[14]

Reformed polemics makes it clear that *ex opere operato* was a crucial concept already in the sixteenth century. It was not merely a concept of technical theology, but a mode of expression that had been commonly used for a long time, and then had acquired official validity at the Council of Trent. For the anathema of Trent concerns those who deny that the sacraments contain the grace that they signify, who deny that they grant grace to those who do not place obstacles in the way,[15] and in addition, those who deny that grace is granted *ex opere operato* (on the basis of the work wrought), and who declare that belief in the divine promise is sufficient by itself to obtain grace.[16] We encounter this definition everywhere in official statements and in theological expositions, since the *opus operantum* has thus been officially determined.[17]

It has become clear that the intent of this definition was

14. See my article on *ex opere operato* in *GTT*, 1953. Cf. also Polman, *Onze Ned. Geloofsbelijdenis,* IV, 79ff.
15. Denz. 849.
16. Denz. 851.
17. Cf. the statement in the encyclical *Mediator Dei (Ecclesia docens),* p. 34.

to emphasize that the working of the sacraments is "objective," and does not depend in any way upon the recipient. The pope, for example, says of the sacraments: "These have therefore an 'objective' efficacy which truly makes our soul the participant in the divine life of Jesus Christ."[18] Not through our working, but through the working of God, are they efficacious.[19]

We now touch upon a central point, for it is undeniable that the Reformation has also placed great emphasis on this objectivity, as we shall see later. The Roman Catholics have often complained, however, that the Reformed camp has not understood the real meaning of *ex opere operato,* and that it has incorrectly given a magical interpretation to it. Furthermore, Reformed criticism of the *opus operantum* is seen as a violation of the objectivity of the sacraments, and as a clear symptom of a completely subjectivistic disposition, which caused the Reformation to make the sacraments dependent on the subjective belief of the recipient. Roman Catholics often emphasize infant baptism in this connection, which supposedly reveals even more clearly than other sacraments the objective and independent working of the sacraments.[20]

The intent of the formula *ex opere operato* is sometimes explained by contrasting it with *ex opere operantis,* which means an efficacy that comes from the belief of the recipient.[21] The sacraments do not work in that way. They are effective by virtue of the work wrought, objectively. This is what distinguishes the sacraments of the New Covenant from those of the Old Covenant. The latter worked *ex opere operantis,* while the sacraments of the New Covenant work *ex opere operato.* This also distinguishes the sacraments from the sacramentalia, whose working also depended upon the recipient.[22] The sacraments of the Old Covenant signified and promised salvation, and this promise had to be accepted in faith in order to have a saving effect. The sacraments of the New Covenant, however, do not just signify and promise salvation, but contain it and distribute

---

18. *Ibid.,* p. 35.
19. *Ibid.* Cf. G. de Gier, "De waardering voor offer en sacrament," in *Onrust in de zielszorg,* 1950, pp. 45f.; P. Schoonenberg, "De apostolische Geloofs-belijdenis in de Katholieke Kerk," *Geloofsinhoud en Geloofsbeleving,* 1951, p. 175.
20. Schmaus, *Kath. Dogm.,* IV, 1, p. 65.
21. *Mediator Dei,* p. 34.
22. Cf. Schmaus, *op. cit.,* p. 106.

it.[23] Scholasticism,[24] and after that Trent, speak in this spirit of the efficacy of the sacraments.

Why, then, did the Reformers so unanimously reject *ex opere operato?* Already in his *Loci Communes* of 1521, Melanchthon contends against those who teach that the sacraments in themselves have the authority to justify men. "They attribute to the sacraments of the New Testament the authority to grant justification. That, of course, is an error, for justification comes only with faith."[25] This criticism is also found in the Confessio Augustana, which emphasizes, against Rome, the necessity of faith. It is directed against those who teach that the sacraments justify *ex opere operato,* and that in the use of the sacraments belief in the forgiveness of sins is not necessary. It is said that the sacraments require belief, "and that they are correctly used only if they are received in faith, and thus strengthen faith."[26] The Apology points in the same direction when it says that the Roman Catholic doctrine is actually a Jewish view, namely, that we are justified by a ceremony without faith.[27] The Apology is concerned about faith and belief in the use of the sacraments, because the promise will do us no good if it is not accepted in faith.[28] It becomes evident also that the sacrament is seen in connection with the Word, the promise of God. In the sacrament we have the *verbum visibile,* the sign of the promise. Because of that connection between Word and sacrament, the *Apologia* can affirm: "That is why we say that belief is necessary for the correct use of the sacraments.... For the divine promise cannot be understood without belief" (p. 205).

It is striking that so much agreement exists between Lutherans and Reformed precisely in the rejection of *ex opere operato.* Both continually point to the relation between Word and sacrament, and therefore to the relation between faith and sacrament (cf. *Inst.,* IV, XIV, 14). This is not because they both subjectivize the sacraments, but because they both have a

---

23. See, e.g., Thomas Aquinas, *Summa Contra Gentiles,* IV, 57.
24. According to Schmaus, the expression comes from Peter of Poitiers (1205), and the terms *ex opere operato* and *ex opere operantis* occur first with Wilhelm van Auxerre.
25. Melanchthon, *Grundbegriffe der Glaubenslehre* (ed. F. Schad, 1931), p. 217.
26. *Confessio Augustana,* Art. XIII.
27. *Apologia,* Art. XIII (Müller, *op. cit.,* p. 204): "Sine bono motu cordis, hoc est, sine fide."
28. "Promissio est inutilis, nisi fide accipiatur" *(ibid.)*

correct insight into them. Calvin, for example, rejects the contrast between the sacraments of the Old and the New Covenant, as if the latter actually would supply grace if belief were not present (*Inst.*, IV, XIV, 23); and he objects to the *ex opere operato* not only because it is incorrect, but because (as he remarks) it contradicts the very nature of the sacraments.[29] The long controversy has made it clear that Rome really fails to appreciate this profound remark of Calvin, which represented the heartbeat of the Reformation. Why, one could ask, was the nature of the sacraments as instituted by God affected by the doctrine of *ex opere operato?*

In order to answer this decisive question, we must observe what Rome means by the "objectivity" of the sacraments. This question is very important, because Rome seems to be standing firm against all those who want somehow to make a divine institution dependent on man's subjectivity. This brings us to the most critical point of the whole controversy. Could it indeed be true that the Reformation, with its emphasis on faith and the *sola fide,* has thus affected the objectivity of the sacraments?

Was not Rome correct when it affirmed that salvation comes from above, solely from God; and must not the Reformation, in spite of its *sola gratia,* learn from Rome's sacramental doctrine? The Roman Catholic expositions would have us think so! They point out that the *ex opere operato* makes it very evident indeed that God is the cause of grace, as *causa principalis,* and that he is this *causa principalis* in the sacraments as *causa instrumentalis.* In Thomas Aquinas' discussion of whether the sacraments are the cause of grace, he answers that the sacraments of the New Covenant produce grace.[30] Thomas means this in the strict sense of the word, for in this connection he argues against those who say that the sacraments are administered.[31] For in the latter case, the sacrament would be no more than a sign of grace, while according to Thomas the

29. *Inst.*, IV, XIV, 26: "quicquid de opere operato nugati sunt sophistae, non modo falsum esse, *sed pugnare cum sacramentorum natura.*"
30. *S.T.*, Q. 62, Art. 11: "Utrum sacramenta sint causa gratiae." "Necesse est dicere, sacramenta novae legis per aliquem modum gratiam causare." Cf. Polman, *op. cit.,* IV, 75.
31. "Quidam tamen dicunt quod non sunt causa gratiae aliquid operando sed quia Deus sacramentis adhibitis, in anima gratiam operatur" *(ibid.).*

sacraments not only signify grace but also contain it.[32] That is the basis on which Thomas maintains the truly causal character of the sacraments.[33] Ultimately God, as *causa principalis*, is the worker of grace.

In themselves and apart from God, the sacraments would not be able to communicate grace, because that which is communicated implies a similarity to the divine nature, to which corporeal signs are not suitably proportional. But these signs derive their ability to communicate grace from God's standing behind them, and because he employs the sacrament as *causa instrumentalis* in such a manner that it really produces grace. The sacrament is an instrument in God's hand, and therefore is the cause of grace. These considerations form the background of the Roman Catholic sacramental doctrine. This *causalitas* is the basis for the *ex opere operato,* for against the background of the *causa principalis* (God), grace is infused through the corporeal sign.

That is why this causality is mentioned in many sorts of pronouncements.[34] One can say that the sacraments "in themselves" possess efficacy "because they are acts of Christ himself."[35] They are the source and cause of grace,[36] and therein lies the core of the doctrine of the *opus operantum*. But we are not yet fully informed about this typically Roman Catholic doctrine. For one could think that this strong emphasis on the objectivity of the sacraments and the objectivity of this *causalitas* (as opposed to the dependence of the sacrament on the recipient) would lead to a sacramental doctrine that defends the irresistibility of the sacramental effects. Otherwise, why should Rome have so vigorously attacked Reformed "subjectivism"? Following this reasoning, many have called the Roman Catholic doctrine of the sacraments magical, drawing a parallel with the

---

32. "...quod sacramenta novae legis non solum significant sed causant gratiam" *(ibid.).*
33. Mannens, *Theol. Dogm. Institutiones,* III, 180ff.
34. E.g., the encyclical *Ad Catholici Sacerdotii (Ecclesia docens* 43): "The bearer of the sacred consecration is the distributor of the divine graces, of which the sacraments are, so to speak, the sources." Christ is "present in the sacraments through his power which he infuses in order to make of them efficacious instruments of sanctification" *(Mediator Dei,* p. 27).
35. *Mediator Dei,* p. 36.
36. Trent defines baptism as *causa instrumentalis* of justification (Denz. 799). Regarding Schillebeeckx' considerations on causality, see my article in *GTT,* 1953.

Jewish interpretation of the offering, which never required man's belief.[37] The *ex opere operato* was then understood as a matter-of-fact working from above, whereby human subjectivity did not enter into the picture at all.

Nevertheless, we must now recognize that the Roman Catholic not only rejects this reproach of magic, but that he also faces a problem of subjectivity in the sacraments. This is already apparent in the pronouncement of Trent, which not only poses the *ex opere operato,* but also speaks of the problem of the obstacle.[38] It is impossible, therefore, to speak simplistically of the Roman Catholic sacramental doctrine as "magical."

In spite of her appeal to the objectivity of the sacraments *ex opere operato,* Rome has developed a theory of the relation between "subject" and "object." The question is raised whether, after all, a certain disposition is necessary on the part of the believer, a certain *conditio sine qua non,* without which the sacraments lack the expected effect. It is pointed out in reply, that a subjective disposition *is* necessary for the working of the sacrament.[39] Rome never intended to rule out this disposition in an objectivistic manner,[40] but only to deny that this necessary disposition is either causal or meritorious. That is why Rome teaches that the grace of the sacrament is not granted *ex opere operantum,* that is to say, on the basis of any activity of belief or disposition of the believers. In spite of all the criticism from the Reformed side, Rome wants to defend the gratuity of grace.

This, however, raises the question about the meaning of this necessary disposition. How is it connected with the *ex opere operato,* the absolutely objective structure of the sacrament, which works independently of the recipient? And how is it possible that the Reformed doctrine of *sola fide* is called subjectivistic, while the subjective disposition (the placing of no obstacles) recognized by Rome apparently has no such consequence? If, according to Trent's definition, an obstacle is placed in the way, no sacramental sanctification occurs. In such a case one speaks of the unfruitfulness of the sacraments. Evi-

---

37. For examples see *ibid.*
38. Denz. 849 *(non ponentibus obicem).*
39. Contrary to the apologia of Melanchthon, it is denied that Scholasticism ever had taught that the subjective disposition was unimportant (Pohle, *Dogmatik,* III, 63).
40. Denz. 898.

dently the working of the sacrament *ex opere operato* is not irresistible, for the *Decretum pro Armenis* already contends that the sacraments contain and bring grace to those who receive it "worthily."[41] This definition is more positive than the one of Trent (no obstacle), but in both cases the crux of the matter is the necessity of a certain disposition. The sacraments simply do not work *ex opere operato* in the sense that they always infuse grace from above in an infallible manner. There is an "if," and it is precisely that "if" that creates the real problem in the Roman Catholic doctrine of the sacraments.

According to Rome, the sacrament is not devaluated under any circumstances; but if the necessary disposition is not present, the infusion does not occur. The sacrament remains unfruitful; indeed, "it even leads to destruction."[42] "He who receives a sacrament while in an attitude of turning away from God, uses a sign in an antigodly manner while its purpose is to serve the glorification of God and the salvation of men. He misuses in a self-exalting manner that which is a revelation of divine love and which therefore must be accepted by man in love."[43] It is evident, from expressions like these, that the "efficacy" and "objectivity" so emphatically urged against the subjectivism of the Reformation turn out to be more complicated than could at first sight have been expected. Suddenly all the old issues reappear; the "solved" problem of the relation between subjectivity and objectivity returns again, but now — against the background of the *ex opere operato* — in a still sharper form.

As we saw, Trent defines the disposition negatively: placing no obstacle in the way. This negative definition is certainly not accidental. It is something altogether different from what the Reformation meant by the relation between faith and sacrament, for Rome declares emphatically that true belief is not necessary for the fruitful reception of the sacrament, although there can be an obstacle in the soul that prevents the fruitfulness of the sacraments. But why should this obstacle be of any consequence, in the light of the divine causality of the sacraments? The crux of the matter here is an absolutely necessary disposition that nevertheless does not affect the objectivity of the sacraments. In order to understand Rome correctly at

41. Denz. 695.
42. Schmaus, *op. cit.,* p. 80.
43. *Ibid.,* p. 81.

this point, one cannot be satisfied with a single word of definition. On the one hand, emphasis is placed on the objectivity
of the sacraments, while on the other hand the disposition and
the necessary preparation of grace are indicated. In this synthesis between *ex opere operato* and disposition lies the center of
the Roman Catholic doctrine. Simple antimagical polemics disregards this synthesis, and hence is all the more irresponsible
because it is precisely this synthesis that fits so well into the
characteristically Roman Catholic mode of thinking. This mode
does not simply pit objectivity against subjectivism, nor sacra-
ment-magic against human activity. It does not place the absolute gratuity of grace in opposition to the meritoriousness and
the preparation of man. It rather synthesizes and connects these
contrasting and contradictory elements, and precisely in so doing
it places itself against the Reformed doctrine of the sacraments.

In its emphasis on the objectivity of the sacraments, we
recognize the objective aspect of Rome's doctrine of the Church.
The sacraments are thus anchored in the Church and in the
priesthood. But this portrayal is not complete, for there is still
the aspect of disposition. There is also an activity, a disposition
of the believers, a human striving, an attitude. This disposition
can be defined positively *(Decretum pro Armenis)* or negatively
(Trent). In both cases there is a condition that must be fulfilled if the fruitfulness of the sacraments is to become a fact
and supernatural grace is to be infused into the soul. These
two aspects in the Roman Catholic sacramental doctrine maintain a strange equilibrium. The negative definition of the necessary disposition turns out to be not completely negative after
all, because, for example, the fact is that the recipient is willing
to receive the sacrament. "Of necessity insufficient (apart from
the sacraments of penance and marriage) is the so-called neutral
(habitual) intention to receive a rite of the church," although
— except with the sacrament of penance — "a definite moral disposition" is *not* necessary.[44]

Supernatural grace is prevented from entering man's soul
only when an obstacle is placed in the way. It is possible, says
Schmaus, that the door is opened again later or rather, that the
door is later opened from the outside, because the resistance is
taken away, and then occurs what first could not happen (in
spite of the efficacy of the sacraments) : the infusion of grace.

44. *Ibid.,* p. 80.

Those who understand even slightly the Roman Catholic doctrine of salvation will not be surprised by this synthesis between subjectivity and objectivity, for it involves ultimately the same motive that pervades the entire doctrine of salvation, namely, the synthesis of grace and freedom, or, one could say, the problem of human co-operation in salvation. Objectivity and disposition work with each other, as do grace and freedom, and preparation and the act of God; and they limit each other. In the doctrine of *ex opere operato* the problem of preparation arises, and the problem of co-operation in the process of salvation. It is the same problem that played such an important role in Scholasticism, when, for example, Peter of Poitiers employed the image of the man who decorated and prepared his house for the reception of an important guest, but who with all his endeavor could not cause the guest actually to enter his house, since that entering depended upon the personal freedom and choice of the guest.[45] The cleaning of the house signifies an attitude much the same as the one that causes man to prepare for justification by the grace that comes to him in the sacraments. These conditions, says Rome, do not threaten the reality of grace,[46] for the *conditio sine qua non* is the decorated house, and if that condition is fulfilled, grace enters in. In this way the Roman Catholic doctrine of salvation can on the one hand emphasize grace, while on the other hand it leaves room for this activity on man's part, even in the negative definition. In the doctrine of the sacraments all this obtains this form, that the *dignitas* of the sacrament (one could say: of the guest) is maintained; but its validity is no longer present because the condition — preparation and disposition — is not fulfilled.

Thus Rome can come to a synthesis and reject the reproach of magic. Indeed, the Roman Catholic doctrine of the sacraments is more complicated than that; it shows us a characteristic symptom of the *complexio oppositorum,* the unity of opposing parts, which belongs to the essence of Roman Catholicism.[47] There is a linking of two aspects: grace works objectively through corporeal elements while at the same time that grace

---

45. Cf. A. M. Landgraf, *Dogmengeschichte der Früh-Scholastik* (1952), I, 1, pp. 249ff. ("Die Gnadenlehre").
46. Especially in Thomistic theology (Diekamp, e.g.), the influence of the epistles to the Romans and Galatians is very evident (Diekamp, *Dogmatik*, II, 539).
47. Cf. F. Heiler, *Der Katholizismus*, p. 621.

is not always realized. Van de Pol writes that the Roman Catholic doctrine often seems contradictory to Protestants, but that the Catholic experiences this harmoniously, and that he will never think in terms of an arbitrary selection of contradictory elements.[48]

Nevertheless, it is impossible to see how the Roman Catholic objectivity of the sacraments can be squared with the problem of disposition, and we can only conclude that the objective power, richness, and efficacy of the sacraments, together with the human disposition as necessary condition, are connected in a religious, opaque way as church doctrine. The connection lacks transparency especially because it involves the infusion of supernatural grace. Though Rome acknowledges a certain relation between the sacraments and the recipient of the sacraments, she interprets this as a relation between subjectivity and objectivity, and these two are, so to speak, placed in dialectical opposition. The problem lies in this, that grace is objectively infused through the sacraments, that the sacrament is not dependent on the subjective disposition of the recipient (the polemics against the Reformed), while at the same time this disposition becomes a condition in the full sense of the word, because the soul is sanctified only if the disposition is present. The independent objectivity of the sacraments, which contain and cause grace, leads nevertheless to a distinction between their *validity* and their *dignity*.

This is a particularly interesting development, because of the peculiar fact that the distinction between the validity and the dignity of the sacrament occurs already in Augustine and later in Calvin, where it plays an important role. It is mentioned in the Reformation in connection with the unworthy use of the Lord's Supper; however, the characteristic element of this distinction in Roman Catholic thought lies in the fact that it denies the irresistibility of the sacraments, although these sacraments have been made independent of the recipient. Hence arises the problem of the efficacious working of the sacraments in the hand of God, which is *nevertheless* resisted. It is of course true that the Reformation also directed its attention to the relation between God's work and ours. Calvin, for example, struggled to understand the connection between the two in the light of faith, as well as the relation between sacrament

48. Van de Pol, *Het Chr. Dilemma*, p. 167.

and belief. But in Calvin this relation was removed from the Roman Catholic framework. He did not operate with the scheme of subjectivity-objectivity, nor with the idea that supernatural grace is infused through corporeal signs. He reached beyond the *ex opere operato* and the problem of disposition. He refused to accept the dilemma implied therein, but rather pointed to a third possibility, which did not harbor a compromise between subjectivity and objectivity.

Even beyond the pale of Reformed theology, people have had an inkling of this third possibility. We think especially of the *tertium* of the Old Catholics, as Jans defines it: "The term *ex opere operato* for the working of a sacrament is misleading. On the other hand, efficacy may not be made dependent on the recipient."[49] We may be giving the impression that rejection of the Roman Catholic synthesis between subjectivity and objectivity will again be caught in a vicious circle, since the Reformers themselves made the distinction between the efficacy and the dignity of the sacraments more than once. But the Reformed view of the sacrament — and this is essential — denies that it is caught up in a vicious circle, for it sees the relation between faith and sacrament as a specific relation that does not imply a construction of "balance," but rather a reference to the mystery of the sacrament, which is understood and acknowledged in its objectivity through faith.

There must be a good reason why Roman Catholic theology from Trent up to now (e.g., Pohle, Bartmann, Diekamp, and Schmaus) has interpreted the Reformed doctrine of the relation between faith and sacrament in a subjectivistic manner. There seems to be only one — though adequate — explanation for this peculiar fact (especially peculiar in the light of the Roman Catholic concept regarding subjectivity and objectivity). The explanation is this: "belief" in the Reformed doctrine is interpreted in the light of the disposition-scheme in Roman Catholic sacramentology. This is most clearly revealed in Diekamp's "discovery" of an antinomy in the Reformed doctrine. This antinomy, he thinks, lies in the relation between faith and justification. "According to the Protestant doctrine, justification is the work of fiducial belief, and therefore comes after it. However, that is contradicted by the Protestant declaration that fiducial belief must be the firm trust of the individual that his sins are

49. P. J. Jans, "De middelen der genade: de sacramenten," *VT*, 1951, p. 32.

forgiven; according to that statement, justification should come first."[50] This criticism is typical and illustrative, for it represents Reformed thinking in a manner that can only be called misapprehension and misinterpretation. It is based on the presupposition that according to the Reformed view justification is the work of faith, a thesis that flagrantly contradicts the doctrine of the *sola fide*.

The *sola fide* maintains precisely that this "efficacy" of faith is impossible. We read, for instance, in Article 22 of the Confession of Faith that true faith, which is evoked in us through the Holy Spirit, comprises Jesus Christ and all his benefits. "Through faith" has nothing to do with a creative function of faith, but is essentially the radical exclusion of every creation. Precisely in order to avoid this misapprehension, the Confession adds that *sola fide* does not mean that it is really our faith that justifies us.

The significance of the confessed *sola fide* is not hereby denied, but only clarified and safeguarded against misunderstanding. The intention is to say that faith is in no sense a human given which as "present" disposition lays the foundation for justification. It is a decisive element in the Reformed doctrine that faith is so exclusively directed toward the grace of God that the concept of a creative or meritorial character of faith is never considered. That is why the Confession could say in Article 22 that faith is "only an instrument" with which we embrace Christ. It is "an instrument that keeps us in communion with Him in all His benefits." This faith is not a human contribution to salvation, but it exists and has its unshakable structure in the exclusion of such a causal connection. That is why Diekamp's representation of the Reformed doctrine of correlation is so incorrect. The antinomy of which he speaks would really be present if faith were creative in character, for in that case faith would have to direct itself toward that which it had itself first created. And in that case no answer could be given to the question of what is temporally first, faith or justification.

It seems to be impossible for Rome to see the Reformed doctrine differently. It cannot interpret the *sola fide* doctrine otherwise than as a doctrine that sees faith as a preceding, present disposition which enables man — because of that presence — to work justification. But the Reformed doctrine of

50. Diekamp, *op. cit.*, p. 542.

faith can never be understood in this manner. Faith can be understood only in connection with its directedness and its content, with the recognition of the *extra nos*, with its essential exclusion of all merit, or, to say it differently: with its resting in the grace of God. From that angle, the whole sacramental problem changes. The difference between Rome and the Reformation does not lie in a slight mutation of the question about subjectivity and objectivity, but in an altogether different outlook on objectivity. For the Reformation, the objectivity of the sacraments could no longer depend on the efficacy of infused supernatural grace. For this kind of objectivity had led Rome to posit the strange phenomenon of an obstacle that could still prevent the sacraments from being valid.

In the Reformation, especially with Calvin, the relation between Word and sacrament again came to the fore in the religious-personal concept of *usus sacramenti,* which posited an altogether different relation from that suggested by *ex opere operato* and the disposition. That is what Calvin had in mind when he said that the *opus operantum* was contradictory to the nature of the sacrament (*Inst.,* IV, XIV, 26). The relation between faith and sacrament stands in the light of the connection between Word and sacrament, and thus the *sola fide* obtains its full significance in the sacramental doctrine as well. For the objectivity toward which faith is directed in the sacraments is not different from that when man encounters God in his Word. Because of the relation between Word and sacrament (as sign and seal of the word of promise), the sacraments involve the same directedness of faith as is involved in the doctrine of justification. The sacraments are no longer independent new fountains of grace, utilizing a new causality of grace, but by virtue of the Word the sacraments acquire great significance in man's personal relation to God.[51]

"I say only this: God uses means and instruments which he himself sees to be expedient, that all things may serve his glory, since he is Lord and Judge of all" (*Inst.,* IV, XIV, 12). The

51. It is clear that this "personal" is not meant in contrast to the "communion," a consideration which would affect the essence of the sacrament. The word "personal" intends only to maintain the relation between the sacrament and the Word of the living God, and stands over against the substantial infusion, which does not require faith, but, through the negative character of disposition, acquires an impersonal character. Cf. *Inst.,* IV, XIV, 17.

core of the problem cannot be better defined than by asking about the significance of the sacrament as *instrument*. This definition occupies an important place in the Reformed sacramental doctrine,[52] as indeed it does for Rome as well.

One of the happiest aspects of the controversy concerning the sacraments in the sixteenth century is the fact that Calvin did not fall into the abyss of one-sided reaction. In his rejection of *ex opere operato* he did not devalue or neglect the signs that God gave to his people. Rather, he indicated the significance of the outward signs so clearly that he was warned not to overestimate the sacraments and so, by taking the sacraments as instruments, to end up with a sacrament that works as *opus operatum*.

Bullinger, for example, repeatedly stated that *instrumentum* was too strong a word, and he urged instead that it was the Holy Spirit who granted grace.[53] But Calvin, while attempting to remove misapprehensions, maintained the "instrumental" character of the sacraments in the sense that God uses them, and that, through the qualification of the signs through the Word, they acquire significance in the acts of God. Because the signs are taken up into the acts of God, it is impossible, says Calvin, that they should only be outward and empty signs.

Calvin takes his point of departure from the veracity of God's promise, and therefore also from the veracity of the sacraments. He speaks of the "integrity" of the sacrament, which the whole world cannot violate, and with respect to the Lord's Supper, for instance, he says: "And this is the wholeness of the Sacrament, which the whole world cannot violate: that the flesh and blood of Christ are no less truly given to the unworthy than to God's elect believers"; and he adds: "At the same time, it is true, however, that, just as rain falling upon a hard rock flows off because no entrance opens into the stone, the wicked by their hardness so repel God's grace that it does not reach them" (*Inst.*, IV, XVII, 33). Calvin can write elsewhere: "Man's unworthiness does not rob the sacraments of their significance. Baptism remains the bath of regeneration even though the whole world was faithless; the Lord's Supper remains the distribution

---

52. Cf. E. G. van Teylingen, "Sacramentum-Instrumentum," *VT*, XVI, 1946.
53. "Sacramenta illa (dona) non exhibent aut conferunt, ceu exhibendi et conferendi instrumenta, sed significant, testificantur, et obsignantur." H. Grass, *Die Abendmahlslehre bei Luther und Calvin*, 1940, p. 187.

of Christ's body and blood, even though there was not the slightest sparkle of belief left."[54]

In this emphasis on the integrity of the sacrament we are
struck by a parallel between this consideration, given by Calvin,
and the Roman Catholic distinction between the efficacy and
the dignity of the sacrament. Are we dealing with the same concept here? Does Calvin also end up with a synthesis between
efficacy and disposition?

The answer to these questions must be negative; that becomes clear when we see Calvin's words function in the full
context of his doctrine of the sacraments. For Rome, the
distinction between the efficacy and the veracity of the sacrament functioned against the background of infused supernatural
grace as the essence of the sacrament. For Calvin and all of
Reformed theology, the background is altogether different. There
is much more depth in the sacrament because the gate to the
Word and the promise has not been shut.[55]

The sacrament no longer has the function of infusing supernatural grace, but can only be understood in connection with
the Word of promise. That is why it can be taken up into
the personal sphere of God's promising Word, thus allowing
for a relation in which subjectivity does not compete with objectivity, but in which the subjectivity of faith rests in the
Word of God. There is a receiving of the sacrament which is
altogether different from the receiving of supernatural grace.
The sacrament is directed toward faith, in order to nourish
and strengthen it. That is what Calvin always emphasizes; and
when he describes the sacrament in this manner, it is clear why
in his definition of the sacrament he takes up the conjunction
between sign and signifying matter in the relation between faith
and sacrament. He speaks continually of the integrity of the
sacrament, but this integrity is linked with the context in which
God has given the sacrament, a context which is respected and
acknowledged by faith. The relation between Word and sacrament makes it possible for Calvin to issue such bold statements
as, for example, when he says that the sacraments are given as
truly to the unworthy as to the believers.

The integrity of the sacrament is immediately dependent
upon its relation to the Word of promise. It is not an objec-

54. *Commentary* on Ezekiel 20:20.
55. Cf. O. Noordmans on richness and poverty in connection with the
sacrament (*Natuur en Genade bij Rome,* 1949, p. 12).

tivity in itself, but it can and must be understood objectively
if it is seen in all the connections and in the context in which
God has placed it.[56] The sacrament can never be qualified by
the difference between believers and unbelievers, but only
through its institution by God and according to his purpose. The
objectivity of the sacrament does not lie in the fact that "grace"
is given equally to believers and unbelievers, but in the veracity
of the sacrament as it was given and intended by God, namely,
as veracious and trustworthy sign and seal of his Word.

In adhering to this objectivity, Calvin reminds us of Augustine, who wrote that the sacraments depend on nothing and
that the grace which they portray is not undone by unbelief
or man's unworthiness (*Inst.*, IV, XVII, 34). Calvin overcomes
the tension between *ex opere operato* and the disposition by
exposing the relation between faith and sacrament, and the
relation between Word and sacrament. On the one hand, he
can write that "unbelievers communicate only in a visible
symbol" *(ibid.)*. This is not contradictory to what he says about
the objectivity of the sacrament, but it does accentuate the
relation between Word and sacrament and the greatness of God,
who gives this sign so that it may be accepted and understood
in faith. This sacrament is useless apart from faith, and that is
why Calvin can write: "But what is a sacrament received apart
from faith but the most certain ruin of the church?" (*Inst.*, IV,
XIV, 14). They give nothing and are of no advantage whatsoever "unless received in faith" (IV, XIV, 17). On the other
hand, however, it is impossible because of the relation between
Word and sacrament that the sacrament, as administered according to the command of God, would ever decay into false
appearance, and would lose its objective structure.

Dangers threaten here from two sides. On the one hand,
the sacrament, through its relation to the Word, can be made
into a sealed offer of grace and thus strong emphasis can be
placed on its "objective structure." According to this view, which
is based on the conditional promise, the sacrament is seen as
a portrayal and confirmation of this promise, which makes it
impossible to understand why every act of preaching should not
be accompanied by the sacrament. It can be inferred with complete plausibility that, if the sign confirms the Word, it may

56. Cf. Polman, *op. cit.*, p. 155: "The sacrament may not be detached from
the connections in which God himself has placed it."

always be added to the Word in order to strengthen the trustworthiness of the promise. Why should not the veracity of God's Word be surrounded with signs? But this trend of thought disregards the fact that the sacraments have been instituted for believers and that they serve the strengthening of faith. Hence by the above-mentioned reasoning, one can innocently be led to a false "objectivity" of the sacraments, which detaches these sacraments from the living context in which God has placed them. Those who disregard the directedness of the sacrament toward faith, and so misconstrue the essential relation between faith and sacrament, could then still speak only of an "objectivity" in itself, which is accepted by one person but not another because only the former possesses the "condition" of faith. This sort of view will never be able to contribute more than a pendant to the Roman Catholic problem of *ex opere operato* and disposition.

On the other hand, the danger exists that the relation between faith and sacrament is determined from the point of view of faith, thus leading to a "seeming-sacrament" if faith is not present. Calvin carefully avoided this danger because he discovered, through the relation between Word and sacrament, an integrity in the sacrament that could never be affected by lack of faith. We must be fully aware, however, that it cannot be the intention of our reflection to comprehend the relation between faith and sacrament in a logical scheme which makes transparent the objectivity of the sacrament as well as the involvement of faith with sacrament. For with regard to the signs of God, the concern lies with the miracle of the Holy Spirit in our hearts, in which the integrity of the sacrament and the veracity of God's promise are acknowledged and accepted. And precisely because this insight is given through and in faith, Calvin protests against the view that maintains that the sacraments justify and bring grace as long as man does not place the obstacle of a mortal sin in the way.[57] As far as Calvin is concerned, this view affects the relation between Word and sacrament, and violates the mystery of the gift of the Spirit. It is then no longer possible to escape the problem of subjectivity and objectivity competing against each other, and one

---

57. *Inst.*, IV, XIV, 14. Cf. D. J. de Groot, "Het effect van het gebruik der sacramenten voor ongelovigen volgens Calvijn," *VT*, 1936, pp. 144-149.

cannot avoid, in the end, the problem of an efficacy that cannot penetrate into man's heart.

Only if we see the objective structure of the sacrament in connection with the relations "Word-sacrament" and "faith-sacrament" can we fruitfully speak of God's veracity also in the sacraments. It is interesting that this procedure does not result in a system where the whole sacrament-relation has been logically placed in transparent categories, but it does allow one to speak of the sacraments in a manner that does not deviate at the door of the hearts of the believers. Those who look steadily at the relation between Word and sacrament, and between Word, sacrament, and faith, can point to the *usus sacramenti* in which reference is made to the veracity of the Word of promise, and in which man is called to accept the sacrament in faith. This dual outlook in the Reformed doctrine of the sacraments takes the place of the synthesis in the Roman Catholic doctrine. The Reformed doctrine of the sacraments was never intended to function as a new gnosis, but only to do justice to the depth and the richness that lie in the sacraments.

The Consensus Tigurinus delineates clearly the relation between Word and sacrament and between faith and sacrament. This is all the more significant because the correspondence between Calvin and Bullinger on the "sign and thing signified" preceded it. The fundamental structure of Calvin's doctrine of the sacraments is most sharply revealed in' this Consensus because Calvin not only opposes Rome in it, but also takes care to avoid a spiritualistic over-reaction. The result of the correspondence is mainly that Calvin and Bullinger declare together that a distinction must be made between the sign and that which is signified, while at the same time the truth of the sacrament may not be separated from the signs.[58] On the one hand, simple identification is opposed; on the other hand, the connection is indicated. This twofold aspect does not harbor a contradiction, but is linked with that twofold relation between Word and sacrament and between faith and sacrament. Those who through faith accept the promise, receive also Christ with his gifts.[59] The sacraments in themselves work nothing (Art. XII), and one should not blind himself by staring at the signs

---

58. "Quare etsi distinguimus ut par est, inter signa et res signatas, tamen non distinguimus a signis veritatem."
59. Consensus Tigurinus, Art. IX.

(Art. XI), because water, bread, and wine do not in themselves administer the Christ (Art. X), nor do they give us participation in his gifts. But faith refuses to separate the sign from that which is signified, for without the promise the sacrament cannot be imagined.[60] That is why the sacrament is revered, and why the power and the efficacy of the sacraments must be looked upon in faith.[61] Faith will never speak of useless, vain, and mere signs, although one can speak and preach critically and warningly of their uselessness if they are not accepted in faith.

In the relation between faith and sacrament and between sacrament and promise, we understand in faith that we receive the gift of Christ (Art. XII). God makes use of the sacraments as means while the power to act lies with him (Art. XVIII). Everything is directed at the *usus sacramenti*. That which is accepted in belief, becomes opaque apart from faith. Either the sacrament is detached from the Word, or the sacrament is subjectivized. Only in faith can the sacrament become simple, not in the rational sense, but in the simplicity of faith which learns to rest in the veracity of God's promises. Because the sacrament is grounded in the Word, even unbelievers come into contact with the veracity of the promise (Art. XX). If they show disdain for the sacrament, they are despising the rich promise that attends it, namely, that it brings us into contact with the living God. And the whole problem of sign and signified is once again illuminated by the Consensus when it says that grace is so little connected with the act of the sacraments that their fruit is sometimes received after the act (Art. XX), when a reminder is given of the baptism of children and the celebration of the Lord's Supper. On the Roman Catholic interpretation of the sacrament such a view regarding the temporal moment is, of course, impossible because the infusion of grace is thought to be essential for the sacrament.[62]

The Confession of Faith also contains profound observations about the connections in which the sacrament is placed according to God's ordinance and intent. A distinction is made here be-

---

60. Art. X: "vis et efficacia sacramentorum recta fidei via."
61. Art. XII: cf. the connection between sign and that which is signified in Art. VIII.
62. See on Consensus Tigurinus: H. Grass, *op. cit.*, pp. 186-190; E. Bizer, *Studien zur Geschichte des Abendmahlsstreites im 16. Jahrhundert,* 1940, pp. 243-273; Polman, *op. cit.*, pp. 119f.

tween the sacrament and the truth of the sacrament, while it is said at the same time that the sacraments have been joined to that which is signified. Faith lives in the connection between sign and that which is signified; but Judas and Simon the magician, who received the sacrament, did not receive Christ who is signified by it, for "He is only administered to believers." Indeed, everywhere in the Reformed confessions we find the confession of both the objectivity of the sacrament and the necessity of faith.[63]

There is no logical solution here which can also be understood apart from faith. Anyone who attempts such a solution by separating subjectivity from objectivity, then trying to relate them with some such concept as meritorious co-operation, has simply failed to appreciate the true nature of the sacrament. Those who, on the other hand, fully acknowledge the relation between faith and sacrament and between Word and sacrament, are no longer surprised about the close connection the Reformed doctrine of the sacraments continually indicates between "sign" and "that which is signified." When faith speaks of this connection, it is confessing the veracity of God. But apart from this confession of faith, there are only insoluble difficulties.

It need not surprise us that our reflection on the relation between faith and sacrament has repeatedly led us to the same questions that were discussed in the relation between faith and justification. Both ultimately involve the nature of faith, indicated in the expression *sola fide*. One of the richest and profoundest discoveries of the Reformation is its separation of faith from any kind of merit. In this way automatism and superficiality can be avoided, while at the same time there is no spiritualistic evaporation of the sacrament. It is therefore not without reason that the Belgic Confession can speak of God's working in the sacraments: "... so He works in us all that He represents to us by these holy signs" (Art. XXXV).

These holy signs are not merely jogs for the memory, whose only effect is psychological. No, the sacrament may not for a moment be detached from the Giver of the sacraments. The signs, instituted by divine sovereignty and therefore filled with the power of his hand, are of great significance for faith. When we speak, therefore, of correlation between faith and sacrament, we do not refer to that modern sense of correlation in which God and man are interdependent. The Reformed concept of cor-

63. See, e.g., Confessio Helv. Post. (Müller, pp. 208ff.).

relation is altogether contrary to mutual interdependence, but rather acknowledges the sovereign promise of God which founds the whole correlation and which is acknowledged in faith. Faith thus holds fast to the signs, and it rests in the Word of promise. Faith knows that it may not rashly handle the conjunction of sign and that which is signified, as Israel could not rashly rely on the presence of the ark in the fight against the Philistines. We think also of the word that God spoke to David in another war against the Philistines: "When thou hearest the sound of march-ing in the tops of the mulberry-trees . . . thou shalt bestir thy-self; for then is Jehovah gone out before thee to smite the host of the Philistines" (II Sam. 5:24). The simple sign becomes a means in God's hand, and the sign is understood in faith, and the struggle is won, because one can and may rely on the veracity of God in that sign. In faith, the sign, the simple element, is known by virtue of the Word of God, and in faith that sign be-comes the way to victory.

We now come to a topic which is raised especially in the writings of Kuyper, namely, the so-called special grace of the sacrament. Against the background of a sharp devaluation of the sacraments, Kuyper asked "which (sort of) grace comes to us by means of the sacrament." In response he argued sharply against the concept that the sacrament only *reflects* grace. Reflection is not sufficient: "What you need is the anointing of grace itself."[64]

The sacrament is "a means, ordained by God, to bring us grace." Not until we are able to see that clearly, shall we hungrily seek the sacrament, and find more in it than "only a portrayal of a *tableau vivant*" (p. 464). Kuyper is especially critical of the Zwinglian interpretation of the sacraments. He speaks of Zwingli's "deplorable representation," according to which, in reaction against Rome, he saw the sacrament as a mere sign (p. 430). He characterizes Zwingli's theory regarding the Lord's Supper as possessing "sober simplicity" and as "intellectual," but also as "barren and mendacious" (III, 148). He would rather err with Luther in consubstantiation than with Zwingli to let go of all mystery in the sacrament *(ibid.)*. "Mere sign, that is, a lack of feeling for the mystery." It is Zwingli's error that he denies any working of grace in the Lord's Supper (p. 124). The sacrament is reduced to the level of any phenomenon that we experience as

64. A. Kuyper, *E Voto,* II, 463.

edifying, such as the starry heaven, a death bed, or a praying child.[65]

In opposition, Kuyper teaches emphatically that the sacrament does not just portray something, but that it also does something, that it carries with it a working of grace which cannot be separated from the essence of the sacrament. Hence the question arises wherein that specific working of grace is situated. For Kuyper wants to speak of a "sacramental grace which works also in baptism as a separate working of grace with individual character, which cannot be put on a line with any other."[66]

Kuyper emphasizes that the sacrament does not serve to evoke belief, but to strengthen it.[67] This does not, however, destroy the uniqueness of the sacramental working. For, he says, it is essential to the sacrament that "at the moment of baptism or of the Lord's Supper, a twofold act occurs, the one on earth through the administrator, and the other through Christ in heaven who has instituted the sacrament."[68] It is this second act which counts in the determination of sacramental grace. If this working from heaven does not accompany the administration of the sacrament on earth, the sacrament is not present; there is then nothing left but an appearance.

Baptism, for example, is "mere dead form" when Christ does not accompany it with the working of his grace from heaven. It is form without essence.[69] In baptism, says Kuyper, there is a working of the Holy Spirit which "can be distinguished from other workings of the Spirit"; for the nature of this working Kuyper points to I Corinthians 12:13. It is not enough that personal grace works in us. Grace does not receive its full justice if it involves only the individual man. It must place us in connection with that body to which we organically belong (p. 541). There must be a connection between personal life and the mystical body of Christ, and it is sacramental grace that gives that to us in baptism.

This does not mean, Kuyper continues, that baptismal grace effects that connection between us and the body of Christ, for that connection has already been made in regeneration. One cannot

---

65. Kuyper opposed the externalization of the sacraments and sought their vindication (*Voor een distel een mirt*, 1891, Foreword).
66. *E Voto*, II, 541.
67. Cf. *Voor een distel een mirt*, 1927, pp. 39ff.
68. *E Voto*, II, 534ff. and *Voor een distel een mirt*, p. 33.
69. *E Voto*, II, 535.

have been regenerated without being simultaneously made a
member of the mystical body of Christ (p. 542). But that bond
of life must become a bond of faith, and our faith must enter
into communion with the mystical body of the Lord. Communal
awareness must be awakened; the believer must disavow the false
communion of sinful mankind and cast his lot with the veracious
and pure communion of the body of Christ. Through grace, our
personal belief must receive the habitude by which we enter into
communal faith. This grace is the sacramental grace which we
receive in baptism.

This is the strengthening of our faith, that it now joins itself
to communal faith in the body of Christ. The faith that has
already been implanted is strengthened "by taking it out of its
solitariness and by leading it into the communion of Christ's
body" (p. 544). Even if a person had already confessed before
his baptism that salvation is in Christ, and even if he were already
incorporated in Christ, he makes the real transition only through
baptism (ibid.). Then, for his own believing consciousness, he
goes from the unreconciled to the reconciled, from sin to ransom,
and from wrath to favor.[70]

Kuyper also adheres to a specific sacramental grace in the
Lord's Supper. As we saw, he rejects Zwingli's views. "The Reformed stand with Rome, Luther, and Calvin against Zwingli in
their adherence to a divine working of grace in the sacrament."[71]
The issue is "the enrichment of our soul with the life of grace"
(p. 132), and Kuyper attempts to determine the specific element
of that working of grace in the Lord's Supper. This working
is trinitarian in nature (pp. 133ff.), but the richest and most
glorious working is brought about by the Holy Spirit (pp. 145,
153). Here, too, Kuyper makes mention of the mystical body
of Christ (pp. 161ff.), for in the Lord's Supper one is joined to
the body of Christ (p. 165). This does not mean that the Lord's
Supper works regeneration, which is presupposed, but its working
stands against the background of the transition from death to
life, a transition which has already taken place. It is not the
normal communication of grace, such as is given in the preaching of the Word and in prayer (p. 161) — that would make the
Lord's Supper superfluous — but something else happens. Kuyper
agrees that the Lord's Supper strengthens man's faith, but that

70. Cf. E Voto, II, 553ff., and Locus de sacramentis, p. 130.
71. E Voto, III, 127.

happens "in this specific manner, that it makes the vitality of the mystical body of the Lord (who is the Head) tingle in us, who are the members of this body" (p. 167). It is a very different working, and its strengthening effect is very great *(ibid.)*.

The transition from solitariness to communion with the body of Christ is the fundamental element in Kuyper's doctrine of sacramental grace. One could speak of the social aspect of the sacraments.[72] And Kuyper's exposition strikes us in that it reveals a remarkable tension between the subjective and the objective elements. Objectively speaking, (presupposed) regeneration already implies communion with Christ's body. One receives baptism as a member of the body of the Lord.[73] That which is lacking lies therefore in the realm of our consciousness and awareness.

There is a relation between sacramental grace and our faith, and herein lies Kuyper's agreement with the Reformed interpretation of the sacraments as strengthening of faith. But, concretely speaking, this sacramental grace is something unique and specific. In "the joining with the communion" a materially new element is introduced for the sacraments in addition to infused grace. But it is hard to see why the specific element of sacramental grace should be associated with the difference between solitariness and communion, since this solitariness does not in any case belong to true faith, and therefore can never be (in relation to God) even a temporary response to his revelation. How then can the concepts of solitariness and communion explain the nature of a specific sacramental grace given by a unique working of the Holy Spirit?

In spite of Kuyper's reservations, it is difficult to understand how one can still maintain that the sacrament points wholly and exclusively at that offering of which the Word has spoken.[74] The purpose of the sacrament is to make believers rest in Christ's fulfilled work, and the strengthening of faith consists precisely in that. This is not like strengthening a *habitus* which is already present in man, as one ordinarily speaks of strengthening. In the sacramental strengthening of faith the believer looks to the promise, and joyfully accepts that promise. For this faith is "the

---

72. Cf. J. M. Spier, "De doopsgenade bij Kuyper," *Bezinning,* 1948.
73. *E Voto,* II, 556.
74. Cf. the Consensus Tigurinus (Art. VII): the sacraments "nihil aliud significant, nisi quod verbo ipso annunciatur" and "quod ore Dei pronunciatum erat, quasi sigillis confirmari et sanciri."

instrument that keeps us with Him in the communion with all His goods."[75] That is why one never can point at a "plus," as though the sacrament grants a completely separate and new sacramental grace.

To reject special sacramental grace does not devalue the sacrament, but only serves to point out that the working of the sacraments rests essentially upon belief in salvation, which belief is strengthened by the sacraments. The sacraments do not provide a separate grace having nothing to do with belief. Nothing is added to the *sola fide;* nothing is more "real" and mystical than the relation of faith. Rather, the very aim of the sacrament is to make the believer live that faith in all aspects of his life.[76]

At this point there was a difference between Kuyper and Bavinck. Bavinck held that the sacrament provides a benefit, but not an entirely new one, for the gift of the sacrament lies precisely in the fact that faith is directed toward all the richness of Christ's benefits. "There is no grace conveyed by the sacrament which is not conveyed by the Word.[77]

Bavinck also correctly relates the sacrament to the incorporation in Christ. Without mentioning Kuyper, but in obvious reference to his exposition, Bavinck writes: "Incorporation into the body of Christ also takes place through faith, and it receives its sign and seal in the sacrament of baptism. Baptismal grace exists, and according to Scripture and the Reformed confession can only exist, in *declaratio* and *confirmatio.*"[78] This *declaratio* and *confirmatio* presuppose faith, which is the only way to maintain fully the decisive significance of faith. Kuyper did not err because he rejected so vehemently Zwingli's exposition of the sacrament and made a plea for the acting of God in the sacrament. But when he posited a specific sacramental grace, he understressed the role of the sacraments in the strengthening of faith and thus weakened the relation between faith and sacrament. We may appreciate Kuyper's motive, but we may not speak of a specific sacramental grace unless we mean that benefit of the

---

75. Conf., Art. 22.
76. Cf. the Geneva Catechism of 1545 (Müller, *op. cit.,* p. 147): "fidem in nobis inchoatam esse nequaquam sufficit, nisi continenter alatus, et magis in dies magisque augescat. Ad eam ergo tum alendam, tum roborandam, tum provehendam sacramenta instituit Dominus."
77. Bavinck, *Geref. Dog.,* IV, 497.
78. *Ibid.*

Holy Spirit by which he strengthens our faith so that it comes to rest in the fulness of salvation in Christ.

Clearly, then, the truly Reformed concept of the sacraments allows for the power and the efficacy of the sacraments. It does not reduce the sacrament to a *nudum signum*, a useless and vain sign, which can perhaps have some psychological effect but which cannot function in God's acting.[79] Calvin has repeatedly pointed out that the sacred sign does not deceive, for that would be contrary to God's veracity. This non-deceiving is directly connected with the working of the sacraments. While Bullinger worries about the *per sacramentum*, Calvin rejects the *per sacramentum* if it implies the automatic inclusion of grace in the sign but accepts it in the light of the conjunction that is founded in the Holy Spirit and accepted by faith.

Bruining has written that Calvin stands with Zwingli in his exposition of the sacraments, because he does not appreciate the sacraments as means of grace, but only as representations of grace.[80] But that gives an altogether incorrect view of the Reformed position. Calvin is quite strong in his language when he gives attention to the conjunction that corresponds to faith: *"sacramenta continent, conferunt gratiam."* This implies neither the exclusion of grace from the sacrament, nor some automatic connection between sign and that which is signified. The point becomes clear when we consider that Calvin had rejected the above-mentioned definition of the sacraments in 1536. When, later on, he believed it to be acceptable, he was thinking of the living, personal relation between the Holy Spirit and faith, and he could — to prevent misunderstanding — add in the historical situation: "but it is a rather dangerous way of speaking and for that reason it may be sufficient either to look away from it, or to soften its harshness by means of a sensible explanation."[81] It is obvious what Calvin means by a sensible explanation, namely, the explanation according to which the sacrament is neither subjectivized nor objectivized, but which grounds the conjunction between the sign and the signified firmly in the acts of God. This is to reject the automatic conjunction which depersonalizes the sacrament, but also to reject the notion of the

79. Bizer, *Studien zur Geschichte des Abendmahlsstreits im 16. Jahrhundert,* 1940, p. 261.
80. A. Bruining, *Verzamelde Studien,* I, 86ff.
81. Dankbaar, *De sacramentsleer van Calvijn,* 1941, p. 42. Cf. Consensus Tigurinus, Art. XVIII.

mere sign in itself, for through the Spirit because of its institution by God the sign is full of efficacy with respect to faith.
That is why the *per sacramentum* and the *cum sacramento* can
be accepted simultaneously without involving us in contra-
dictions.

Some have remarked that there is a parallelism between a
heavenly and an earthly act in the Reformed sacramental doctrine. Beckmann even saw a consequence of Platonism here.
"What, then, is the essence of the sacraments for Calvin? It is
in the strict sense of the word a marvelous, God-directed parallelism of a heavenly and an earthly act. . . . In this divine-human
parallelism lies the depth, the disquiet, and the problematics
in Calvin's sacramental doctrine. On the one hand stands the
symbolum with its mysterious content as *testimonium, sigillum,
pignus,* as *testificatio, repraesentatio;* and, because it is God's
symbolum, it corresponds to an *exhibitio,* a heavenly *veritas,* for
God is veracious and what he affirms, he holds to. But only
from the point of view of God, according to his will and good
pleasure is it such a symbol, only in so far as it is *instrumentum,
organum, vehiculum gratia, adminiculum fidei, adjumentum ad
percipiendam gratiam,* not in itself as though it possessed any
power in itself. God has not deposited his grace in the earthly
sacrament."[82]

This parallelism, in which Beckmann is indeed approaching
the essence of the sacrament, has nothing to do with Platonism,
however. Calvin is not concerned with constructing a systematic connection, but with the acts of God by which he strengthens faith through divinely qualified signs. Beckmann's so-called
parallelism is nothing but the correlation between faith and
sacrament, in which the sign can never be detached from the
Giver of the sacrament. Beckmann describes this correlation ex-
cellently: "For Calvin there is here no point of rest, but only
the perpetual movement between God and man, Spirit and
faith, *figura* and *veritas,* etc. Only in this connection can the
essence of the sacrament be revealed to clarify the instrumental
and grace-mediating character of the sacrament."[83] Perhaps it
is better to speak only of movement in this context, rather than
of disquiet, for it is precisely in this movement that rest is
brought about. One does not place his trust in isolated signs, but

82. J. Beckmann, *Vom Sakrament bei Calvin,* p. 35.
83. *Ibid.,* p. 39.

accepts those signs that are in God's hand for the strengthening of that faith which must be strengthened in order to rest fully in the promise.

This rest stands, in spite of the interpretations that repeatedly threaten it. The efficacy of the sacraments has often been misinterpreted, either by objectivizing them, or by making them dependent upon the subject. The mystery of the sacrament can be understood, however, only if both of these concepts are rejected. For God's acting differs from the objectivity of things in this world, and faith is something other than a subjective disposition which can be investigated as to its presence or absence. That is why Calvin can write that, apart from faith, the sacrament is nothing but a certain ruin for the Church. That is no subjectivizing of the sacrament, but a reference to the mystery of the sacrament, which can be understood only in the way of belief, and which in that way displays its full power. Those who expect more from the efficacy of the sacrament do not understand that thus they do not esteem the sacrament more highly, nor do they really strive after more reality, for this striving must alienate them from the one reality that the sacraments are designed to secure: the reality of salvation.

CHAPTER FIVE

THE INSTITUTION OF BAPTISM

BEFORE WE begin our discussion of baptism, we must remind ourselves that historically the *institution* of the sacraments has always been a prominent question. It is easy to see why this should be true of baptism. If baptism were nothing more than one of several customs and rites instituted by man to express certain religious thoughts and concepts, it could boast of a venerable tradition and would fit nicely into certain anthropological theories, but it would have no decisive significance for the Christian faith. For that decisive element cannot lie in what man does, but in what God does and grants. Precisely because throughout the centuries baptism has been directly connected with admonition, sealing, and assurance, the institution of baptism is of primary importance, for here the question arises whether it is man who speaks, or whether it is God who comes to meet man with his divine authority.

Throughout the centuries, the Church has answered this question no less positively than with respect to the institution of the Lord's Supper. Baptism was not seen as a ceremony that somehow originated in man's mind, but as an ecclesiastical rite instituted by Christ himself. Thus, the Church has refused to base her confession of baptism on any psychological or historical contingencies. She has rather pointed to a certain concrete act in history, an act of Jesus Christ. When she spoke of the divine institution of baptism, she meant nothing other than the institution by Christ himself. The unanimity of the Church on this point was undoubtedly based on the clear New Testament command to baptize in Matthew 28:19. Until people began to doubt the authenticity of this word and increasingly to deny it, there was no difference of opinion regarding the institution of baptism by Christ.

It is not sufficient, however, that the historical institution of baptism should be accurately established and the person who instituted it accurately identified, unless it is further understood that these facts are absolutely essential to the nature and validity of baptism. It would be wrong to adhere to the institution just because it has become common practice in the course of history, while forgetting its relation to the Christ who suffered and died for our salvation. The sacraments, including baptism, are by virtue of divine institution involved with the New Covenant, with the coming of the Kingdom of God in the Messiah. Being historically founded, they are therefore also dated in the history of salvation. Baptism and the Lord's Supper are signs that proclaim the all-sufficiency of the work of Christ.

To be sure, there is a connection between the sacrament of the New Covenant and the signs of God in the Old Covenant, especially circumcision and the passover; but the Christian tradition has nevertheless emphasized strongly the institution of the sacraments by Christ himself, thus indicating the importance of his historical appearance and work. They are the sacraments of the New Covenant, the sacraments of the Christian Church. They were seen as the signs of salvation in the Messiah, of the Kingdom that had come. They are immediately linked with the word that was spoken by Christ: It is finished. Detached from this finished work, they lose their decisive significance. They are signs of the reconciliation which became historical reality in the Messiah. He himself is the meaning, the truth of the sacraments, "without which they would be nothing."[1] Only his authority can give a solid basis to baptism (and the Lord's Supper); and this authority is not merely formal, because he founded them, but also material, determining their content. Institutor and institution can never be detached from each other. It is Christ's sacrament that requires our attention.

Having established this important connection, we must now notice that baptism is not a completely new act having no analogy with Israelitish and pagan practice. It is important that John the Baptist already performed the act of baptism which, according to the express testimony of the New Testament, was also by divine authority. Hence the question has often been raised, what is the relation between John's baptism and the baptism instituted by Christ? Some have replied that they are

1. Conf., Art. 35.

very closely connected, even identical with each other, while others maintain that they are sharply to be distinguished.

The question about the relation between the two baptisms arises because of the significance that the New Testament attaches to the baptism of John. It is not at all regarded as a human production, or as an arbitrary, ritual formality. In a debate between Jesus and the Pharisees, the Redeemer himself speaks of the origin and thus of the authority of the baptism by John. "The baptism of John, was it from heaven, or from men?" (Mark 11:30). This question was the response to another question about Jesus' own qualifications (Matt. 21:23), while Christ's counter-question is not answered by his opponents. Behind the "ignorance" lies cold calculation. The answer "from heaven" would evoke the problem of their unbelief, while the answer "from men" would evoke a conflict with the crowd. But in the clash regarding Jesus' own qualification, the question of origin is posed in connection with that baptism which preceded the baptism instituted by Christ. We remember the publicans who were baptized by John, and who thus, according to the Word of Scripture, justified God, while the Pharisees and the Scribes "rejected for themselves the counsel of God, being not baptized of him" (Luke 7:30), a new reference to the relation of John's baptism to the will of God. The rejection of the baptism of John stands on a line with the rejection of the will of God.

This divine origin we find emphatically attested in the gospel story about John's activities. He did not call himself the Baptist by his own initiative, but he knew himself called to this activity of baptism by virtue of God's command. He declares emphatically that he was sent to baptize with water (John 1:33). The Pharisees' critical questions regarding his qualifications to baptize did not make him hesitant for a moment; they are answered in his reference to the One who is greater, the Messiah of God. John's baptism is immediately connected with the coming of the Messiah: "That he should be made manifest to Israel, for this cause came I baptizing in water" (John 1:31). There is therefore a close interrelation between John's baptism and the coming of the Kingdom of God, of which John himself has announced the approach (Matt. 3:1).

All this does not imply that John's baptism is identical with the baptism instituted by Christ. The very fact that the confession of the Church spoke of the institution of baptism by

Christ prompts us to reflect more closely on the connection between the two. To that end we must first pay attention to the baptism of John. This baptism was preached in a specific and critical situation as a baptism of repentance unto the remission of sins (Mark 1:4). It took place on the level of absolute seriousness, of eschatological, judicial seriousness, as becomes clear from John's sharp address to the Pharisees and Sadducees: "Ye offspring of vipers, who warned you to flee from the wrath to come? Bring forth therefore fruit worthy of repentance" (Matt. 3:7, 8).

The purpose of John's baptism was evidently to inaugurate a radical change, a radical repentance, an inner change of life, a confession of sins in the light of the Kingdom now approaching. The way which John must pave for the coming Messiah is a way through the wilderness — a way of contrition and repentance. All of his work points toward the coming King, a King who also stands in the center of John's baptismal activity. The baptism is dated, directed, and subservient to him who had to come, while John himself had to decrease (John 3:30). John's preaching and baptizing is significant only as a witness in this historical situation, where he is placed as the forerunner of the Messiah. His activity cannot be described in general categories, because it is determined uniquely by the testimony of him who is now coming, the Lamb of God, the testimony of him who comes after John, but who is before him (John 1:15).

This involvement of John the Baptist with the Messiah is essential to all his activity. It is activity with respect to the Kingdom of God.[2]

"An essential part of John's testimony is his own negative

---

2. This is rashly denied by Rudolf Otto (*Reich Gottes und Menschsohn*, 1940, p. 48), who regards Matt. 3:2 as a redactional insertion, and thinks that the words of John himself begin with Matt. 3:7. Otto appeals to Luke 16:16 to show that John did not preach the Kingdom of heaven, but only announced the coming judgment and wrath of God (p. 48). In this way he explains the vexation of John against the absolutely new message of Christ, and comes to regard "Jesus in contrast to John" (pp. 55ff.). Marsh says correctly: "He made no claim to manuscript for his action and it should be recognized at once that the evidence of the manuscripts is entirely in favour of the genuineness of the words" (H. G. Marsh, *The Origin and Significance of the N. T. Baptism*, 1941, p. 83). It is clear that Otto's interpolation-view, without basis in the text, decisively influences all of his interpretation of the Kingdom of God.

testimony about himself."[3] Seldom have disciples so completely misunderstood their teacher as did the disciples of John, who, by honoring him in independence, misunderstood the significance of his calling and thereby obscured the core of his message.

Clearly John's baptism is to be understood in the context of the history of redemption. But this does not answer all our questions. Many interpreters have gone on to distinguish sharply between John's baptism and Christian baptism. Roman Catholic theology, for instance, maintains that John's baptism worked *ex opere operantis* (depending upon belief and repentance), while Christian baptism supposedly works *ex opere operato*.[4] Hence John's baptism is thought to be inferior to Christian baptism: it did not give or contain grace, as Christian baptism does. And it is thought that this contrast is warranted by the gospel itself, in which John declares that he baptizes with water, while Christ would come and baptize with the Holy Spirit and with fire (Mark 1:8). Markus Barth also takes note of the contrast between water baptism and baptism with the Spirit. John's baptism, he says, is not a real sacrament in the sense of the later sacramental doctrine, but a sign pointing toward the real baptism, according to the coming remission which would become reality in the death of Christ. John could not grant real remission in his baptism, but he could only pave the way toward remission, the remission that is found in the Messiah. "Remission cannot be the gift or the effect of John's baptism, because only with the arrival of the coming One is it brought about, and bestowed by him together with the gift of the Holy Spirit."[5]

On the other hand, there are those who maintain the identity of John's baptism with Christian baptism. Bavinck points out that they agree in sign and in that which is signified, and that Lutherans and Reformed have been willing to admit, at most, a difference in degree.[6] He believes that the difference between baptizing with water and baptizing with the Spirit does not distinguish between John's baptism and Christian baptism, but between John's baptism and the outpouring of the Holy Spirit on Pentecost. John's baptism was also a baptism to repentance

3. M. Barth, *Die Taufe ein Sakrament?*, 1951, p. 111. Cf. Luke 3:15 and John 1:25, and John's self-distinction with respect to the Messiah, John 1:21.
4. E.g., Thomas Aquinas and the Council of Trent.
5. Barth, *op. cit.*, p. 125.
6. Bavinck, *Geref. Dog.*, IV, 476.

unto the remission of sins, and as such it conforms essentially to Christian baptism. The difference in degree of which Bavinck speaks refers to the fact that Christ has taken over baptism from John, has had it administered by his disciples, and has made it mandatory for all believers from all nations.[7]

Calvin, too, calls the ministry of John "completely the same" as the one which later was committed to the apostles. It is the same baptism: unto remission of sins. Calvin objects to the "subtle reasoning of Augustine," who thought that sins were forgiven *in hope* through John's baptism, while the baptism instituted by Christ did away with man's sins in reality (*Inst.,* IV, XV, 7). The only difference, according to Calvin, lies in the fact that John baptized in him who would come, while the apostles baptized in him who had already revealed himself (*ibid.*). There is, of course, a progress in the gifts of Christ after the resurrection, but that cannot be employed to indicate differences regarding baptism. It is incorrect, says Calvin, to infer from the relation between baptism by water and baptism by the Spirit that John's baptism differed from the one instituted by Christ.[8] In the comparison between these baptisms, the crux of the matter is the comparison between the two persons, John and Christ. John did not want to give himself any credit (I baptize with water). Therein, says Calvin, John stands on the same level as those who baptize now, for they, too, can in themselves administer only the outward baptism. In other words, Calvin is interested in the relation between the human instrument (John and the others after him) and Christ as the Giver of the baptism with the Spirit. Man is always the administrator of the outward sign, while Christ gives the effect of the sign.[9]

Kuyper also holds that the distinction between water baptism and Spirit baptism may not be used to differentiate between John's baptism and Christian baptism. He, too, points out that Christians also baptize with water. Nevertheless, Kuyper is not willing to place the two baptisms on the same level.[10] As he sees it, John's baptism was nothing but a baptism with water. It was not accompanied with a working of the Holy Spirit, and therefore did not serve as an instrument for the Holy Spirit. If John's baptism were placed on the same level

7. *Ibid.,* p. 478.
8. *Comm.* on Acts 1:5.
9. *Ibid.*
10. A. Kuyper, *E Voto,* II, 511ff.

as Christian baptism, says Kuyper, one would have to conclude that our baptism is also nothing but a baptizing with water in which the Holy Spirit does not work, so that one could not possibly speak of a sacrament.

Why did the Holy Spirit not accompany John's water baptism? Because, answers Kuyper, before Pentecost there was no direct working of the Holy Spirit even in the baptizing of Jesus and the disciples., The Spirit was not yet, so that the working that comes with baptism did not exist until the outpouring of the Holy Spirit. John's baptism was a baptism with water and therefore only a part of real baptism. Baptism with the Spirit had later to be added to the baptism with water. John was not thinking of two baptisms when he contrasted his baptism with the baptism with the Spirit, says Kuyper, but he referred "to the two indispensable constituent parts of one and the same baptism." According to Kuyper, John and Jesus administered a baptism together, John with the sign of water, Jesus with the working of the Holy Spirit. Jesus could do that after he had been glorified, so that all baptisms before the Ascension must be distinguished from Christian baptism. The efficacy that actually belongs to baptism with water did not come until the day of Pentecost, while "now this efficacy accompanies baptism with water immediately."

Kuyper distinguishes between John's baptism and Christian baptism more clearly than does Bavinck. While Bavinck merely speaks of a universalizing of John's baptism, Kuyper emphasizes the progress to the glorification of Christ and the outpouring of the Spirit, and he links this aspect of the history of redemption to the specific feature of Christian baptism. Thus he can characterize John's baptism with water by analogy with every water baptism of later times, and he can say that baptism becomes real baptism only through the accompanying work of the Spirit.

In general it can be said that the place of John's baptism in the history of redemption has received much attention of late. Herman Ridderbos, for example, does not recognize a contrast between the two baptisms, "but baptism as commanded by Christ to the disciples is nevertheless no continuation of John's baptism." The difference between the Old and New Covenants is also valid with respect to baptism. While John looks

11. *Ibid.,* p. 514.

forward to the fulfilment of the Kingdom of God, as something that is to come, Christian baptism represents the fulfilment proper[12] and it forms the visible manifestation and sealing of that which has arrived with the coming of Christ. Christian baptism is the baptism of the Kingdom that has come, and it is a sign of this kingdom; John's baptism could only point toward its coming.

One is reminded here of Augustine's view (forgiveness "in hope"), which Calvin criticized as being too "subtle." But this aspect of "hopefulness" need not make John's baptism inferior, as long as we place it in the context of a historical development from John to the fulness of the Kingdom in the Messiah. Then we are able to recognize that John's baptism carried a significance beyond that which was seen by its believing and repentant subjects; its further significance rested upon the subsequent coming of the Kingdom for the world. For it cannot be said that John's baptism is simply identical with later Christian baptism. This does not imply that John's baptism possessed only an "outward" meaning, but it does emphasize that John's baptism is *dated* and can be understood correctly only in that light. Thus we find John himself saying: ". . . that he [Christ] should be made manifest to Israel, for this cause came I baptizing in water" (John 1:31).

All of John's activity had been critical in a very specific sense. He called to conversion and baptism. But this baptism did not serve to mark a change from gentile to believer; rather, it was a baptism of Israel itself.[13] Without denying Israel's special position as the elect people of God, John combatted a certain misunderstanding of that election as it was expressed in the words: "We have Abraham to our father" (Matt. 3:9). John's preaching, like Christ's (John 8:33ff.), is directed against such pretension: "I say unto you, that God is able of these stones to raise up children unto Abraham" (Matt. 3:9). Any appeal to the covenant of God with Abraham apart from faith

---

12. H. Ridderbos, *De Komst van het Koninkrijk*, p. 335.
13. That is why it is not possible to deduce John's baptism from proselyte-baptism. Although there may be a connection in the exterior rite, the two are qualitatively different. See, e.g., Carl H. Kraeling, *John the Baptist*, 1951, pp. 102ff.; H. G. Marsh, *The Origin and Significance of N. T. Baptism*, 1941, pp. 8f.; F. Gavin, *The Jewish Antecedents of the Christian Sacraments*, 1928, Lecture II; Kittel, *TWNT*, I, 535ff.

and obedience is fundamentally irreligious. Hence Israel is called to repentance, conversion, and baptism. It is a call full of eschatological seriousness: the axe lies already at the root of the trees (Matt. 3:10; cf. vv. 7, 12). The Kingdom that has come nigh urges an ultimate decision, to true repentance and turning about. Only in this way can the Kingdom be entered without fear, a Kingdom of God's grace and judgment. The judgment is preached with special clarity by John. The way through the wilderness must be paved.

The rite of baptism is the sign of this eschatological serious-ness, in which God's mercy goes beyond his judgment for him who in repentance approaches the Kingdom. This baptism is not merely an external rite; as sign, and connected with the preaching of baptism to repentance, it stands in direct relation to the remission of sins by the grace of God. It is understandable that the Church should have seen a close connection between John's baptism and Christian baptism, for both of them imply a relation between repentance and remission, and both are signs of God's grace in purification. Hence there could be no principal difference between them; both signify a participation in the salvation of Christ, which is the only salvation taught in the Old and New Testaments. This is not to deny, however, that this salvation became a historical reality at a given point in time with the coming of Christ.

It is wrong, therefore, to *identify* John's baptism with Chris-tian baptism, since this would neglect the temporal relations in the history of redemption. On the other hand, John's baptism does involve true repentance and is indeed a sign of the com-ing salvation of God.

John's baptism is the baptism of the coming Kingdom. It is not merely an "external" rite, nor is it "inferior," except in the chronological sense (cf. Matt. 11:11). The "lesser" of John's baptism corresponds to the word of the Baptist that he himself must decrease while Christ must increase. John was essentially a herald, whose value lay in his preparation for the coming King. That is why we may not, with Kuyper, say that the water baptism of John is the same as the later baptism with water, lacking only the added gift of the Holy Spirit. Nor may we adopt the Roman Catholic causal interpretation, which contrasts *ex opere operantis* with *ex opere operato*. Neither of these views does justice to the historical aspect of redemption, from the prelude to the actual coming of God's Kingdom. Both

tend to externalize John's baptism, which contradicts its direct
linkage with repentance and conversion and with the remission
of sins.[14]

One can say with Bavinck that Christian baptism (instituted
by Christ before his ascension) joins itself to John's baptism
and "expands" itself to other nations. But that expansion does
not become possible and real until the great historical change
has occurred to which John refers: the coming of the Kingdom
of God and the gift of the Spirit which is implied by that coming. It is understandable, then, that in the history of baptismal
interpretation there have been so many variations regarding
the relation between John's baptism and Christian baptism. On
the one hand, some paid too much attention to the different
places of the baptisms in the history of redemption, and thus
would not speak of their identity. Others, however, looked at
the context in which John's baptisms stood, noticing its sign
and that which it signified, and accordingly placed full emphasis on the agreement between the two baptisms. The two
views do not exclude one another; rather, they belong together.

All the faithful who lived before the coming of God's Kingdom participate in the treasures of that Kingdom, i.e. the remission of sins. Christ's work is fully historical in nature, but
its efficacy is not bound to a certain time. In this respect —
participation in the remission of sins — John's baptism is inferior to Christian baptism. Therein lies the relative value
of the opinion of those who so emphatically defend the "identity"
of the two baptisms. But this agrees fully with the view of
Augustine, who attempted to indicate the redemptive-historical
difference between the two baptisms with the locution "in
hope." He did not thereby oppose the *reality* of remission in
John's baptism, and hence Calvin's reproach, that Augustine
used "subtle" reasoning, is unjustified. So, too, was Coccejus
incorrect when he said that in the Old Covenant the salvation
of Christ was only a matter of *paresis* and not yet of *aphesis*.

The sign in both John's baptism and Christian baptism is
the water of purification. To understand it, we must see that
it is more than a mere "illustration" of something. We must

14. Stromberg points out that in Acts 2:38 and Luke 3:3 "the essence of
   Christian baptism and the baptism of John is identically portrayed"
   (*Studien in der Christlichen Kirche der ersten zwei Jahrhunderte*, 1913,
   p. 52).

rathér consider the total context in which God has placed it
when he instituted this sign.

By his sovereignty, God has elevated the use of water above
other arbitrary parables or symbolical acts. He has, further,
revealed that this symbolical washing possesses real efficacy in
the total economy of God's acts. The importance and compelling
power of this sign lies in the power and trustworthiness of the
Word of God, in the preaching of baptism unto repentance.
The baptism of water is a portrayal of purification. This is
already indicated in the Old Testament: "I will sprinkle clean
water upon you, and ye shall be clean: from all your filthiness,
and from all your idols, will I cleanse you. A new heart also
will I give you, and a new spirit will I put within you; and
I will take away the stony heart out of your flesh, and I will
give you a heart of flesh" (Ezek. 36:25f.). These earlier wash-
ings do not reduce the significance of the baptismal act, because the simple image of purifying water acquired (through
God's divine selection and election) great significance. Since
it is God who has selected the symbol, we never shall be able
to speak of it as "unimportant." The continuity of this symbol
in the history of redemption becomes visible when Peter speaks
of all the things that have happened throughout the country
of the Jews: "beginning from Galilee, after the baptism which
John preached; even Jesus of Nazareth," in which Peter harks
back to the beginning of the Messianic era (Acts 10:37).

The relation between John's baptism and Christian baptism
can be understood only in the light of redemptive fulfilment.
The contrast between *ex opere operantis* and *ex opere operato*
is a caricature of this fulfilment. It does not originate in the
category of fulfilment, but in the sacramental interpretation
which attaches a "causality" of grace to the sacraments. Over
against this construction, John's baptism must be seen and interpreted in its direct relation to Christian baptism; and it is
fully understandable that the Reformers, opposing the Roman
Catholic theory of contrast, pointed to the continuity between
the two baptisms as manifested especially by the sign and the
thing signified. We must remember, of course, that the relation
between the baptisms can be seen fully only in the light of the
fulfilment of the Kingdom of God, which receives its historical
realization in the historical work of Christ.

In the midst of the fulfilment of the Kingdom stands Christ's
command of universal baptism. This baptism is the royal sign

of the richness of the Kingdom at hand. The institution of this sign is preceded by the royal proclamation: "All authority hath been given unto me in heaven and on earth" (Matt. 28:18) .[15] Just as John's baptism had raised a question about John's qualifications, so now Christ's qualification stands in focus. Before the Ascension Christ gives this sign of God to the Church, a sign of particular power through his divine institution and his involvement with the Kingdom.

In the institution of this baptism, the sign cannot be detached from the preaching of the gospel. The command to baptize is joined firmly with the command to preach. Both the sign and the preaching refer back to the accomplished salvation which now is carried into the whole world. Behind Christian baptism, as behind the Lord's Supper, stands the cross of the Lord of the Church, the cross and the resurrection. The preaching, which no longer will be limited to Israel, will be accompanied by this sacred sign of baptism, and therein it will stand beside the Lord's Supper. That is why both baptism and the Lord's Supper are the signs, the sacraments, of the Kingdom that has come. They are Christian sacraments in the full sense of the word. They have been instituted by Christ. The Old Testament analogies that preceded them were directed toward that which now has become reality.

Some have expressed surprise that the baptism by water was not ended after the outpouring of the Spirit on Pentecost. The reason for this surprise can usually be traced to a "spiritualist" point of view, which discovers an opposition between the workings of the Spirit and the visible sign. But the contrast between "outward" and "inward" is a false one. The historical progress of the acts of God is clearly not to be grasped with these categories, as is shown by the fact that from the very beginning of the Christian Church we encounter baptism with water.

On this latter point, Flemington has asked: "How was it that when some six weeks after the death of Jesus his followers came together to live as an organized community, they seem unhesitatingly to have agreed that any fresh adherents to their number must enter by the gate-way of baptism."[16] Many believe that somehow Jesus Christ himself stood behind this immediate practice of baptism, but the question has been raised whether

15. Cf. K. Barth, *Auslegung von Mattheus* (on ch. 28:16-20), p. 11.
16. W. F. Flemington, *The New Testament Doctrine of Baptism*, 1948, p. 117.

authority for this could be found in the command to baptize as found in Matthew 28:19, or whether Christ's authority was merely postulated to justify actual Church practices. More than once people have chosen for the "post late" view on the basis of objections against the authenticity of the command to baptize: they say that it could not possibly have been uttered by Christ, but that it must have been a later formulation of the Christian Church, a sort of baptismal dogma which was carried into the New Testament, and which therefore is not a sufficient basis for the confession of the Christian Church that baptism was instituted by Christ.[17] The arguments vary in approach and nature, but they focus especially on the fact of the apostolic baptismal practice, in which other formulas for baptism are supposed to have been used, and on the fact that the passage in Matthew already uses the trinitarian formula for baptism.[18]

These objections against the authenticity of Jesus' command to baptize in Matthew 28 show clearly that textual criticism is not the real issue. The argument is a material one, involving words by Christ. Van Bakel asks, for example, why Jesus did not give the command during his human life.[19] Here he fails to realize that the situation in Matthew 28 is completely new in terms of the history of redemption. These forty days are the period after the resurrection and before the ascension, in which Christ speaks emphatically of the *exousia* which now is given unto him (Matt. 28:18). He gives his command when he takes leave from his disciples, and this command is therefore grounded upon the factuality and the absoluteness of his fulfilled work. Hence baptism is now given as a universal sign for all nations.[20]

---

17. Cf. *ibid.*, pp. 105ff.; M. Barth, *Die Taufe ein Sakrament?*, pp. 527ff. The arguments are mainly still those of Kirsopp Lake and Conybeare: "For many centuries the passage was accepted without dispute; within recent years, however, the critical study of the N. T. has made it difficult to read the verses as an exact record of actual words of Jesus" (Flemington, p. 105). "The struggle concerning the oldest text is not yet decided" (M. Barth, p. 527).

18. Cf. H. A. van Bakel, *De oorsprong van den Christelijken Doop*, 1913, pp. 4ff. Cf. also J. H. Scholten, *De doopsformule*, 1869, ch. 1.

19. Van Bakel, *op. cit.*, pp. 20f.

20. Van Bakel attempts to show that the perspective "for all nations" has no place in the gospel. "The gospel of Matthew knows only the mission in Israel" (*Oorsprong*, p. 6). To be sure, Matt. 8:11 speaks of those

It is strange that the authenticity of Jesus' command to baptize is often denied while at the same time — in view of the immediate baptismal practice of the Church — the authority of Jesus Christ is thought to stand behind Christian baptism. Flemington, for example, concludes that Jesus evidently intended that "the entry into the community should be accomplished outwardly by the rite of water-baptism."[21] He substitutes this "intention," then, for the command to baptize as given in Matthew 28, and thus, without the support of scriptural references, seeks to maintain the universal significance of baptism. To this speculation we reply that it is not permissible to argue from what was only possible, particularly since the situation in question is completely determined by the newness of the authority bestowed upon Christ. The command to baptize is not an isolated command, but is closely linked with the preaching of the Lord and his Kingdom. Christian baptism does not merely perpetuate an existing rite, but it accompanies the spreading of the gospel throughout the world according to the command given to the apostles. The message of salvation must be carried into the world of the gentiles (cf. Mark 16:15). The witnessing of the apostles is based on what now has happened, the witnessing that will reach the ends of the earth (Acts 1:5).

Luke says regarding Christ's speaking with his disciples between resurrection and ascension that he spoke about "things concerning the Kingdom of God" (Acts 1:3). The command to baptize was given in that same period by him whom God had made Lord and Christ (cf. Acts 2:36), and herein rests the universality of the message which goes out to all nations. The factuality of salvation in Christ through cross and resurrection leads to the new situation of the apostolate.[22] The witnesses to

---

who will come from East and West, and we read in Matt. 24:14 that the gospel of the Kingdom will be preached in the whole world, but the first word is said to the Jews only to put them to shame before the pagan officer, and the last word is inserted. The connection between gospel and world is lost via emendation, while with the command to mission, an appeal is made to the evidence that Christ could have done that equally well while he was still living, for instance, in his words in Matthew 10. The speculative nature of such a line of thinking becomes very evident here.

21. Flemington, *op. cit.*, p. 128.
22. This does not undo the words of Matt. 10:1-4. For an interpretation of this passage in the light of redemptive history, see H. N. Ridderbos, *Korte Verklaring* on Matthew, II, 261.

Christ's resurrection now go out into the world to make the nations his disciples. This is the context in which the Church appealed to the authority of Christ in the institution of Christian baptism. The appeal was correct, because it respected the new situation in which Christ proclaimed his program for his holy Church throughout the world.[23] Christ's decisive authority is not that of a vague and general omnipotence, but the authority of the crucified and resurrected Lord.

The question whether Christian baptism is from God or from men has therefore a definitive answer. The sacred sign is forever lifted above all arbitrariness. It is and remains the meaningful sign of the accomplished salvation and of all the richness of blessing comprised in that salvation. Faith lives by it and in it. Every form of spiritualism must bow before the fact that the community of the New Testament did not dispense with water baptism when the Spirit was poured out. Rather, baptism immediately took its place as a divine, legitimate given in the reality of the Church. The Word is heard in joyful discipleship and baptism is administered and accepted (Acts 2: 37-38).

The New Testament gives no warrant for the contrast between sign and Spirit, for the sign stands in a *serving* relation to the salvation in the Lord. Those who accepted the Word were baptized when they saw that the Kingdom consisted in a new discipleship to the new Lord, as the eunuch asked to be baptized when he learned of the Man of Sorrows (Acts 8: 36). Baptism is the powerful sign of the Kingdom of God and of the Spirit, of purification through the blood of Christ, of regeneration and new life.[24]

In the light of this fulness of the accomplished salvation in Christ, the crucified and resurrected Lord, the argument against the authenticity of the baptismal command on the basis of its

<hr/>

23. Cf. Grosheide, who points to the aorist: "that is the command that Jesus gives now for ever" (*Commentaar op Mattheus*, p. 375).
24. We point out that the background of the problem of baptismal recognition lies in the earnestness of the fact that in baptism we do not just come into contact with an ecclesiastical rite, but with a signifying and sealing by God. That is why the problem mentioned can only be satisfactorily discussed in connection with the *locus de ecclesia*, as Church of Jesus Christ. A solution which affects the essence of baptism in its divine institution will not do. Therein lies a parallel with the problem of intercommunion, of which we shall speak later.

trinitarian formula is no longer valid.[25] Rather, we should recognize that Matthew 28:19 is a rich revelation regarding baptism in the context of the trinitarian fulness of God. Baptism is now related clearly to the Father, the Son, and the Holy Spirit. Undoubtedly there is progress here in the trinitarian revelation, for, although Christ had also spoken of the Father and the Holy Spirit before his resurrection, he speaks now in this explicit form of Father, Son, and Holy Spirit. Since textual criticism provides no evidence whatsoever that this passage is a later interpolation,[26] it is clear that the objectors have simply applied human standards to divine revelation. Their method rests on "a priori assumptions when reading the gospel."[27]

There is much difference of opinion regarding the baptizing "in the name" of the Father and the Son and the Holy Spirit,[28] but it is clear at any rate that baptism is here placed in relation to the full communion and superiority of the Triune God, through whom baptism is given its decisive significance in the Kingdom at hand. It is possible for unbelief to isolate baptism from this Kingdom and from the purifying blood of Jesus Christ, and it is possible to detach baptism from the symbolic power which is founded on its sacred institution. But this perversion, which leads to the neglect of God's signs and to the undermining of the certainty of salvation, cannot destroy the value of God's sign of the richness of his kingdom, which was given through the *Kurios* when he ascended into heaven to send the Comforter to his Church on earth, the Comforter who will lead it in all its life, including its witnessing to its Lord, who has all power in heaven and earth.

The sacred, visible sign does not in any way subvert the comfort of the believer. The New Testament warns urgently against the "wisdom" of man, assuring us that in baptism God confirms his salvation with inviolable signifying and sealing power, for comfort in all temptation and doubt. Those who think baptism to be inferior because "external," while the work of the Spirit is "internal," want to be wiser than God himself, and wiser than the Lord Jesus Christ, who places the nations within the reach of his reconciling grace through calling and

---

25. Cf. H. N. Ridderbos, *op. cit.*, p. 262.
26. Cf. Grosheide, *op. cit.*, p. 376.
27. *Ibid.*, p. 262.
28. Cf. Oepke in *TWNT*, I, 537.

admonition, command and comfort, and who is with his Church
for ever and ever.

We now wish to discuss a question directly related to the
institution of baptism, namely, whether baptism is *necessary*.
Because, as we have already seen, Jesus Christ himself is the
content and the veracity of the sacraments, there is good reason
to ask about the urgency and the necessity of the use of the
sacraments.

In this connection we find repeatedly in Reformed theology
the statement that the sacraments are not necessary for the
obtaining of salvation. This is not said about the sacraments
in general, but with respect to *salvation*. The intention of the
Reformers is clear: they wished to deny the Roman Catholic
doctrine that the sacraments are necessary because they infuse
supernatural grace. Reformed theology opposed this view by
stating that the divine promise comes already in the Word and
can be accepted in faith. What the Reformers presupposed, then,
was their own view of the relation between Word and sacrament.[29]

Everything depends, of course, upon the meaning of "necessity." Concretely, it is easy to see how a Church that believes the
sacraments to be "unnecessary" may lose its appreciation of
them and may even neglect them. It is therefore good to reflect
on the necessity of the sacraments in the light of their divine
institution and on their great significance because of the institution. Clearly, in the light of their divine institution by Christ,
one will not easily speak of the sacraments' non-necessity. Granted
that sacramentalism is an error, we should not allow polemical
interests to threaten our vision of the whole truth. And we can
escape that danger by speaking without hesitation of the necessity of the sacraments in the light of their institution by
Christ.[30] Even in those churches where the non-necessity of the
sacraments for salvation is emphasized, men continue to speak
of the command of God and of our calling to use the sacraments.
Furthermore, neglect of the sacraments led to the use of the
term "disobedience," which presupposes a certain necessity of
the sacraments. Only if we honor their institution by Christ

29. Cf. Bavinck, *Geref. Dog.,* IV, 511.
30. Think of the manner in which Calvin speaks of baptism in his com-
    mentary on John 3:5: "Verum quidem est, baptismi neglectu arceri nos
    a salute, atque hoc sensu necessarium fateor."

fully, can we speak polemically of the non-necessity of the sacraments.

The danger of devaluation is not imaginary, since believers always run the danger of stressing what is immediately "necessary" for their salvation; and if they are told that the sacraments are not necessary for salvation, they might easily conclude that they are relatively unimportant.[31] We must therefore be careful. On the one hand, we must maintain the polemic against Rome; but on the other hand we must speak emphatically of the necessity of the sacraments in the light of the institution by God.

That institution was, after all, not a work of divine arbitrariness, but an occurrence significant for God's guidance of his Church. When we consider that the sacraments are pledges of God's grace and signs of his promise, we shall be able to speak all the more seriously of the necessity of the sacraments, for this necessity is directly connected with our weakness, smallness of faith, and unbelief, the very reasons for which God has ordained the sacraments. The thesis of the non-necessity of the sacraments can be correctly posed only in an antithetical context, and only if it is followed immediately by a no less positive posing of the necessity of the sacrament. Only then shall we have honored the institution of the sacraments.

It has been said that not the absence of the sacrament, but contempt for the sacrament, makes one guilty in the eyes of God.[32] That means on the one hand that God's grace can be infused in the individual who for some reason is deprived of baptism, while on the other hand there can be a disdaining of the sacrament in the light of its institution by divine command. While Rome inconsistently makes exceptions which cannot be reconciled easily with the above-mentioned theory of infusion of grace, Reformed theology has emphatically maintained this distinction, not because "necessity knows no law," but in the light of the nature of the sacraments in distinction from the Word of promise. In this connection, reference has

31. Cf. Heppe, *Die Dogm. der ev. ref. Kirche*, 1861, p. 431, where it becomes clear that the danger of devaluation is not imaginary.
32. Cf. H. Bavinck, *Geref. Dog.*, IV, 511: *privatio baptismi* versus *contemptus baptismi*. This term occurs also in F. Junius, *Opuscula theol. selecta* (ed. Kuyper, 1882, p. 265). Junius speaks of the sacraments "non esse necessaria simpliciter." Cf. also A. Schweizer, *Die Glaubenslehre der ev. ref. Kirche*, 1847, II, 598.

often been made to Mark 16:16, "He that believeth and is baptized shall be saved; but he that disbelieveth shall be condemned." It is pointed out that the two parts of the sentence are not quite parallel, since belief is connected with baptism while the warning of destruction involves only unbelievers.[33]

Although we cannot discuss here the critical issues pertaining to Mark 16:16, it is clear at any rate that this text cannot be appealed to by those who think baptism to be relatively unimportant. The warning is against unbelief, and the promise of salvation is given to those who believe *and* receive baptism. Here we have further insight into what is meant by the non-necessity and the necessity of baptism.

In this light we can, without exaggeration, agree with Marcel's expression "the necessity of baptism" and with his dictum: "baptism is a duty."[34] Baptism is not left up to the whim of the believers, who then determine whether they need this condescending act of God's strengthening and sealing. On the contrary, when God institutes the sacrament for the strengthening of faith he thus ends all dispute. The question whether this sacrament is necessary is illegitimate in the eyes of Christian faith. The only proper question is that uttered by the eunuch: "What doth hinder me to be baptized?" (Acts 8:36). This is no negative approach to "unimportant" baptism, but an eager seeking of the sign of God through which one can travel his way with gladness.[35]

In the textually disputed verse (8:37) that follows, Philip replies, "If thou believest with all thy heart, thou mayest." This does not warrant the conclusion that the ancient Christian Church left baptism to arbitrary decision. Rather, it points to the fact that no obstacle prevented executing the unbreakable and meaningful connection between believing and being baptized.

Because of this connection by virtue of God's command, one can and must speak of the necessity of baptism. The desire for God's sign is not dependent on the state of one's belief, whereby the believer himself determines whether he needs strengthening of faith through the sacrament. The seeking of the sign cor-

33. Cf. Bavinck, *loc. cit.*
34. Marcel, "Le baptême. Sacrement de l'Alliance de Grâce, *La Revue Réformée*, 1950, p. 134; cf. also p. 40.
35. Cf. O. Cullmann, *Die Tauflehre des N. Testaments,* 1948, pp. 65ff.

responds to the granting of the pledge of God's goodness in the struggle with man's heart. One can ask for a sign out of unbelief, as the Pharisees did who wanted to try Jesus, but one can also desire the sign in order to honor in it God's institution and to rest in God's salvation. To be sure, we shall have to maintain our protest against every evaluation of baptism that pushes the Word of promise to the background; but those who see baptism in its institution and in its connection with the progress of the life of faith, will have to speak emphatically of the necessity of baptism. Thereby they will be in complete agreement with the practice of the Church, which warns against the disdain of the sacrament. The non-necessity of the sacrament in polemics has nothing to do with the superfluousness of the sacrament,[36] which either practically or theoretically always turns out to depend upon a form of spiritualism. To say that baptism is more or less superfluous is to reveal one's failure to appreciate the richness of God's institution.

The basic issue concerning the doctrine and practice of baptism is not simply whether one acknowledges that baptism has been instituted by Christ, but whether one wishes to continue speaking with joy and gladness of the necessity of the sacraments. This is the real touchstone. The Reformed opposition to sacramentalism expressed in its speaking of the non-necessity of the sacrament, evinces not a *lesser* appreciation of the sacrament but a *different* appreciation. When we stress the connection between faith and sacrament, and the related concept of *usus sacramenti,* we base our view on God's goodness. It is faith, desiring the sacraments and making use of them, that will speak of the necessity of the sacraments. The man of faith does not attempt to be wiser than God, who cannot be separated from his mercy and who in mercy has granted the sacrament to weak, sinful man. Only thus will the institution of the sacrament be honored and the way of faith traveled gladly, also because of the sign.[37]

36. Cf. the emphasis in Kuyper, *E Voto,* II, 489.
37. Cf. the well-known distinction between *necessitas praecepti et medii,* as found, e.g., in Marcel, *op. cit.,* p. 40.

CHAPTER SIX

BAPTISM AND FAITH

OUR PREVIOUS discussion about the origin and institution of baptism leads us now to the question of its *significance*. In other words: What place does holy baptism occupy in the Christian faith? This question in turn cannot be separated from the one about its power and efficacy, for the controversies about baptism have always involved its efficacy. We shall speak again of baptism as a sign and seal of God, but first we should ask ourselves whether we have the right to speak in this way. Hence, at the outset we will avoid the dogmatic and confessional term "sign and seal" and turn directly to the teaching regarding the place of baptism in the salvation of God.

The problem is most clearly summarized in the words baptism and faith. These words mark a connection which is altogether decisive for the whole sacramental doctrine. On the one hand, we are confronted with those who hold that baptism could not be essentially valuable for faith. An "external" sign, they say, can possess no real function for faith, which is "spiritual" in nature and directed toward a Person, God himself. On the other hand, however, baptism has been seen as a sign with specific causality in connection with salvation, the grace of God in believers. We saw already that Rome assigns to all sacraments, including baptism, an efficacy *ex opere operato,* a causal efficacy which is absolutely necessary for the obtaining of regeneration, for the transition from the state of sin into the state of grace. That is why Rome maintains that those who do not fully accept the causal efficacy of baptism, in spite of assertions to the contrary, have not escaped the grip of spiritualism.

It is understandable that the controversies about the significance, the efficacy, and the power of baptism are focused

mainly on the New Testament, for it is there that we see baptism, Christian baptism, as instituted by Christ himself, and as
a sign of the Kingdom at hand. Rome has repeatedly appealed
to Scripture, declaring that the New Testament contains clear
proof of the causality of the sacraments, especially baptism.
There is therefore good reason to occupy ourselves with some
aspects of the multiple witness of the New Testament.

Although it is not possible to treat all scriptural references
that have played a role in the controversy about baptism, we
nevertheless want to direct our attention to some central and
decisive passages, asking what the New Testament teaches us
regarding baptism.

We begin with certain passages where baptism is clearly
linked with salvation and regeneration. They include Paul's
words about being baptized into Christ (Gal. 3:27), and about
being buried with Christ through baptism into death (Rom.
6:4); the word about saving "through the washing of regeneration" (Tit. 3:5), about the washing of water (Eph. 5:26), and
Ananias' declaration to Saul (Acts 22:16). Reference has also
been made to the passage in which Christ speaks specifically
of regeneration (John 3:5).

These and other passages are indicated in order to accentuate the great significance and power of baptism. And it is clear
that neglect or disdain of the baptismal 'sacrament flagrantly
contradicts the message of the New Testament. There is evidently a very important relation between baptism and the
salvation of Christ, and the question is raised what the nature
of this relation could be. According to Rome this question is
beyond debate; any interpretation other than hers must be
a mutilation of Scripture's testimony. But there are other voices,
not Roman Catholic, who have also spoken of this causality.
Evidently, then, it is impossible to reject this "causal" exegesis
without further ado, since it is not limited to the Roman Catholic
doctrine, where this causality plays such an important role.

We consider, as examples, especially Heitmüller and Schlier.
The former takes his starting point in Romans 6 as *locus classicus* of Paul's baptismal considerations. According to Paul, he
says, baptism creates in man "a new nature," on the basis of
which the new life can originate and be developed. The person
who is baptized experiences a mystical physical-hyperphysical
communion with Christ: it is a complete new creation, a regeneration. And Heitmüller adds, polemically: "Paul does not

say that this is *symbolized* by baptism, but that it is *effected* by it."[1] Baptism causes a being-in-Christ,[2] an efficacy that implies "deliverance from the powers of darkness" (p. 323).

Schlier follows the same route where the working of baptism is concerned. Sharply criticizing Barth's baptismal views, with their emphasis on the cognitive element in baptism, he emphatically declares that the New Testament contains no warrant for the idea of cognitive efficacy; "rather, baptism according to its nature is in the New Testament an act that, performed causally, effects the salvation of the baptized person," as, he thinks, the New Testament shows very clearly. "And how should we otherwise explain the texts in which baptism and baptismal water are mentioned with the dative, instrumental ablative, or with an instrumental preposition as the means through which salvation is received?"[3] He refers especially to Titus 3:5 and John 3:5, and concludes that he who denies the causality of baptismal water must also deny the causality of the Spirit.[4] For the definition of the New Testament baptismal doctrine he, like Heitmüller, makes use of the famous term *ex opere operato*.[5] He sees baptism in the New Testament as completely *causa instrumentalis* of grace, so that every symbolical interpretation must be rejected.[6]

We are not concerned here about the issue of symbol versus reality, but with the question whether the New Testament indeed warrants the view of baptism as *opus operatum,* as cause of grace. The very closeness of the connection which we encounter everywhere in the New Testament between baptism and faith makes us wonder whether this·seemingly obvious conclusion that baptism is "causal," has not been furthered by some tendentious thinking. For the question cannot be avoided: what function must now be assigned to faith? Heitmüller reveals this tension

1. W. Heitmüller, *Im Namen Jesu,* 1903, pp. 319ff. Cf. also Heitmüller, *Taufe und Abendmahl bei Paulus,* 1903.
2. *Ibid.,* p. 320. Heitmüller says that for Paul baptism was not just symbol, but sacrament.
3. H. Schlier, "Zur kirchlichen Lehre von der Taufe," *TLZ,* 1947, p. 325. Schlier has since joined the Roman Catholic Church.
4. Schlier thinks that the teaching of the Heidelberg Catechism (Q. 72 — not the outward washing with water cleanses from sin, but the blood of Christ) is incorrect, since, he says, this does not form a real contrast.
5. *Ibid.,* p. 326. Cf. also H. Schlier, *Der Brief an die Galater,* 1949, p. 130.
6. Cf. also Schlier, "Die Taufe nach dem 6. Kapitel des Römerbriefes," *EvT,* 1938, pp. 335-347.

when he must acknowledge that Paul also speaks of the relation between faith and baptism, and must even declare that it "is beyond any doubt that Paul places faith first; he does not know baptism without faith."[7] But this does not lead him to correct his *opus operatum* construction. On the contrary, he only concludes as follows: "There is no reason to investigate the relation between baptism and faith here." But in saying so, he bypasses the core of the problem and prevents himself from getting a clear insight into the baptismal doctrine of the New Testament. For this relation between baptism and faith is not at all a "foreign body" in Paul's trend of thought; rather, it is the center of all his views regarding baptism. That which Heitmüller thinks to be inconsistent points precisely at the way in which the remarks in the New Testament regarding baptism can be understood. Paul is not just concerned about an added aspect in this relation to faith, but about baptism itself in definite connections and contexts from which it may not be detached. That is why Paul speaks in Colossians of the believers who are buried with Christ in baptism and then says: "Ye were also raised with him through faith in the working of God, who raised him from the dead" (2:12). Precisely at the point where Heitmüller must acknowledge the close relation between faith and baptism, he should have understood that it is impossible to be satisfied with the *opus operatum*. Dobschütz has criticized Heitmüller on this point, showing that Paul never isolates the act of baptism in such a manner that we could think of an *opus operatum*.[8]

It is certainly no accident that Heitmüller, from his point of view, discovers an inconsistency in Paul. For in acknowledging that for Paul there is a relation between faith and baptism, he touches for a moment upon the profoundness of the New Testament revelation regarding baptism, concerning which the dilemma of symbol versus reality provides no enlightenment at all. The *opus operatum* leaves no room for the relation between baptism and faith; it allows only for the unfolding of the "ontic," which is causally effected by baptism. Those who cannot discover this ontology anywhere in the New Testament, and hence who learn to see the relation between faith and baptism, will

---

7. Heitmüller, *op. cit.*, p. 327.
8. E. von Dobschütz, "Sakrament und Symbol im Urchristentum," *Theologische Studien und Kritiken* (Hamburg), 1905, p. 7.

not (like Heitmüller) find the latter to be an indigestible piece of Paul's baptismal doctrine.

Precisely this relation between faith and baptism forms the background for the varied and many-sided mode of speaking in the New Testament. There is no competition here between the "subjective" and "objective" moments — a concept that has played a tremendous role in the history of baptismal doctrine. The so-called "balancing" of subjective and objective factors is completely ruled out by the New Testament relation between faith and baptism, which does not present two factors standing beside each other, but a recognition — in faith — of what God does in baptism. That is why we must do full justice to this multilateral mode of speaking in Scripture. We may never approach Scripture with an *a priori* scheme, nor are we permitted to start from a subjectivity which has been detached from objectivity, or from an objectivity which has been detached from subjectivity.

In all the questions about New Testament baptism, the center of discussion seems to be Romans 6, a chapter which has repeatedly been quoted for the *ex opere operato* and for the "objective" character of baptism. In Romans 6, Paul is from the very beginning concerned with absolute salvation in Jesus Christ. He speaks also in other epistles of that salvation, sometimes in connection with baptism, sometimes without mentioning it (cf. Col. 2:6ff.). He points to the richness of that salvation in all sorts of connections and speaks of the consequences implied in it. The offer of reconciliation, in which God has made peace through the blood of the cross (Eph. 2:14ff.), stands always in the center of his considerations. His eye is directed toward Christ's great deed of love: "For the love of Christ constraineth us; because we thus judge, that one died for all" (II Cor. 5:14). The important thing for Paul is always the decisive blessing and the power that originates with the cross of reconciliation. His attention is continually directed toward that still recent past of which he speaks with so much emphasis in Romans 5, that Christ died for us while we were yet sinners (5:8). There is a historical occurrence which lies at the base of all Christian life and also at the base of baptism: the cross. The word of the cross is a power of God to salvation for everyone who believes (Rom. 1:16).

Everything that Paul says in his epistles about baptism may never be detached from this foundation: Jesus Christ crucified

(I Cor. 2:2). In this, Paul is at one with the whole uniform kerygma of the New Testament regarding the only cause of our salvation (see Heb. 5:9). This central thought in the New Testament and in Paul is so obvious that anyone who strongly emphasizes the causality of baptism — and the other sacraments — must also continue to emphasize that the cause of salvation is the historical reality of the cross of reconciliation.[9]

Hence it is extremely important how one conceives the relation between that original "causality" of salvation and the "co-causality" which comes to light in the sacraments. There is a danger that the notion of co-causality will introduce insoluble tensions, even leading, willy-nilly, to minimizing of the actual cause of our salvation. That is why it is important to see what Paul actually writes in Romans 6, after stating so emphatically what is the cause of our salvation in Romans 5. Against those who think that much sin entails much grace, and who act as if they have the abundance of grace at hand (let us continue in sin, so that grace may abound), Paul confronts the believers with the inviolable actuality of faith. Where grace holds sway, one can no longer remain in sin. "We who died to sin, how shall we any longer live therein? Or are ye ignorant that all we who were baptized into Christ Jesus were baptized into his death?" (Rom. 6:2-3).

Those inclined to minimize the significance of baptism will certainly find no support in this passage. But it is equally clear that Paul is not concerned to posit a second cause of salvation along with the first (the cross of reconciliation). The absoluteness of baptism depends wholly upon the absoluteness of historical salvation in Christ. In the light of Paul's testimony regarding Christ, how could a relatively new and independent causality ever come to stand beside that first causality, in which the love of God is truly revealed in historical reality? Those who do hold to a second cause — even while acknowledging the *prima causa* — will inevitably begin to place the actual moment of salvation more and more in the second causality which occurs at the moment of baptism. In that moment, for instance, we see with Rome the great event of the transition from death to life through the infusion of supernatural grace. But Paul has no knowledge of such a transition, such a *translatio*, because he is concerned

---

9. See, e.g., Thomas Aquinas on the sacraments and the *passio Christi* (*S.T.*, III, Q. 62, 5).

only with another transition which became reality in the death
of Christ for us (Rom. 5:6).

Paul speaks frequently of how believers are presently involved
with the past time of Christ's death. They are buried with him
into death (Rom. 6:4), their old man was crucified with him
(6:6), and they have died with Christ (6:8).

With him . . . it evidently happened then, at the time of
Christ's death. Paul points to that reality of reconciliation with its
many consequences in Colossians 2. Those who have accepted
Christ and who are rooted in him and confirmed in their faith,
have received all their fulness in him (2:6ff.). They were circumcised in the circumcision of Christ, that is, the baptism —
"having been buried with him in baptism" (2:12). This is no
co-causality, but a specific involvement of baptism with that
tremendous event at the time of Christ's suffering and death. Paul
points repeatedly to that sacred event in the past, so that believers
as reconciled children of God will be without fear in the presence
of God and will have confidence for the future. When did the
life of reconciliation take over their lives? For the answer, Paul
always points to the reconciliation. "You, I say, did he make
alive . . . having forgiven us all our trespasses; having blotted out
the bond written in ordinances that was against us, which was
contrary to us" (2:14). The believers are led to that window
which opens forever upon the prospect of peace with God
through the reconciling suffering and death of Christ. All of
Paul's epistles are in agreement in this, as they are in agreement
with the rest of Scripture. But it is especially significant for us
here that Paul, in connection with this great historical event,
speaks also of baptism.

To be sure, Paul can also speak of communion with Christ
without expressly mentioning baptism, but that does not eliminate the fact that this baptism is linked with the death of Christ.
This connection is expressed in relational terms: being baptized
into the death of Christ (Rom. 6:3) — an expression that shows
the complete involvement of baptism with the death of Christ.
It is impossible to deduce an *ex opere operato,* or a "causality"
of grace, from this. Baptism is completely dependent, and its
richness and profound significance lie precisely in this fact. To
say at this point that baptism is *also* necessary is to miss the exclusive significance of the cross of reconciliation. Nor do we, by this
judgment, make baptism unimportant; rather, we stress the

essential value and significance of God's sacred ordinance according to which baptism is called holy, sacred.

Baptism cannot be called important because of a supernatural
infusion of grace which exalts the moment of baptism above the
"appointed time" of Christ's suffering and dying. This is a dis-
tortion of the New Testament; it makes baptism the true cause
of supernatural grace, as if a second cause were necessary after
the grace of God had appeared in Jesus Christ and peace was
brought through his blood. This is not the teaching of Romans
6 and Colossians 2. Paul is not referring to the time of baptism,
but to another moment, another time, of which baptism is the
living, efficacious sign. Nothing happens in and through baptism.
Rather, baptism is meaningful only through its pointing at
another event in which those who were dead in their transgres-
sions are truly reconciled, in which the accusations written
against them are blotted out. That is why it is so significant
when Paul writes that we are baptized into Christ Jesus and into
his death. The significance of baptism is so great because it is
God's sign which involves Christ. Against "antinomian legalism"
Paul can say: Do you not know that all of us who were baptized
into Jesus Christ were baptized into his death?

The appealing power of this call to sanctification is historically based on that event, and Paul's word "with" reveals the
profoundest mystery of Christ's love. We were crucified *with*
him and died *with* him (Rom. 6:6, 8). This involvement with
Christ has drawn much attention, the more so since Paul spoke
so emphatically in Romans 5 of a certain "distance" from Christ.
Christ died in due season (5:6), while we were yet sinners (5:8),
died for the weak and ungodly (5:6). How shall we reconcile
this distance with the involvement of Romans 6? Is it not precisely the purport of the gospels that nobody was with Jesus in
his last struggle on the Mount of Olives, and that Thomas' plan,
"Let us go, that we may die with him" (John 11:16), was not
fulfilled, while Peter's "Even if I must die with thee, yet will I
not deny thee" (Matt. 26:35) was not fulfilled either? None of
the disciples was able to be awake with him (Mark 14:37) and
he was left by all (Matt. 26:56). How, then, do we understand
dying with him, being crucified with him, and being buried
with him?

It is the mystery of Christ's suffering and death that the distance of Romans 5 — the loneliness of his solitary act of fulfilment
— does not contradict the "with" of Romans 6, but coincides with

it, because precisely this loneliness of reconciliation reveals itself
in the profoundest communion of the believer with his love. The
"with" of Romans 6 is not the same as Peter's and Thomas'
"with." It is not the "with" of the contemporary who was in contact with him (see Luke 5:9), but a being "with him" in the
meaningfulness and efficacy of his suffering and dying. It is the
involvement of a sinful life in his uncomprehended love.

In the wake of Kierkegaard, some have spoken of our contemporaneity with Christ and of being a disciple contemporary
with Christ. Cullmann has called this a failure to appreciate the
"redemptive-historical *(heilsgeschichtliche)* significance of the
present";[10] although we participate and share in the fruits of
Christ's work, he says, "we cannot go back to him in order to
come within reach of salvation." This criticism, which is quite
correct, reveals the romantic and uncritical aspect of this current
"fad."[11] Paul does not intend to diminish the temporal distance
to the cross,[12] but to express the real and effective significance of
the cross for us. The cross is a historical fact, but in that fact, in
which God acts in the life of his Son, God's reconciling acts become historical reality. Moreover, one cannot say that the cross
was a fact that would be applied only later on to believers, since
this event was directed toward believers when it took place. They
themselves were fully involved as the objects of reconciliation.
Therein lies the profound interrelation between Romans 5 and 6.
Romans 6 does not speak of an event that is related chronological-
ly to what is indicated in Romans 5. Rather, both speak of the
one reality of reconciliation. Christ died for the ungodly "in
due season," and "we died with Christ"; the relation between
these two is not primarily one of time, but of *meaning*.

Now it is in terms of this meaning of the cross for believers
that Paul brings up baptism. He does not say that there was first
the causal power of the cross of reconciliation, and thereafter the
causal power of baptism, however agreeable this may be to the
view that baptism infuses supernatural grace at the great moment
of transition from death to life — a transition made "possible,"
be it granted, by the death of Christ. The notion of a possible

10. O. Cullmann, *Christus und die Zeit,* 1946, pp. 128f., 148f.
11. Cf. A. Nygren, *Der Römerbrief,* 1951, p. 175. Cf. also Barth's criticism of
    Kierkegaard, *K.D.,* III, 2, 578ff.
12. Think of I Thess. 4:14, where in an altogether different context the
    moment of distinction is sharply revealed. Cf. R. Schnackenburg, *Das
    Heilsgeschehen bei der Taufe nach dem Apostel Paulus,* 1950, pp. 145ff.

reconciliation, later to be made actual by another agency, can never help us to understand baptism correctly. Romans 6 is precisely the passage that brings beneficial order into so many confusions in the history of the dogma (first and second causality, possibility and reality). For it is clear that baptism is meaningful only when related to the cross, to what once happened. The "with" of Romans 6 refutes the second causality of grace. This does not make baptism a mere *nudum signum,* one of several illustrative portrayals. On the contrary, because of its involvement with the cross baptism is God's specially ordained sign, which derives its power from this relation to the cross.

We are now in a position to explain why Paul in certain contexts can speak of salvation in Christ without mentioning baptism. It is not because he devaluates baptism, for competition between them does not and cannot exist. He can even say to the Corinthians: "For Christ sent me not to baptize, but to preach the gospel" (I Cor. 1:17). Such a statement is meaningful as a warning against overestimating the practice of baptism, which can actually destroy the sacrament by giving it independent status. So, later on, he reminds his readers of the warning to Israel, when all the fathers were under the cloud and walked through the sea and were baptized unto Moses; but God was not well pleased with most of them (I Cor. 10:1ff.). They overestimated the sacrament, detaching it from all the connections and contexts in which God had placed it, as Israel detached the ark and the temple from the presence of God and therefore had to do without the blessing. Thus the sacrament lost its relation to reconciliation and to true faith.

The fundamental fact about baptism will always be its involvement with the death of Christ. That is made clear in Romans 6 and throughout the New Testament — so clear, indeed, that even those who hold that baptism works *ex opere operato* want nevertheless to express these undeniable connections. They try then to place a connection between baptism as the supernatural infusion of grace and the cross of Christ. Ultimately, we are confronted here with the same problem that we will meet later with respect to the cross and the offering of the mass. One must take notice each time of the relation between the decisive "then" and that which happens now in the believers.

Among Roman Catholic theologians, Odo Casel is especially sensitive to this problem. In his so-called doctrine of the mystery, in which he speaks also of baptism, he appeals in particular to

Romans 6. He seeks the involvement of baptism with the cross by urging that, although Christ's suffering and death occurred only once, this event is now "continuously present in sacramental efficacy," namely, "in the mystically real Now."[13] At its core, Casel's view is a reaction to the so-called doctrine of the effect, which says that Christ's work is important to us now only in its effect. Casel, however, maintains that the *passio Christi* is itself actually present, not in the historical sense, but *in mysterio*. The historical redemptive event does not merely send out its radiating influence, but is really present *in mysterio*.[14]

The remarkable thing in the discussion around Casel is that everyone is busy with the problem of involvement. Most of the criticism is directed at Casel's opinion that in Romans 6 the crux of the matter is the physical death of Christ. Monden, although he criticizes Casel, holds that baptism deals with the "ontological" conforming of the Christian to the dying and rising Christ, and "this contemporaneity, ideally implied in Christ's dying on the cross, becomes real through baptism."[15] In this scheme we discern once more the categories of "possible" and "real" and, in spite of the criticism directed at Casel, we also see here an emphasis on that real contemporaneity which occurs in baptism. This event is accentuated more and more, for the infusion of supernatural grace in baptism is the beginning of ontological similarity. Casel's "presence of the mystery" is really not decisive for the issue that occupies us here. Neither he nor his critics avoid the scheme of "ideal and real"; for both, Christ's work becomes valid only when grace is infused through baptism. But Paul is not concerned with an ideal contemporaneity in the cross which is realized later; he speaks, rather, of a "dying-with-Christ," "buried-with-Christ," and "crucified-with-Christ" which offers a decisive foundation for the call to sanctification and the radical turning away from antinomianism. He speaks of what happened in the death of Christ. This death does not create the possibility of reconciliation and of grace, but is the historical revelation of that grace. It is not a possibility which

13. K. H. Schelke, "Taufe und Tod. Zur Auslegung von Röm. 6:1-11," in *Vom Christlichen Mysterium*, 1951, p. 10.
14. Cf. L. Monden, *Het misoffer als mysterie*, 1948, p. 30, where he discusses the biblical evidence, especially Romans 6. Cf. R. Schnackenburg, *op. cit.*, pp. 139-144.
15. Monden, *op. cit.*, p. 76.

is later realized through our faith or through infused grace,[16] but in this death lies the reality of salvation toward which faith is directed and of which baptism is the divine sign. To suppose that baptism merely realizes a posssibility is to rob salvation of its decisive significance and to place the power and reality of reconciliation in the shadow. It does not help, later on, to admit that salvation was effected "only once." The consideration "only once" is a decisive argument not only against the Roman Catholic doctrine of the Lord's Supper, but also against its baptismal doctrine.[17]

In its defense of Roman Catholic baptismal doctrine, the school of the "mysterious presence" has also appealed to Paul's words in Romans 6:5: "For if we have become united with him in the likeness of his death, we shall be also in the likeness of his resurrection." The word *homoiōma* is the crux of the matter. According to this school, dying with Christ and rising with Christ and thus becoming like him actually takes place in baptism. They conclude that this dying with Christ is possible only if Christ also dies in baptism, albeit not in the historical manner of Golgotha, but *in mysterio*. As Monden puts it, presenting Casel's view: "One does not die and arise with somebody, if that somebody does not die and arise together with us, as actually and really as we ourselves die and arise. Therefore, a real, actual dying of Christ is continued in baptism and in the whole sacramental order."

Other Roman Catholic theologians take issue with this concept of "becoming in the likeness of Christ's death." They hold that this text cannot possibly mean that our dying with Christ would imply the actual presence of Christ's death in his physical reality. These theologians point out — and in doing so come closer to Reformed exegesis — that Romans 6 refers not to a "mystical" dying of Christ in the moment of baptism, but to Christ's death in the past.

Cools, for example, confronts the "concept of mystical death" with an altogether different interpretation of Paul's statement. Although he acknowledges that Paul speaks of a contemporaneity,

---

16. Cf. M. Barth, *Die Taufe ein Sakrament?*, pp. 272-74, 278. See also Karl Barth, *K.D.*, IV, 1, 313, in his criticism of Thomasius.
17. It is important to realize that in both it is a matter of the so-called *applicatio*. This concept is useful in theology, depending on its definition. One can easily do injustice to what happened in the past, however, if the concept is used wrongly.

he declares that Casel has misinterpreted Paul's meaning. Baptism does not involve a mystical dying of Christ, but his historical dying. Cools points out that the same thought occurs in Paul at another occasion when he is not speaking of baptism, and concludes: "It is therefore a matter of the historical, concrete, real death on Calvary, and nothing warrants the thought that our sins have been taken away at another moment, at which Christ supposedly died in a mystical manner, a moment unknown and unmentioned by Paul."[18]

It is clear that the arguments of Cools and others against Casel are very strong, because they point to the connection of Paul's words in Romans 6 and Romans 5 with the death of Christ. It is precisely this outlook on the past to which Paul repeatedly refers in his epistles. Besides, in Romans 6:9 Paul explicitly adds that Christ was raised from the dead and dies no more, since death has lost its power over him. This passage altogether prohibits a "mystical death" of Christ. That is why the criticism directed against Casel could pave the way to a better interpretation of the text, and of the involvement of baptism with the death of Christ. To be sure, these Roman Catholic theologians retain the view that baptism is the moment at which supernatural grace is infused; nevertheless, they do recognize the connection between our baptism and the suffering and dying of Christ, a connection which, in Casel's theory, is increasingly replaced by the contemporaneity of our death with the mystical death of Christ in baptism.

Actually, of course, this text directs our attention to the efficacy of the communion which is revealed in the reconciliation of Christ. It is not a historical fact which later must be brought into connection with believers, but a reconciling act in which they themselves are involved because it was directed toward them, and in which they participate in faith with all the consequences which are therein implied for sanctification.[19]

In the light of the New Testament teaching that baptism is

18. R. P. Cools, "La présence mystique du Christ dans le baptême," in *Memorial Lagrange*, 1940, pp. 295-305. Monden thinks that Cools goes too far, especially when he says that Casel's view is made impossible by the text (Monden, *op. cit.*, p. 77).
19. Polman, *Onze Ned. Geloofsbelijdenis*, 1953, pp. 218ff. See also Karl Stürmer, *Auferstehung und Erwählung*, 1953, pp. 132ff., 55ff.; J. Schneider, *Die Taufe im N. T.*, 1951, pp. 43ff.

directed toward believers, it is perfectly understandable that Paul should repeatedly stress the connection of salvation with *faith*.

The full righteousness of Christ is received through faith (Rom. 10). Believers have received the Spirit through the preaching of faith (Gal. 3:2), they are the children of God through faith in Jesus Christ (Gal. 3:26), while Christ dwells in our hearts through faith (Eph. 3:17). De Beus is therefore correct when he writes that the sacramentalist interpretation of baptism "does not square with Paul's view regarding faith."[20] Only when the involvement of baptism with Christ's death and with faith is fully honored, can justice be done to its function in the life of believers according to Paul and the whole New Testament.

For baptism is the event in which man, having come to faith, makes a public transition from paganism and the old life of sin and death to a new life in communion with Christ. It is "an act of admission into the church,"[21] which follows automatically upon the faithful and believing listening to the gospel. Precisely here is the concrete connection between faith and baptism which makes it utterly impossible to isolate baptism from the connections in which God placed it.

Even after Paul has already been taken into Christ's service and has received his commission, he still hears the words of Ananias: "Stand up, be baptized and cleansed of your sins."[22] It is nothing but rationalizing and schematizing when this is seen as the *opus operatum* resulting in infused supernatural grace. We must reject the dilemma posed by this view between *opus operatum* and mere symbolism. For baptism is neither of these: it is the sign given by God, which has rich and profound meaning in the acts of God, and which safeguards the baptized person in the temptations and doubts of his own heart. Therein lies the significance of baptism for believers, and therein lies the reason that Paul can give an urgent warning in the light of this baptism

---

20. De Beus, *De oud-Chr. Doop en Zijn voorgeschiedenis,* II, 149.
21. W. T. Hahn, *Das Mitsterben und Mitauferstehen mit Christus bei Paulus,* 1937, p. 132.
22. Cf. Flemington, *The N. T. Doctrine of Baptism,* p. 59: "St. Paul looks back to baptism as that which marked for each Christian the inauguration of the new age, the transition from the old life to the new. Everything began for the convert when he came up out of the water and robed himself afresh in his garment. It was really nothing less than a putting on of Christ" (Acts 22:16).

when he speaks of what turns out to be the real thrust of Romans 6: the newness of life.[23]

It was once asked — critically and polemically — whether we are regenerated by the resurrection of Jesus Christ from the dead, or whether this resurrection only prepares, while grace is then granted — for the first time — in baptism.[24]

This question raises a profound problem for baptismal doctrine. The same writer says correctly that baptism is not "a second work through which his work becomes beneficial for the believer."[25] That would once more make baptism an independent something, leading us back to the notion of infused grace. Nevertheless, with this latter view in mind, Roman Catholics repeatedly accuse the Reformed of no longer being able to attach to baptism its profound significance and content. By this they mean that baptism is no longer the real transition from death to life, the beginning of salvation. Admittedly, the Reformed view was sometimes weak; Zwingli, for example, feared to call the sacraments "means of grace" or to say that God acts in baptism. Cullmann also speaks of such an exaggerated fear.[26] But it is clear that no such fear is to be found in Calvin, for instance, who continued to emphasize that act of God.

It all depends, however, on what one means by this "new" act of God. It may never be construed against the background of a mere "possibility" of reconciliation which Christ acquired for us. But there is another sense of "new" that acknowledges completely the historical reality of reconciliation, namely, when that new element in baptism is related to belief in Christ's offer of reconciliation. Barth has contrasted the causal aspect of baptism with the cognitive.[27] One can indeed say that baptism is related to the cognitive, to the knowledge of faith, but one must be careful that this cognitive aspect is not subjectivized and thus opposed to the objective. For it is precisely a cognition of God's own acts in reconciliation. It is not necessary, in opposing so-called realism, to fall into the abyss of spiritualism. For we are baptized not by human whim, but by divine command.[28] Hence it is possible to speak of baptism as sign and seal.

23. Cf. Nygren, *Der Römerbrief*, p. 176.
24. H. Werner-Bartsch, "Die Taufe in N.T.," *EvT*, VIII, 83.
25. *Ibid.*
26. O. Cullmann, *Die Tauflehre des N. T.*, p. 29.
27. K. Barth, *Die kirchliche Lehre von der Taufe*, pp. 18-19.
28. Cf. Oepke in *TWNT*, I, 538.

In I Corinthians 6:11 Paul admonishes the Church concerning baptism: "... but ye were washed, but ye were sanctified, but ye were justified in the name of the Lord Jesus Christ, and in the Spirit of our God." Here the act of God and the act of the believers are inseparably connected: "therein speaks the desire, the act, which issued forth from the Corinthians themselves."[29] In this act, they were aware that they were to be the mere objects of the love of God. That is why their act is full of consequence. Those who do not live in sanctification forget the significance of their baptism. Were we not baptized into the death of Christ, and did we not die with him? Because their baptism is related to this historical salvation and this reconciliation, in which their life was involved, Paul can hark back to baptism, not as an isolated moment of infusion of grace, but as a transition in the indivisible harmony of faith, baptism, communion with God, and isolation from the world.

We need not be surprised, then, when Paul writes that Christ gave himself up for the Church in order to sanctify it, "having cleansed it by the washing of water with the word" (Eph. 5:26). These last three words make untenable any attempt to divorce faith from baptism, faith from word, or faith from cross. Nor, in the light of the New Testament, may we simplistically oppose the notions of symbol and reality. It is no overestimation of baptism to say with Flemington: "For Paul baptism was far more than a highly dramatic means of preaching the gospel. In baptism itself something happened."[30]

Because faith and baptism come together in a single act, one can say: "the symbolism was not only expressive but also effective."[31] For baptism is more than a human act, more than an expression of subjective faith, more than a human testifying. It is the reality of the instituted sign which through its very institution is related — in a manner willed and set by God — to the assurance of salvation. That is why, for instance, Ephesians 5:26 does not warrant the deduction of *ex opere operato*, as some still do. One can speak of the "effect" of baptism only in the light of the fulness of relations in which it is placed.

In this connection the remark of the Heidelberg Catechism is important, which says that the Holy Spirit "not without great

---

29. Grosheide, *Comm.*, p. 205.
30. Flemington, *op. cit.*, p. 82.
31. *Ibid.;* cf. J. Schneider, *Die Taufe im N.T.*, 1951, p. 53.

cause" calls baptism the washing of regeneration and the washing away of sins.[32] Not without great cause: that indicates that the language is deliberately chosen. Some have supposed that these expressions are merely a "sacramental mode of speaking" — *as if,* so to speak, our sins are washed away by baptism.[33] But the Catechism does not say this. The language is not exaggerated but accurate; it should be taken quite seriously, as is shown by the appeal to the Holy Spirit. Baptism is a divine sign, accepted in faith to full salvation on the authority of the Spirit. Thus one receives the divine authentication "that we are spiritually cleansed from our sins as really as we are outwardly washed with water."

We may certainly not disregard those passages of Scripture to which people in the course of the centuries have appealed to prove the causality of baptism, for they undoubtedly have great significance for baptismal doctrine. But neither should we detach them from context. Titus 3:5, for example, is frequently cited by Rome to prove its own view. (This is the same text of which the Catechism says that the Holy Spirit does not speak that way without great cause.) .But Rome then separates the passage from the correlative connections in which it comes to us. Having done so, she finds "evidence" for a second causality after and along with the first causality, which supposedly lies in the cross of reconciliation.

Much ink has been spilled about this statement of Paul, especially on the question whether Paul actually intends to speak of baptism here, or whether he is only using the image of washing by water. The Catechism adopts the first view, which of course is not exegetically decisive. Paul speaks of the appearance of Christ's and God's kindness and love for man, and then he says that God has saved us "through the washing of regeneration and renewing of the Holy Spirit, which he poured out upon us richly, through Jesus Christ our Saviour." In the center stands the richness of grace that has appeared. That grace is directed toward us, not because of the works of righteousness, but because of mere kindness.

32. Q. 73; cf. Q. 71, where it is said that Scripture thus indicates baptism, with reference to Titus 3:5 and Acts 22:16.
33. On "sacramental phraseology," cf. Heppe, *Dogmatik,* pp. 428, 436; Bavinck, *Geref. Dog.,* IV, 461; T. L. Haitjema, *Dogmatiek als apologie,* 1948, p. 298.

It becomes ours through the washing of regeneration and through the renewing of the Holy Spirit. Bouma thinks of baptism, and refers to Ephesians 5:26 (the Church cleansed by the washing of water with the word). He wonders how this saving must be understood. What is involved, he says, is a divine act of saving from destruction, a benefit portrayed in a twofold manner: as rebirth and fruit.[34] He then asks about the relation. He does not believe that according to Paul regeneration occurs by means of baptism; such an interpretation would be jumping to a conclusion, "for nothing else is said of that regeneration and renewal than that they stand in an unspecified relation to the administered baptism."[35] Bouma does not deny the connection which is indicated by *dia*, but he does deny that this is self-evidently the sort of causality indicated by *ex opere operato*. If this text really were a *locus classicus* for the Roman Catholic baptismal doctrine, baptism would acquire a saving character in the full sense of the word.

Bouma points out that this exegesis causes great difficulties in connection with the possibility of *losing* grace, a possibility that is essential to the Roman Catholic baptismal doctrine. For the salvation in question is full and complete, not something that can be lost again. Titus 3:7 reads: "That, being justified by his grace, we might be made heirs according to the hope of eternal life." As Bouma points out, Rome does not attribute *this* salvation to baptism, and hence this text would prove more than even Rome can accept. Nevertheless, repeated appeals are made to this *locus classicus* to provide a basis for the *ex opere operato*. The only way to avoid the difficulties sketched above is to abandon the causal scheme of baptism that occasioned them. Paul speaks with "great cause" about baptism in the light of those connections in which he sees it, connections with the cross and with faith. He can link baptism to regeneration and renewal through the Holy Spirit using the word *dia*, but not in the sense of an isolated causality. Rather, baptism is the event that lifts the one cause of salvation high above doubt and obscurity. The cross of reconciliation and the appearance of the Redeemer form the absolutely dominant central point. That is why this statement of Paul can be quoted to oppose spiritualistic superficializ-

---

34. C. Bouma, *Comm.*, p. 441.
35. *Ibid.*, p. 442.

ing of baptism, but not to show that grace is infused through this sign.[36]

Scripture speaks in various ways about the purification that comes with salvation, not always in connection with baptism. In every case, however, the mercy of God is the true central point. If we understand this fact, then we perceive not discord but harmony between Titus 3:5 and these other passages. We hear, for example, of Christ's blood that cleanses from sin (I John 1:7), and of the sprinkling with his blood (I Pet. 1:2). It is never the case that in Scripture one text competes with the other. All the light that shines for man comes from the one point, and it is from that point that the harmony is revealed.

Baptism does not compete with purification, the Word does not compete with baptism. Thus, Christ can speak of this purification of being washed and thus coming to participate in him, and of the purity of his disciples (John 13:9f.) in connection with his act of foot-washing as well as the word which he has spoken to them (John 15:3). All of which shows that baptism is part of a complex totality, from which it must be artificially abstracted if one attributes to it alone a special infusion of grace.

Another passage used to support the causal theory of baptism is John 3:5, where Jesus says to Nicodemus that a man must be born *of water* and the Spirit to enter into the Kingdom of God. Jesus' conversation with Nicodemus is about the miracle from above, the new creation by which one enters the Kingdom of God. This regeneration is linked with the Kingdom and with the Messiah, whose coming and working is mentioned in John 3:14. A person must believe in him so that destruction will be turned away and life eternal may be found (3:16), while God's love is the foundation of regeneration (3:16). This is the context in which we must interpret "born of water and the Spirit."

According to Grosheide, the water can only refer to baptism, since the term would be difficult to understand if that were not the case.[37] But this shows that we may not rashly draw conclusions from words used in connection with salvation. Here again, we read words (of water and the Spirit) which point at the connections in which baptism is placed. Through the coming of the

---

36. It seems impossible to deny that Paul in Titus 3:5 is speaking of baptism. Cf. Stromberg, *Studien zur Theorie und Praxis der Taufe*, p. 6. Cf. also Flemington, *op. cit.*, pp. 101-05.
37. Grosheide, *Commentary on John*, I, 211; cf. C. Bouma, *Korte Verklaring*, I, 106. Cf. also Bultmann, *Das Evangelium des Joh.*, 1950, p. 98.

Messiah, baptism would become the sign of the Kingdom that had come. This baptism could be known in its full significance only through the coming of the Messiah.

Again we are confronted with a linking of regeneration, purification, baptism, and faith, a linking which is characteristic of the whole New Testament, and by which this word spoken by Christ also becomes fully intelligible. If we ignore these connections we will have to posit two causalities, one for water and one for Spirit, and then say that they are related as primary to secondary cause. This is, of course, a possible theory of baptism, but it introduces a distinction into the text which is not at all warranted. On the view defended here, however, it is understandable that John can speak of regeneration in Christ (I John 5:4) and of being in God (I John 4:3), without mentioning baptism. This is because the problem of baptism does not lie in the relation between two causes, but in another relation, namely, between baptism and salvation, or, to say it differently, in the involvement of baptism with God's salvation in Jesus Christ.

We turn now to another controversial text, I Peter 3:21. After Peter states how the inhabitants of Noah's ark were "saved through water," he adds: "which also after a true likeness doth now save you, even baptism."

Once again we must avoid rash conclusions, the more so since Peter connects baptism with Christ's resurrection, concerning which he had already said that God in his mercy had regenerated us by the resurrection of Jesus Christ from the dead (1:3). Moreover, in I Peter 1:23, he speaks of regeneration "not of corruptible seed, but of incorruptible, through the word of God, which liveth and abideth."

It is clear that, if the richness of salvation is defined in so many ways, Peter's word "baptism saves" may not lead to hasty conclusions irrespective of the context. It is necessary to realize with how great emphasis Peter speaks of the work of Christ. He speaks of regeneration by *(dia)* Christ's resurrection (1:3), through faith (1:7), through the gospel which is preached (1:12), and of having been redeemed from the vain manner of life through the precious blood of Christ as of a lamb without blemish and spot (1:18-19). Christ is revealed "for your sake, who through him are believers in God, that raised him from the dead" (1:21). Christ's suffering and dying stand central in the background. Christ "bare our sins in his body upon the tree ... by whose stripes ye were healed" (2:24-25). Christ, being right-

eous, died once for us, the unrighteous, in order to bring us to
God (3:18).

Christ's redeeming work dominates the whole of Peter's
epistle, and we must interpret his words regarding baptism in
this connection, even though they have repeatedly been dragged
into discussions of the "instrumental" character of baptism.
Peter speaks first of the saving of Noah and his family and then
he says that few were saved through water (3:20). And when
Peter now says that baptism is the counterpart of redemption
from the flood, it is clear that the difference between "through
water" and "by water" may easily begin to play a role in the
interpretation of this text. Greijdanus[38] does not like the reading
"through water" because the following verse says that baptism
also *(kai)* saves us now; hence he concludes that for Peter the
water of the flood-judgment was a water that saves. Wohlenberg
also writes that "by water" "must be taken instrumentally, as
is also made necessary by the antitype in v. 21a."[39] In contrast,
Markus Barth prefers the translation "through water." It is
especially in Barth that we see a close relation between his
exegesis and his dogmatic point of view. He does not believe that
there is an instrumental power in either the water of the flood
or the water of baptism. In the flood, salvation was not through
the water, but from the water and through the ark (cf. II Pet.
2:5). Hence the counterpart does not warrant any conclusion
in favor of the instrumental function of baptism. It is clear that
Barth's rejection of baptism as sacrament and his subjectivizing
of baptism makes him lean toward the exegesis "through water,"
because with this translation he can remain critical toward the
instrumental theory of baptism. That does not mean, however,
that every preference for the translation "through water" is the
sign of a prejudiced dogmatic stand. The translation "through
water" has more than once been preferred by those who did not
at all object against the instrumental character of baptism.[40]

It is therefore not necessary to make a definite decision with
respect to this difficult problem, since the important point for the
doctrine of baptism is preserved either way, namely, that saving
occurs by way of baptism. But there is no doubt where Peter
stands on the question of a new *causality* of the saving water.

38. Greijdanus, *Comm. ad loc.*
39. Zahn (Wohlenberg), *Comm.*, p. 115.
40. E.g., in the translation of Canisius.

Those who quote him here in favor of *ex opere operato* are indulging in forced exegesis from a dogmatic point of view that isolates baptismal causality from the conjunction between faith and baptism so characteristic of the New Testament.

Not only does this manner of exegesis encounter objections from other parts of Scripture, but also from Peter's epistle itself. It is striking that the expression "baptism saves" stands in the same verse (3:21) where Peter also says that this baptism is "the interrogation [appeal, RSV] of a good conscience toward God." This shows clearly that one cannot read the New Testament's baptismal passages in terms of the infusion of supernatural grace without meeting difficulties, for Peter speaks here of what could be called the subject's side of baptism as well.

That does not imply a subjectivizing of the sacrament, as Markus Barth infers incorrectly from these words. But Stromberg is correct when he says that this indication of baptism as an appeal *(eperōtēma)* shows "that the author is far from applying a magical interpretation to baptism."[41] The fact that Peter, immediately after speaking of saving through baptism, can easily speak of the subject's side of baptism, indicates the relational connections of the sacrament; he is neither objectivizing nor subjectivizing baptism.[42]

Although it is not permissible to expound on one epistle in the New Testament by means of another, we may note the parallel to Peter's words in Hebrews 9:14, where we read that Christ's blood which was offered without blemish unto God cleanses our conscience from dead works to serve the living God. We also recall Hebrews 10:22, which speaks of drawing near to God with a pure heart in fulness of faith, "having our hearts sprinkled from an evil conscience: and having our body washed with pure water."[43] It can indeed be said that baptism saves, if this statement is not detached from the context in which it is placed in Scripture. Spiritualism has always disregarded such emphatic words in Scripture, and therefore has called forth just criticism of its oversimplification. God's signs are not merely external symbols; he has graciously instituted the sacraments for believers so

41. Stromberg, *op. cit.,* p. 7.
42. The exact nature of the "appeal" in I Peter 3:21 may be passed by here. M. Barth understands it as prayer that saves and as testimony of faith. His argument is typical of his devaluation of baptism as a sacrament.
43. Grosheide thinks baptism is meant; Barth does not.

that they would fully live in salvation, obtained by Christ, and therein would honor God's grace.

For those who gain more and more understanding of the connections that are laid in Scripture, Scripture's words regarding baptism imply no threat to the absolute sufficiency and "causality" of Christ's reconciling work. On the contrary: it is precisely those words that provide a powerful testimony to that sufficiency. And such words also provide a defense against the thought of Markus Barth, who rejects baptism as a sacrament.

Barth, apparently reacting to the sacramentalist interpretation of baptism, defines baptism (as sacrament) as "an objective means to salvation of God, or as a guarantee of the preaching (of the gospel)."[44] This reaction is even more evident when he says that baptism may not be changed into a "small and uncertain competitor of the Lord Jesus Christ." This latter statement is, of course, quite correct; but over against that, he asserts that the heart of baptism is an act of the believer. "Christ's message in baptism is not brought primarily to the baptized person, but through the baptized person, the one who baptizes, and the Christian community, it is brought to the whole world." Here is another instance of what has happened so often in the history of the sacramental doctrine, that in reaction to realistic sacramentalism, one falls into the abyss of Zwinglian symbolism and spiritualism. Barth's error does not issue from his opposition to the fatal idea of competition, which corrupts all connections between baptism and cross, but from his subjectivizing of the sacrament and his rejection of the act of God in the sacrament. Evidently he sees no other possibilities than objectivizing and subjectivizing, and he chooses the latter. That is why he cannot appreciate baptism as an instrument, for he first has interpreted this instrumentality as "second causality."

It is at precisely this crossroads that another way must be taken in the light of the New Testament. We see that way in the rejection of *ex opere operato* and simultaneously in the rejection of spiritualism. Or, in other words: in the rejection of the false dilemma between baptism as involved with man's act of faith, and with the act of God. In the New Testament we find no contrast between having oneself baptized and being baptized. There was no reason for Zwingli to plead for the sacrament as exclusively an act of the believer. The Reformation

44. M. Barth, *op. cit.,* p. 521.

spoke of means of grace and of the instrumental character of the sacraments without implying any form of competition with the sufficient offering of Jesus Christ.

Precisely because it honored fully the involvement of baptism with the cross, the Reformation could speak of this instrumentality. In the relation between faith and baptism the Reformers found the meaning of the conjunction between sign and that which is signified. One might suppose that this word "conjunction" introduces a dogmatic aspect, but nothing is further from the truth. For "conjunction" only indicates that undetachable connection that we find in the New Testament between baptism and faith. It is a connection that reaches far beyond subjectivizing and objectivizing, because faith is not a co-factor contributing to the reality of salvation. In its very essence, faith eliminates the idea of competition. In this conjunction between baptism and faith, only one light shines, the light of the sacrifice that was brought once for all (Heb. 9:26). The conjunction between baptism and faith is not a synthesis between subjectivism and objectivism, but a rejection of both in the prospect of God's salvation.

CHAPTER SEVEN

THE SACRAMENTS AS SIGNS AND SEALS

REFORMED theology speaks of the sacraments as signs and seals. This designation can only be understood against the background of the distinction between Word and sacrament. The sacraments are signs and seals with the Word, of the promise of God; as the Heidelberg Catechism formulates it, "the sacraments are ... appointed of God ... that He may the more fully declare and seal to us the promise of the gospel" (Q. 66). It is striking in how many different ways the Reformed sacramental doctrine speaks of the significance and intent of the sacraments. We read, for example, that they have been designed to direct our faith to Christ's sacrifice and that the Holy Spirit assures us by the sacraments that the whole of our salvation stands in that sacrifice (Q. 67). In Article 33 of the Confession of Faith we hear of the sealing of God's promises and of the sacraments as pledges of God's benevolence and grace toward us, and as "visible signs and seals," while Article 34 says that the sacrament of baptism serves us as a testimony that God will be our God forever, and that he wants to make something clear to us with it, namely, that which the sacrament indicates.

In all these definitions, the element of comfort and certainty comes clearly to the fore, as it does also in the form for baptism. The dipping in or sprinkling with water teaches us something. The impurity of our souls is signified so that we may be admonished. We also hear of witnessing and sealing. It is said of the Father that he witnesses and seals, and of the Son that he seals, and of the Holy Spirit that he assures us, while the word addressed to the parents mentions God's ordinance in baptism to seal for us and our children his covenant. In the prayer, the sealing and confirmation are mentioned as reason for gratefulness in connection with God's acceptance of us as his children.

It is clear that in all these modes of expression, no sharp and

134

consciously scientific distinctions are intended that as such could be handled in dogmatic reflection. Their focus, however, is uniformly the certainty of believers, toward which baptism is directed. They receive assurance of salvation and rest in the fulness of the Lord's promises. This is already true in Calvin, who points so emphatically to the nature of the sacraments when he says that the purpose of the sacrament is one of "confirming and sealing the promise itself, and of making it more evident to us and in a sense ratifying it." It is not so much the strengthening of God's own Word, as the strengthening of our faith in that Word (*Inst.*, IV, XIV, 3).

The sacraments are testimonies of the grace of God and "are like seals of the good will that he feels toward us, which by attesting that good will to us, sustain, nourish, confirm, and increase our faith" (IV, XIV, 7). In that, says Calvin, consists the office of the sacraments. All these motifs occur often throughout the Reformed tradition on the sacraments. They could be summarized in the definition that the sacraments are signs and seals of God's promises in order to strengthen our faith (cf. *Inst.*, IV, XIV, 9).

This does not mean that these signs and seals can in themselves perform the miracle of strengthening our faith. They cannot be detached from the power of God and from the working of the Spirit, who convinces us *in* the sacrament. The administration of the sacraments does not fulfil its function with regard to our salvation unless the Spirit as "teacher" sends his power, the Spirit "by whose power alone our hearts are penetrated and affections moved and our souls opened for the sacraments to enter in" (*Inst.*, IV, XIV, 9). If it were not for this working of the Spirit, says Calvin, the sacraments would have no effect on us. Calvin says that he wants to make a distinction and "distribution" between the Spirit and the sacrament. He means that the working of the sacrament cannot be explained or demonstrated by "natural" evidence, for only the operation of the Spirit can fill the sacraments with power *(ibid.).*

The various Reformed definitions of the sacraments show that their doctrine cannot be described adequately as "symbolic," even though many have done so. In the Reformed view, the sacraments are not simply illustrations and depictions, but signs *and seals* of God's promise. The Heidelberg Catechism shows that clearly when it says that God wants "to assure us by this divine pledge and sign that we are spiritually cleansed from our sins as really as we are outwardly washed with water" (Q. 73).

Only if we respect this emphasis can we understand that precisely this designation of the sacraments, as signs and seals, contains a rejection of the symbolic interpretation. It manifests a reaching beyond symbolism, and hence is incompatible with the theory of so-called *nuda signa,* as we can clearly discern, for example, in Calvin's struggle against Zwinglian symbolism.[1] Calvin insists here that the *signum* must be connected with the sealing of God's promises.

The words "seal and sign" refer, then, to an act of God: he signifies and seals by his promise. Nor may the signifying and sealing be separated from each other, for both concern one act of God. It is possible, of course, that man in his unbelief may receive the outward sign without desiring or receiving the "truth" of the sacrament, without receiving Christ who is signified by the sacrament;[2] and the Confession says that the sacraments are nothing at all without their truth, namely, Christ;[3] but it is clear that this "nothing at all" can never be said of the sacraments as institutions of God, and it is also clear that this term indicates the uselessness of taking the sacraments without faith. This warning does not reduce the sacraments to *nuda signa,* for he who does not receive the "truth" of the sacrament has nevertheless been confronted with baptism as sign and seal; and precisely therein lies the basis of the serious sin of misusing the sacraments.

It is probably clear by now that the formula "sign and seal" is of great importance for Reformed sacramental doctrine. Moreover, the addition of "seal" to "sign" is the really significant aspect of this doctrine, for it indicates that the symbol has been taken up into the whole of baptism and that it is undetachably connected with the acts of God. By itself, the sign could be an illustration and nothing more than that; but when the sign has been incorporated into the sealing act of God to strengthen our faith, the sign receives its specific significance, for then it is ordered in sharply defined relations. The sign is an indication in which there is nothing arbitrary because it is founded by the institution of God.

1. See, e.g., Calvin, *Opera selecta,* II, 273. Cf. also Consensus Tigurinus, *passim.*
2. Conf., Art. 35.
3. *Ibid.*

It has been said that Calvin in his further description of the sacraments went much further than the words "sign" and "seal" admit, and more "than his definition would make us expect."[4] Here Bolkestein confronts us with a very important question, namely, whether the designation "sign and seal" may indeed be called sufficient. Bolkestein's theory is that Calvin's statements involving sign and seal issue largely from his polemics against Rome, but that when Calvin turns to argue against Zwingli and the spiritualists he uses stronger language. There he says that the truth of the sign, that which is signified, cannot be separated from the sacrament. Hence the sacrament is always efficacious.

Now it is true that such strong statements are common in Calvin and that in many respects they even determine his sacramental doctrine. That does not mean, however, that Calvin here initiates a second line of thought. Rather, it is precisely herein that Calvin confronts us with the profound meaning of "sign and seal." For the sign and seal cannot exist in themselves, and Calvin sees them in the living and dynamic connection of the acts of God, which involve faith and which grant the gifts of salvation in the true *usus sacramenti*.[5] Hence Calvin's line of opposition against Zwingli is not a second line, nor does it present a trespassing of the limits of the definition of the sacrament, but it belongs undetachably to what he understands by the "sign and seal" of God.

When Bolkestein says that the conceptions of sign and seal are very important for Calvin, but that they are not sufficient for him, then it all depends how we must understand such a statement. For Calvin is not so much concerned with conceptions as with the mystery of the sacraments, and with their reality as it is indicated by the mystery. That, I think, is the reason why Bolkestein is incorrect when he says: "Not only with Calvin, but also with those who followed him, we see that the limits of the concepts 'sign' and 'seal' are repeatedly trespassed. It is evident that they are unable to interpret the full context of the sacraments."[6] Such a statement can be maintained only if sign and seal are again detached from the living God. Because Calvin never does that, one can say of him that

4. M. H. Bolkestein, "Repraesentatio bij Calvijn," *NedTT*, 1952, p. 572.
5. Cf. Conf., Art. 33.
6. Bolkestein, *op. cit.*, p. 278.

the sacrament is correctly defined and described by the designation sign and seal, as it is done in Reformed theology and
the Reformed confessions. No "plus" is necessary, for it is the
act of God toward which faith is directed and to which it adheres in order thus to receive that richness of which Calvin
so emphatically speaks.

It is interesting that Bolkestein calls Calvin's two conceptions of the sacrament "symbolic representation" and "effective
presentation" respectively. The latter, presumably the "plus"
factor, is where Calvin goes beyond the merely "cognitive"
aspect of the sacrament, designated by "sign and seal."[7] But
that is certainly not the case. For Calvin the granting of salvation does not come separate from the sign and seal. The
dualism mentioned does not exist. Bolkestein gives the impression that "sign and seal" refer to something merely symbolic,
and then he explains: "If the concepts of sign and seal fall under
the symbolic representation, the concept of [effective] presentation goes beyond that, and it is precisely this concept that takes
us to the heart of the sacrament."[8] We believe that this interpretation devaluates Calvin's use of "sign and seal" to something symbolic in the illustrative sense. But that is impossible
for Calvin with respect to "sign," and even more so with respect
to "seal." The whole point of "sign and seal" is precisely what
Bolkestein calls "presentation," because Calvin does not speak
of sign and seal *in abstracto,* but of the signs and seals of faith,
which finds rest in them because of what they mean.

It is therefore incorrect to say that Calvin trespasses the
limits of the concepts sign and seal, and it is also incorrect to
credit Luther with correcting Calvin by going beyond a merely
"cognitive" sacramental doctrine.[9]

Bolkestein rejects the latter view, of course, because he thinks
that Calvin holds the "effective presentation" theory. But Calvin
does not hold it as a "plus" factor, which goes beyond "sign
and seal." Rather, according to Calvin it belongs to the essence
of the sacrament that the signs are instrumentally (not abstractly) interpreted in the light of the correlation between

7. *Ibid.,* p. 280.
8. *Ibid.,* p. 281.
9. Bolkestein quotes here *(ibid.)* the article of G. C. van Niftrik, "De
kinderdoop en Karl Barth," *NedTT,* II, 18ff., in which Van Niftrik states
that the definition of the sacrament as sign and seal is unsatisfactory. However, see Bolkestein's note on Van Niftrik, *ibid.,* p. 181.

faith and sacrament. Calvin has thus arrived at a harmonious concept of the sacraments, although it is not at all a rational systematics in which all elements of the sacrament occupy a logical, evidential place. His mode of speaking — in a harmonious manner — issues from his acknowledging the connection which God himself has laid between sign and that which is signified in the presence of faith.[10]

There is therefore good reason to maintain the designation of the sacraments as signs and seals.[11] That does not mean that a good description of the sacraments guarantees a pure, believing understanding of the sacraments and a good and worthy use of them; but it makes it possible, when teaching the doctrine of the sacraments, to explain what they are. The two words taken together make clear that the sacraments are symbols, but not symbols that stand by themselves.

It can hardly be denied that this designation of the sacraments is linked to the human custom of attaching a seal to a

10. The problem mentioned by Bolkestein, of the "plus" of effective presentation, touches the core of the sacramental doctrine. What Bolkestein indicates as "plus" (*de exhibitio*) is definitely essential in the sacramental doctrine of Calvin and the Reformed, and we want to reject the view that this is a "plus" consideration which enriches the interpretation of the sacrament as sign and seal.

Another question is the one that Polman posed in connection with Calvin's sacramental doctrine (*Onze Ned. Geloofsbelijdenis*, IV, 111-14) regarding the "temporary definition of the sacrament." Polman treats here of the manner in which Calvin speaks of the sacrament as coinciding with the visible sign and then again of the signifying matter as incorporated into the definition of the sacrament (p. 114). Polman points to the Confession as parallel, where we sometimes get the impression that the sacrament is only the visible sign, and then again that the outward and the inward action are incorporated into the definition of the sacrament (Art. 35). This, I think, touches upon a different problem from the one of the "plus" of Bolkestein. Polman says correctly that regarding the question "whether the sacrament is only a testimony or also an efficacious organ of the Spirit" Calvin adhered to the latter view. That Polman does not intend to introduce a duality with that "also" between testimony and organ appears from his exegesis of that sacrament at many places. That is why this problem is different from Bolkestein's. Cf., e.g., Polman, *op. cit.*, IV, 135, and especially p. 137 where he says that Calvin "has maintained on the one hand the God-willed conjunction between sign and the thing signified, and between sacrament and the truth, while on the other hand he has not for a moment subjectivized the sacraments from the side of faith.

11. G. C. van Niftrik, *Kleine Dogmatiek,* 1953, p. 280. Cf. also W. F. Golterman, "Teken, symbool of chiffre?" *NedTT*, III, 439.

certain document, and that this general custom forms the background for the use of this concept in Scripture. When the
sacrament was designated in the church as "seal," it was done to
emphasize its trustworthiness. Men were confirmed and stimu-
lated by the manner in which Scripture spoke of seal and sealing, and it is hardly surprising that the Church started very
early to make use of the designation "seal."[12] When we study
the concept "seal" and "sealing" in Scripture, we discover that
it can be used in a wide and general sense. That general use
we find, for instance, in I Corinthians 9:2, where Paul writes
to the Church: "for the seal of mine apostleship are ye in the
Lord." The context makes it clear that Paul speaks of the
recognition of his apostleship by the Corinthians. They are
the seal in and through their recognition of Paul's apostleship.
The word *sphragis* is used in a general sense with a strong
accent on the trustworthiness, the authenticity, and the guarantee.[13]

The use of the word "seal" for the sacrament becomes still
more meaningful when we remember that Paul connects it specifically with circumcision when he writes: "he [Abraham] received the sign of circumcision, a seal of the righteousness of
the faith which he had while he was in uncircumcision" (Rom.
4:11). Here, too, the issue is the sealing, the guarantee regarding the righteousness of faith, that is to say, the righteousness
toward which Abraham's faith was directed. In the seal which
he received, namely, the one of circumcision, he received "the
means of confirmation and of verification."[14] We find a similar
use of the word "seal" in John 6:27: "Work not for the food
which perisheth, but for the food which abideth unto eternal
life, which the Son of man shall give unto you: for him the
Father, even God, hath sealed." This is not the sacrament of
Christian baptism, but a designation of the veracity of Christ's
Messiahship. In the divine sealing lies the emphatic acknowledgment of Jesus Christ as the Son of God, and of his Messianic
dignity. According to Grosheide, the form of the verb ("to
seal") points to a specific act of God; in this connection Grosheide thinks of baptism or of the miracles that Jesus performed

---

12. "Among the many riddles of the oldest Christian baptismal stories, one
    of the most enticing is the designation of baptism as *sphragis*. Heit-
    müller, in *N.T. Studien*, 1914, p. 40.
13. Grosheide, *Comm. ad loc.*
14. Heitmüller, *op. cit.*, p. 46.

as "proof" of his Messiahship. It is clear from the New Testament, then, why the Christian Church began very early to describe that element of trustworthiness and confirmation with the word "seal."[15]

That becomes still more evident when we pay attention for a moment to the manner in which Scripture speaks of "sealing." We think of II Corinthians 1:21-22: "Now he that establisheth us with you in Christ, and anointed us, is God; who also sealed us, and gave us the earnest of the Spirit in our hearts"; and along with that, Ephesians 1:13f.: "In whom, having also believed, ye were sealed with the Holy Spirit of promise, which is an earnest of our inheritance." And finally Ephesians 4:30: "And grieve not the Holy Spirit of God, in whom ye were sealed unto the day of redemption." It appears here that there is a very close relation between sealing and the gift of the Spirit, who is an earnest of our salvation and inheritance. That is especially clear in II Corinthians 1:22, which speaks of an earnest of God's promises (1:20). It is a confirmation *in* the Anointed One, a confirmation by judicial power and guarantee.[16] God himself gives that in the gift of the Spirit, the seal, the earnest of the inheritance, so that here also the element of certainty and trustworthiness stands in the foreground.[17] "God puts his seal on the believers by giving them the Holy Spirit, through which they are sealed as his children."[18]

And finally, we recall Revelation 7:22ff., where we hear of the angel who has the seal of the living God, and of the number of those who were sealed — 144,000. Those who have the seal are spared in the judgment (9:4; cf. 14:1; 22:4). Those with the seal of God stand in contrast to those bearing the mark of the beast on their right hand or their forehead (Rev. 13:16-17; 14:11).

The question may be asked whether in these contexts the connection between baptism and seal becomes visible. Grosheide, who thinks that in the New Testament "seal" does not always imply baptism, believes that II Corinthians 1:22 does have a connection with baptism. This is not inconsistent, as long as we recognize that "seal" is not yet a technical term

15. Cf. Grosheide, *Commentaar op Johannes*, I, 431.
16. Grosheide, *ad loc.*, p. 68.
17. F. J. Pop, *Commentaar op 2 Corinthe*, p. 45.
18. *Ibid.*

designating baptism. It is only a matter of definite contexts, centering on the description of veracity and trustworthiness.

Before we look more closely into the significance of baptism as seal, it is necessary to notice a very special connection which Roman Catholic doctrine finds in the texts that speak of sealing and baptism. We mean the well-known doctrine of the *character indelebilis,* which is certainly one of the most remarkable themes in Roman Catholic dogmatics, especially because of the manner in which the givens of Scripture are treated.

The indestructible mark is, according to Rome, given with the administration of baptism and also with the administration of confirmation and ordination. It is not the same as an infusion of supernatural grace (which is not *indelebilis*), but something else which cannot be defined so easily. For the indestructibility of this character in baptism, Rome appeals to the texts mentioned: II Corinthians 1:22; Ephesians 1:12; and 4:30. Conclusions drawn from these texts became part of the Church's doctrine, especially at Trent, where the anathema is spoken against those who do not accept that in these three sacraments the "character" is stamped into the soul, the spiritual and indestructible sign, from which it follows that they never can be repeated.[19]

It is deduced from these texts that baptism marks the recipient with "a spiritual sign, different from grace" by means of a "spiritual mark imprinted in the soul."[20] The essence of this "character" is indicated in various ways: it is distinguished from supernatural grace because that grace can be lost through mortal sin, something that cannot be said of the "character." It is described as an "ornament of the soul," as a *habitus* or disposition of no small significance, since for the sake of this character, baptism does not have to be repeated even though grace is lost. In the mark lies a certain dedication to the service of the Lord, which is not sanctifying in nature. It is, so to speak, an ontic substratum of grace, something to which grace can always be rejoined. It is acknowledged that the New Testament does not render a clear and independent proof, but it does

19. "S.q.d. in tribus sacramentis, baptismo scilicet, confirmatione et ordine non imprimi characterem in anima, hoc est signum quoddam spirituale et indelebile, unde ea iterari non possunt, A. S." (Ses. VII Can. 9; Denz. 852).

20. *DTC, s.v.* "Charactère sacramental," p. 1701. Cf. Bavinck, *Geref. Dog.,* IV, 464.

contain references "which can be explained along the lines of the dogma and by leaning on tradition."[21]

In connection with the textual references quoted for this character, it is understandable that there were a number of theologians in the Middle Ages (A. van Hales, Bonaventura, A. de Grote) who were of the opinion that the character was grace itself, and that thereby believers were distinguished from unbelievers. This is entirely understandable, since Scripture does not speak in the references mentioned of something neutral which abides even if supernatural grace is lost, as a kind of ontic substratum in the soul; Scripture speaks rather, in a decidedly soteriological and comforting context, of a confirmation appealing to the faithfulness of God, who in the Holy Spirit gives the earnest of the inheritance to come. But Rome detaches the character from this soteriological context and thus makes it a habit which can be isolated from salvation and which continues to exist in the soul even if grace is lost.

It is clear that what Scripture says of sealing lies precisely on the plane of everyday speech, in which seal and sealing indicate the guaranteeing, sealing, and assuring of God's promise. But Rome turns it into a "mark" in the soul which does not assume the continuous presence of grace in the soul. It becomes a "spiritual and indelible mark."[22] To be sure this is connected with the meaning of "seal," but only in the sense of a spiritual dignity. It is an evidence of Christ's taking possession, "once for all," of the baptized person (p. 62), a being-connected-with-Christ (p. 63), a becoming-like-unto-him (p. 65). The character thus forms the foundation for sanctifying grace, and so, says Rome, explains the revival of sacramental grace. When, because of a sinful disposition, a person does not receive supernatural grace in baptism, he still receives the sacramental sign, the character, which remains active since it is an act of God. When the impediments are removed, the character produces grace (p. 66).

Although the "character" is esteemed very highly, it evidently has nothing to do with sealing in its comforting aspect. Paul speaks of that as the Yea and Amen of God's promise, as the dwelling in and the earnest of the Holy Spirit, who keeps and

21. Schmaus, *Kath. Dogm.*, IV, 1, pp. 38ff., 122ff.; Bartmann, *Dogmatik*, II, 219ff.; M. J. Lucian Farine, *Der sakramentale Charakter*, 1904, p. v.
22. A. Janssens, *Doopsel en vormsel* (Serie *Kath. Kerk*, 12), p. 61.

safeguards us for the inheritance and seals us "unto the day of redemption" (Eph. 4:30).

The difficulties of this Roman Catholic doctrine of the *character indelebilis* (of which Thomas himself said that the essence of the mark was difficult to define) [23] have sometimes been resolved by assuming that the Holy Spirit himself is the "character" and that therefore a *qualitas creata* is not the identifying characteristic of the mark. Differences regarding the nature of the mark existed already in Scholasticism.[24] Durandus saw it as nothing but a relation,[25] but generally it was regarded as a reality present in the soul, now and after death. That is a great mystery, according to some even more mysterious than grace itself, "for the latter manifests itself much more in its concrete effects and is also more clearly and decisively described in revelation."[26] In connection with the doctrine of the supernatural, Farine came to see the character as the Holy Spirit himself, not as quality infused into the soul.[27] It is remarkable that he appeals to the same texts for this view that form the basis for the official doctrine of the character. "It is inconceivable that the existence of a metaphysical-qualitative character [in the sense of Scholasticism] could be derived from the same [texts]" (p. 41).

In order to maintain his own position, Farine points out that especially the seal printed on us (II Cor. 1) is identical with the pledge that is in our hearts, namely, the Holy Spirit. It is not something that is imprinted by the Holy Spirit. "There is no mention whatsoever of such a causality of the Holy Spirit." From there, Farine comes to the conclusion: "The Holy Spirit must therefore be the imprinted, divine seal" (p. 43). He points to a similar criticism based on the normal, scriptural usage of these texts in Scotus and Biel (p. 44). But he does not accept their conclusion that therefore the doctrine of the "character" is incorrect. In spite of the rejection of this character as a created reality, we must, he thinks, maintain the doctrine.

Farine has evidently been impressed by the urgent significance of the work of the Spirit, of which the New Testament speaks in connection with sealing. But he now connects his

23. *S.T.*, III, Q. 63. Cf. Farine, *op. cit.*, p. vi.
24. Cf. Bartmann, *op. cit.*, II, 221.
25. *Ibid.*
26. *Ibid.*
27. Farine, *op. cit.*, p. 41; cf. p. 15.

conclusion (that the seal is the Holy Spirit himself) with the Roman Catholic doctrine of the character, which is distinguished from grace. That brings him into great difficulties, for according to Trent the character is an indestructible mark, and that is, of course, also maintained by Farine. He wonders therefore how that is compatible with his interpretation of the seal as the Holy Spirit himself (p. 59). He seeks the solution by supposing that the character comes to everybody but that it is a sign of likeness unto Christ for those who love God. "For the others, however, those who forever have excluded themselves from this communion in love, it is a sign of eternal perdition." In that sense, they participate "in the divine, living Spirit" (ibid.).

The incompatibility between the scriptural light (which connects sealing with the pledge of the Spirit) and the dogmatic church doctrine of the "character" is clearly evident here. The result is that nothing is left of the comfort of the sealing "unto the day of redemption." It is astonishing to be told that the Holy Spirit, who dwells as "character" in the heart, nevertheless provides no divine guarantee to the person who possesses this character. To be sure, there is a kind of "guaranteeing," but it is purely a conditional guarantee. "As pledge and indestructible sign, the character lays the foundation for the complete ransom of the full property, for the just as well as for the wicked" (ibid.). So the earnest of the Spirit is detached from perseverance, because it is not grace itself. The sealing retreats behind the conditional promise, which is and remains present in the "character" in the "reality" of the Holy Spirit.

We now return to the question how we must understand the sacrament as seal. An answer is possible only if we start from the fact that the sign and the seal may never be separated. Nevertheless, that has often been done; the sign as something external was then contrasted with the seal as something internal. The implication was that one could receive the sign without the truth of the sacrament. This is how Article 35 of the Confession of Faith is sometimes read, which also speaks of the wicked who receive the sacrament but not its truth, not Christ, who is signified by the sacrament. But this is a different situation, which Calvin has so vividly described as the vanity and uselessness of the sacraments when they are involved with unbelief. This does not affect the nature of the sacrament as instituted by God. The distinction between sacramental sign and the truth of the sacrament is quite different from the dis-

tinction between sign and seal. To miss this point would lead
one to the conclusion that the wicked have the sign of the
sacrament but that they have never come into contact with
the sacrament as seal. Baptism then becomes a mere appearance, because there is a relation only to the external sign. But
this divests the sacrament of its integrity, although at first it
had been described as sign and seal.

It is understandable ʾthat this approach should have been
taken more than once, for it is a fact that although the sacraments are instituted only for believers to strengthen their faith,
they are at the same time administered in the Church of Christ
on earth to those who actually do not believe. To manage this
problem, a distinction was made between sign and seal, and
the seal and sealing were associated with the work of the "inner
Teacher," with the work of the Holy Spirit in the hearts of
believers. The definition of the sacraments could then no longer
be maintained, with the result that the distinction between the
sacrament as sign and as seal contributed to a serious devaluation of the sacrament and its objectivity.

We learn here that the serious problem of the relation between unbelief and the sacrament may never be solved by separating what God has put together. What man does in unbelief
may never be constitutive for the determination of the sacraments as divine institutions. One can say that, although the
unbeliever receives the sacrament, he does not receive its truth
(Jesus Christ), but it cannot be said that the unbeliever receives the sign but not the seal,[28] for the unbeliever has no
right to harm the power and integrity of the sacrament as
seal and sign. Both the sign and the seal in the one act of
God in the sacrament have bearing on the word of promise;
that, then, which is abandoned with respect to the seal, cannot
be retained with respect to the sign. That is why a distinction
may never be made between the sacrament as sign and the
sacrament as seal for the mere sake of solving a rational difficulty.

Others have found a different solution to the same problem.
They admit that the sign and the seal cannot be separated,
but then they distinguish an "objective" sealing through the
sacrament of baptism from a "subjective" sealing by the Holy

28. Cf. L. van der Zanden, *De Kinderdoop, Sacrament der gelovigen*, 1946,
    pp. 73ff.

Spirit. These two "sealings" happen independently of each other, and then must somehow be reconnected through a combining of objectivity and subjectivity.

More than once, the sealing by the Holy Spirit has been detached in a mystical manner from baptism and given a separate efficacy. In this context, the promise of baptism becomes something "objective" and "external" with a general, impersonal content. It is detached from the "for us," and loses its personal address. The sealing through baptism becomes a general promise which is strengthened and confirmed by the subjective seal of baptism. Behind this interpretation of baptism stands the thought that God's promise is a general promise, valid in itself, implying however an absolute being-directed-toward-us, so that it cannot be understood as a comforting promise either.[29] With that, the divine promise has been undone from its real content, and becomes a general offer of grace.

It is no mystery why this interpretation of baptism should arise. Men realize that the promise and baptism have bearing on faith. Belief is then seen as the subjective factor which individualizes the "general" promise and which gives this promise (sealed in baptism) its directedness and its "for us" character. Faith then acquires a constitutive aspect, even a creative one, because this faith *makes* the sealed offer to be a solace. Through faith, the objective sealing becomes a saving good.

This theory, however, destroys the biblical correlation between faith and promise. Faith receives a totally incorrect function. For in the Bible, faith does not make the general promise concrete, but rather acknowledges what comes to us in the divine promise as divine comforting. Faith does not possess one single constructive and creative moment; it rests only and exclusively in the reality of the promise. It does not create, but rests in the promise, and the sealing is connected with precisely this, that the creative character of faith is radically excluded. Our assurance of salvation is surely at stake here, for if our faith must create, it may also fail to create.

We see now that the mystery of the sacramental doctrine lies in this pure relation between faith and sacrament. This has nothing to do with a subjectivizing of the sacrament by virtue of faith, but it indicates the relation that is implied in the purpose of the sacrament. Faith does not compete with the

---

29. Cf. Bavinck's statement regarding this thought in *Geref. Dog.*, IV, 468.

objectivity of the sacrament; it is rather a believing understanding of the meaning of God's word in the sacrament. Unbelief cannot understand this meaning. The question now arises,
however, whether outside the true *usus sacramenti* baptism has
any meaning at all. The question can also be formulated thus,
whether baptism does not then become a mere outward act
with no significance, an apparent baptism and nothing more.

This matter is extremely important and played a decisive
role in many discussions, so much so that it even became formulated by the Church, which emphatically rejected the idea of
false baptism. In the ecclesiastical controversy among the Reformed Churches, the synod of Utrecht of 1945 stated "that
according to the judgment of the synod, baptism which is administered to those who later in unbelief reject the sacrament
may never be designated as false baptism, because baptism, administered in Christ's Church upon God's sovereign command,
can never be empty and vain." This thesis was posed against
those who thought that the synod favored an interpretation
of baptism that logically contradicted the objective structure
of baptism. It was therefore no accident that at a specific point
in the contention, "false baptism" was concretely discussed.
Nevertheless, this rejection of false baptism has not led to a
reconciliation, because it was thought that, although false baptism was formally opposed, this was not really possible in the
light of the presuppositions. Greijdanus, for instance, has written regarding this thesis against false baptism that there was
no reason to argue about the *words* "false baptism," but that the
idea was actually there in synod's opinion that "baptism is a
full baptism with him who believes; it is not full baptism with
him who does not believe";[30] and he says of the latter: "Even
though one refuses to call the latter false baptism, it is not
full baptism, its content is less, different from that of full
baptism."[31]

With that, Greijdanus thinks, the objectivity of the sacrament is affected, for then one can begin to construe the sacra-

---

30. S. Greijdanus, "De 16 uitspraken van de synode van Utrecht in Augustus
    1945," p. 33.
31. A little further, Greijdanus speaks of two baptisms, a real, full baptism,
    and an unreal, non-full baptism. He declares that the thesis against
    false baptism is directed against the *words* "false baptism" and that the
    problem proper is left untouched.

ment in the light of the contrast between faith and unbelief. And against this view Greijdanus specifically refers to Calvin, who said that baptism remained the water of regeneration even though all the world were unbelieving, as the Lord's Supper remained the distribution of Christ's body and blood even if there were no spark of faith left.

This controversy, which is not at all a new event in dogmatics, has as its background the relation between baptism and the unbeliever, a relation which had received much attention long before it became the cause of a conflict in the Reformed Churches. However, in the ecclesiastical conflict the matter was sharply defined, as is shown by Greijdanus when he writes that the distinction between full and non-full baptism is not found in the first question regarding baptism, nor in the confessional writings, that it is utterly uncalled for, and that the results of this distinction must be called nothing less than disastrous.[32]

It is necessary to see clearly what the problem is here. Perhaps it is correct to say that the whole problem of the sacraments is concentrated in the controversy about false baptism, for if false baptism is admitted, or at any rate a point of view is admitted in which false baptism can only be rejected through inconsistency, one can conclude that the sign, instituted by God, could — within the Church — be nothing but appearance, a meaningless sign, or even a mistake of the Church.

That explains why the controversy about false baptism was at the heart of the discussions, because it touches fundamentally upon the integrity of the sacrament. It must immediately be added, however, that one must be careful in his analysis, precisely because such serious consequences are involved, the more so when false baptism is rejected with an emphatic appeal to the institution of God. Simplistic solutions, employing distinctions that introduce "rational clarity" and nothing more, contribute nothing. The very fact that Article 35 speaks of "the sacrament, but not the truth of the sacrament," indicates that in Reformed theology and its confession an attempt is made to express the relation between unbelief and sacrament as it affects the Church's administration of baptism. Bavinck already touched upon this when he wrote: "Of this baptism, Christ is the administrator. And only if he baptizes and gives the signi-

---

32. See S. Greijdanus, "Mijne schorsing door de Generale Synode van de Geref. Kerken in Nederland," p. 13.

fying matter with the sign, is one truly baptized,"[33] a statement
which finds its parallels in various of Bavinck's other works.[34]

Obviously, everything depends on the meanings of the words
here. It is necessary to say this about Bavinck, but about Greijdanus as well, who before the ecclesiastical struggle about baptism and the covenant made statements much like Bavinck's.
A clear example is found in Greijdanus' exegesis of Romans 6,
where he says that Paul speaks here of "baptism as such" and
then continues: "Not only of water-baptism, but of the full, real
baptism, of the spiritual reality with water-baptism as sign
and seal."[35] A little further, Greijdanus speaks of "connection
and communion with the Lord Jesus Christ as it came about
through real baptism and as it is signified and sealed through
the baptism by water."

The same thought is developed in his commentary on Galatians. "Baptism is here taken as a whole, not baptism by water
alone, without its inner significance, its inner essence, but full
baptism, that is, the connection with Christ and its visible
revelation in the baptism by water which signifies and seals
it."[36] This is the same trend of thought that we found in
Bavinck. It is evident that neither Bavinck nor Greijdanus
intends to devaluate baptism with water when a distinction is
made between water-baptism and real baptism. But of course
such a mode of expression opens up the danger of misunderstanding, for the impression may be given that one is trying
to devaluate baptism with water after all.

On the other hand, it is also evident that neither Bavinck nor
Greijdanus in his commentary wishes to admit the possibility
of false baptism. Both, rather, want to express what Article 35
says of the sacrament and the truth of the sacrament. All such
statements find their basis in that; all want to allow the fulness
of the sacrament in all its connections, especially in the connection between sign and that which is signified. No one wishes
to devaluate the sacrament, as becomes clear when Greijdanus
speaks of baptism as such in Romans 6. It is still *possible* to
speak of a non-full baptism, however, because of the mysterious
fact that one who does not fully acknowledge the historical word

33. H. Bavinck, *Geref. Dog.,* IV, 510.
34. Cf. H. Bavinck, *Roeping en Wedergeboorte,* p. 184.
35. Greijdanus, *Commentaar op Romeinen,* p. 294.
36. *Commentaar op Galaten,* p. 250.

of the covenant and the baptism administered by the Church can distort its actual structure, treating water-baptism as if it were independent of belief or unbelief. On the other hand, one can direct his eye toward the connection between sign and that which is signified and speak, as does Article 35, in terms of a distinction that has nothing to do with a devaluation of the sacrament, but only points to the sin of unbelief with respect to the sacraments.

This last point is relevant not only to baptism, but also to the Lord's Supper. It is strange that with respect to the non-full Lord's Supper (used by the unbeliever) one does not feel the same objection as with respect to the non-full baptism. Nevertheless the problem is the same in principle, and the statement of Article 35 applies to both. We see, then, that there is a danger of quarreling overmuch about words. It may be that the expression "non-full" baptism is unfortunate because it conveys the impression one does not respect fully the objectivity of baptism. But it is quite wrong to infer from such expressions as used by Bavinck and Greijdanus that they teach a "false" baptism. The intention of such statements is more decisive than the choice of words.

It is then highly significant when a Church with great emphasis rejects "false baptism" in response to the criticism that it has subjectivized the sacrament, and when it does so with an appeal to the institution of Christ.[37] It is still possible, of course, to charge that this church is really committed to false baptism by the presuppositions of its sacramental doctrine, as the Lutherans of the sixteenth century said about the Reformed view of the Lord's Supper on the ground that it did not do justice to the real presence of Christ. But one can also look upon it in a different manner. It is also possible that one wants to reflect on baptism only within the limits of God's revelation and that for that reason the notion of false baptism is rejected a priori.

It is of course true that one's presuppositions about the baptismal sacrament may not contradict that. If the Reformed baptismal doctrine did teach that water baptism could not yet be called full baptism, and that one therefore by some roundabout way must come to know whether he belongs to God's covenant before he can apply the promise of baptism to him-

---

37. Cf. my *Gevaren en perspectieven voor ons kerkelijk leven,* 1946, pp. 13ff.

self, then baptism would indeed have been devaluated. But this interpretation surely finds no support in Calvin. This leaves Reformed theology with the serious question of how to interpret "full baptism" consistently with the confessional statement that one can receive the sacrament without participating in the truth of it. This question has never been answered satisfactorily.[38] In so far as it has been attempted, this answer has either come back to the well-known distinction between sacrament and truth of the sacrament, or baptism has been subjectivized in the formula that the giving of the promise is objectively indubitable, while the application of the promise depends on the decision of faith.

If we want to reject this latter formula (as we do), we must admit at the same time that no perfectly rational synthesis can make the objectivity of baptism transparent. Calvin was always aware of this fact and acknowledged it again and again, not in order to flee into a romantic sphere of irrationality, but because he understood that these connections could not be apprehended apart from faith, and that a rational synthesis between subjectivity and objectivity would not do. He was not concerned with a twofold baptism and a twofold Holy Supper in a strange duality which would affect the power and the objective structure of the sacraments. That is why he speaks of *offering (offerre),* both with respect to baptism and the Lord's Supper, because he sees that through the relation between Word and sacrament the integrity of the sacrament is maintained. That is why one cannot speak of a twofold promise, each time with a different content, without violating the integrity of the sacrament and breaking the relation between Word and sacrament. But as long as we hold to the integrity of the sacrament, we can reject emphatically both false baptism and false Holy Supper because they separate what God has united.

Once more, then, the question arises how it is possible that baptism can be administered to those who later reveal themselves as unbelievers. One should not lightly conclude that the sacrament has no meaning for such people. The sacrament is administered here on earth, where it is impossible to know fully the human heart. Because of this fact, it is possible to distinguish between that which belongs to the essence and the

---

38. That becomes evident in Greijdanus when he speaks of the objective basis for faith; cf. *Mijne schorsing,* p. 17.

purpose of the sacrament and that which actually occurs in the administration of the sacrament. In this possible relation between unbelief and sacrament the acts of the Church and the sin of man lie intertwined, and who would think that we can make transparent what sin has made so opaque? And so, lacking the power of logical synthesis, we must rather approach the problem from the pastoral point of view, remembering always that one may never minimize the objectivity of the sacraments, which is based on the relation between word and sacrament.

It is this theme that leads some people to speak (with no attempt at technical precision) of the relation between unbelief and Covenant and baptism. They introduce the notion of Covenant-breaking, and speak of the urgency with which the Covenant promise also comes to those who disdain the Covenant of the Lord in unbelief. This attempt to understand the problem is no proof of the weakening of the objectivity of baptism, but an indication of the fact that the sacrament that was instituted for believers is administered in a world of sin and unbelief.[39]

At this point Calvin's concept of "offering" is relevant, and leads him in a direction principally different from that of Greijdanus. For Calvin does not want to say that in the giving of the sign, the thing signified is received by all, and that in that sense sign and the thing signified are always connected with each other. Greijdanus has objectivized the conjunction between sign and the thing signified, and in doing so he has given a different "point" to the structure of Article 35 and to the Reformed sacramental doctrine. In this manner he has gained clarity at the cost of Calvin's insight in which offering and giving (and receiving) are distinguished.[40] And we see clearly that the controversy about false baptism remains in every sacramental doctrine, and that one can do injustice to the structure of the sacrament with a seemingly clear polemic (full baptism and full Supper).[41]

Closely related to these question is the problem whether baptism is a sealing of the promise or a sealing of believers —

---

39. Cf. Polman, *op. cit.*, IV, 137.
40. The reference to the "offering" in connection with the objective structure of the sacrament, we find not only in Calvin, but also in various Helvetian confessions when they speak of the truth and integrity of the sacraments. Cf., e.g., Müller, *Bekenntnisschriften*, Helv. Conf.
41. See, e.g., S. Greijdanus, *Korte bespreking van het Praeadvies van Commissie I*, p. 7.

a problem that has occupied Woelderink and Oorthuys. Woelderink, who calls the Reformed designation of the sacrament as sign and seal "brilliant," adds immediately: "One thing must be remembered. When we are baptized, not we, but the promise of the gospel is sealed."[42] If this had been understood clearly, he says, the doctrine of presumptive regeneration would never have arisen. "For baptism does not seal us as regenerated people, but it seals to us the promise of the Covenant, that promise wherein undoubtedly regeneration is also implied and on the basis of which we may expect the vivifying Spirit with faith and prayer."[43] Woelderink denies that the sacraments are a seal of infused grace.[44]

Oorthuys starts with the same dilemma.[45] He speaks of pietism, which always points out that originally only adults were baptized. Then it was indeed possible to say that believers were sealed, because faith and conversion were evident. But, he thinks, this historical contingency has affected our conception of the essence of baptism leading us to associate sign and seal with what is present in the believer; thus the sealing is no longer applied to the promise of the gospel.[46]

This consideration undoubtedly contains an important element of truth. Oorthuys attempts here to maintain the objectivity of baptism and its sealing against subjectivism. Woelderink and Oorthuys correctly oppose the view that presumptive regeneration forms the basis of baptism in the sense that one can speak of baptism only as a sealing of assumed regeneration. The correlation between faith and the sacrament thus becomes a relation between the sacrament and grace infused beforehand, while baptism would be the objective sign and seal. But this line of thought threatens the promise of baptism by making it contingent upon already-existing grace. It would evoke a kind of self-analysis altogether different from the biblical mode of self-examination. Such attention to one's interior life cannot fail to weaken one's attention to the Word. Inward grace becomes the basis for baptism, and when it is assumed not to be present, baptism becomes false baptism pure and simple, be-

42. J. G. Woelderink, *Het doopsformulier*, 1938, p. 279.
43. *Ibid.*, p. 280.
44. *Ibid.*, pp. 106, 243ff.
45. G. Oorthuys, *De sacramenten*, p. 61; see also G. Oorthuys, *Doopboekje*, p. 148.
46. Oorthuys, *Doopboekje*, pp. 145, 148.

cause it has been detached from the institution by God and from the promise of God.

But this very real danger cannot be escaped by distinguishing between the sealing of baptism and the sealing of believers by the Holy Spirit. This only raises the problem later on of reconnecting the two elements that were first separated. Moreover, it is a fact that the sealing of the promise functions precisely to seal believers by the Holy Spirit. There is a profound interrelation between the sealing of the promise through baptism and the sealing of believers, for the believer who uses the sacrament as sign and seal in faith, is therein sealed in that sense that he accepts God's promise (sealed in baptism!) to us and rests therein. That is why the sealing of believers by the Holy Spirit is not a separate working of the Spirit, detached from the sealing of the promise through baptism, but is one with it. The Spirit uses the sacraments for the strengthening of faith, to the end that one gains assurance regarding his personal status and finds rest in the trustworthiness of God. Woelderink's and Oorthuys' trend of thought is a strong reaction against subjectivism and mysticism, which make inward grace the basis for a traditionally accepted, but essentially superfluous, baptism. We must agree that such a reaction against the undermining of baptism is necessary, but it is nevertheless possible to speak of the sealing of the believer in baptism in a different manner than happens in subjectivism.

One can say unhesitatingly that baptism is the sign and seal of the promise of God, and at the same time that believers are sealed for the day of redemption in their belief which rests on this promise. This sealing is not based on the fact that interior grace is already present, but man takes his rest in the seal of God. Therein, according to the language of Scripture, the believer is sealed and therein he knows of the safety of his own life. This act of faith does not render the word of promise unstable; on the contrary, it acknowledges that stability and rests in it. That is why there is no contrast between sealing through baptism and the sealing of believers by the Holy Spirit — in the way of Word and sacrament.

When Oorthuys distinguishes the objective promise from the status of believers in order to resist subjectivism, and therefore distinguishes the seal of baptism from the "mark of God on our regenerated state," he has chosen as his opponent a subjectivistic interpretation of the relation between baptism and regeneration. He does not fully recognize, however, that the Reformed confessions speak of the believing use of the sacraments, and also that they speak of salvation in its fulness as it comes to believers through the efficacy of the Spirit. Only here can the contrasts between baptism and regeneration fade away.[47] And that is the only way in which we can understand Article 33 of the Confession of Faith, which says that in the sacraments we are presented with what God gives us to understand through his Word and what he does in our hearts, confirming in us the salvation which he imparts to us.

This is not a subjectivizing of the sacraments or a violation of their objectivity. But it is a rejection of an objectivistic view of the sacraments which objectivizes the promise and detaches it from its connection with faith.

Knowing oneself to be a child of God is thus not a work of self-analysis apart from the sacrament and which only accepts the sacrament as an "outward" sign. This symbolic view stands squarely opposed to the confession of the sealing by the Holy Spirit, who makes use of the sign in order to overcome the resistance of man's heart. Believers are thus truly sealed in the sacrament. The one work of the Holy Spirit which leads to the conquest of all uncertainty stands in an unbreakable and profound relation. Therein, baptism is absolutely eschatologically directed. To be sure, there is in baptism, as in the Lord's Supper, the so-called sign of pledging wherein the believer confesses his belief (I believe, help Thou my unbelief) and thus is distinguished from the unbeliever through baptism. But this subjective act is directed toward the objectivity of salvation and there is therefore never any tension between the two. The purpose of the sacrament is the assurance of salvation, stability rather than instability, proof against doubt, a song of praise about the trustworthiness of God in contrast with the mendacity of man's heart, and a guarded inheritance in the midst of the dangers of this unstable life. Those who do not understand the ways of God because they gaze at the outward sign, live only in their own

47. That Oorthuys' polemics is incorrect appears when he represents the point of view which he criticizes in these terms: "The apostles did not teach us that baptism seals such powerful effects because those who were baptized were believers and regenerated." This suggests that in the baptism which he opposes, grace would be the starting-point of baptism. See for criticism of Oorthuys' view: S. v.d. Linden, *De leer van den Heiligen Geest bij Calvijn,* 1943, p. 186.

wisdom. But those who follow his way will learn increasingly that God uses these pledges of his mercy in the weakness of our faith.

Here, through the efficacy of the Spirit, man's trust is more and more strengthened, and faith rests in what the Spirit himself has said. In this way, it is also understood why the word of promise can come to us in what is usually called the conditional form. That does not affect the sovereignty and trustworthiness of the promise, but it urgently points out to us that this promise and this confirmation can only be understood in the way of faith. This trustworthiness cannot be seen and acknowledged apart from the way of faith. The marvel of the Spirit makes us understand the promise as a directed promise. It is the faith which has heard it from his own mouth. It has nothing to add to this promise, certainly not the application to one's own life. For it was precisely this individual, personal life which was meant and touched by this divine promise. Over against the depersonalization of the sacrament, we must keep our eyes upon the absolute directedness of the promise which in Jesus Christ is Yea and Amen.

In this light, one can fully honor the teaching that the sacrament of baptism is never an empty sign, but that it is connected with the promise of God in such a manner that the nature of this sacrament can never be affected by misuse of it. This is not a matter of objective and subjective factors, but of the call to belief which sees in the signs and seals the fulness of salvation signified and sealed, and which accepts them as signs and seals of God. The sacrament is then not detached from the connections of promise and demand, nor abstracted from the living God, but acknowledged in the intention which God himself has laid in them. That is why baptism stands for us as the sign and seal of the promise of all of salvation. Therein lies the undetachable relation of the baptismal promise with regeneration and the renewal by the Holy Spirit, with justification and sanctification and not in the least — as indicated by Calvin — with the incorporation into Christ's Church.

When belief speaks of baptism, it can speak meaningfully and positively of signified and sealed salvation, as the form for baptism does. If these statements and prayers should be detached from the relation between faith and promise, they may lead one to the opinion that the language is too positive, and one may try to counter this positiveness by beginning to speak of the problem of unbelief. But in doing so, one forgets that these things are said in the light of the conjunction between sign and that which is signified, not in the spatial sense but according to the nature and structure of the sacrament. For in this conjunction full justice is done to the call and demand of the promise, but in such a way that the so-called "conditional" does not become a threat because the voice of God is heard in the promise of the Covenant.

Precisely in the way of promise and demand, it becomes clear that one can speak of the unconditionality of God's promise without in any way minimizing the call in the Covenant. Those who speak *in abstracto* of the unconditionality of the promise, violate the connections between promise and demand and fail to recognize the way in which God leads us to salvation by his promising call and admonishing voice. But one can also speak in a different, nonabstract manner of unconditionality if one accepts the promise of God and if this acceptance is not a consequence to our fulfilling the condition, but a resting in the covenant which is unshakable. That is possible only in the believing use of the sacraments, in which the believer's perseverance becomes visible. We think of the struggle at Jabbok when Jacob says: "I will not let thee go, except thou bless me" (Gen. 32:26).

This perseverance is nothing but the laudation of God in his trustworthiness and in the unconditionality of his mercy. It is the purpose of the sacraments: strengthened faith which no longer doubts in unbelief but which gives the honor to God (Rom. 4:20). Precisely through the condition, this anxiety about the remaining fulfilment of the condition is taken from us, not in superficiality but through trust in him who will not let go of the works of his hand.

Baptism, seen in belief, is thus the sign of the incorporation into Christ's Church, in the holy communion of true believers in Christ, expecting all their salvation in Jesus Christ, being washed with his blood, sanctified and sealed by his Spirit.[48] He is the sign of this transition from the old to the new life which becomes revealed in the Church of Christ through his grace.[49] This seclusion does not issue from proud self-exaltations; it can only be described in the categories of the most humble confession: the purification through the blood of Jesus Christ, the regenera-

48. Conf., Art. 27.
49. Cf. *Inst.*, IV, XV, 1.

tion from above which does not issue from our flesh and blood,
the communion with the *ecclesia militans* and with the Shepherd
of the sheep, as the sheep who hear his voice.[50]

This is nothing else but the miracle of the conjunction. This
conjunction can be affected by superficiality and by misappreciation of the Holy Spirit, if one wants to rest in the sign without
knowing and loving the God of the sign. Then the sacrament
becomes an empty and useless figure, because of the unbelief
which does not understand the meaning of the sacrament and
which disdains it. One thinks here of Israel when it interpreted
circumcision apart from faith and love, and when it took the
ark as a protecting power in the midst of Shiloh's dissoluteness.
In such circumstances the "powerlessness" of circumcision and of
the ark becomes revealed to the gentiles round about. And then
the people can be called an uncircumcised people, and Paul can
say: "For neither is circumcision anything, nor uncircumcision,
but a new creature" (Gal. 6:15).

If we try to draw logical inferences from this statement of
Paul, we miss the point of his admonition. But if we understand
the urgency of these words, we know that there is also a conjunction between sign and that which is signified which is no
usurpation. To this conjunction we are called in the struggle
of life. This is not a theoretical conclusion drawn by the reasoning mind, but the way of the Church in faith and love. In this
conjunction, the call of baptism to salvation is not seen as a
strange matter, as a mechanical addition to salvation, but as a
fulfilment of this richness in the midst of life. He who has not
seen and accepted the connection between baptism and obedience[51] has not understood the sacrament of baptism, nor the
meaning of Romans 6, where Paul lifts the connections between
"sacrament" and ethics above all relativizing.[52] For sacrament
and remission are undetachably linked with each other, and for
that reason also sacrament and confession of sins. That is why
the setting-apart of the believer through baptism as "the mark
of the covenant"[53] is not a false antithesis but a sign and seal of
the mercy of God, and baptism is an incorporation into the

50. Conf., Art. 33.
51. Cf. the form for baptism about the admonition and duty to a new
    obedience.
52. Cf. Hans von Soden, *Sacrament und Ethik bei Paulus* (Marburger
    Theol. Studien, 1931).
53. Conf., Art. 34.

Church of Christ. Here, the sealing by the Holy Spirit is seen in its most beautiful form when in the change and instability and the smallness of faith of Christian life the confession is spoken because of God's trustworthiness: "and that I am and ever shall remain a living member of the Church."[54]

54. H.C., Lord's Day 21.

CHAPTER EIGHT

INFANT BAPTISM

IT CANNOT be denied that the practice of infant baptism rests upon a definite confession, not mere ecclesiastical tradition. Though the New Testament did not give an explicit order to baptize children, it was nevertheless felt that the baptism of children was fully legitimate in the light of the confession of God's Covenant. That is why the opposition against infant baptism has incited heated controversy both in the past and recently. When the Anabaptists opposed infant baptism, the Reformers agreed that they failed to appreciate the significance of God's Covenant; and when Barth criticized infant baptism, the defense was often linked up with the basic tenets of his theology.

The controversy about infant baptism is not just a theologians' quarrel, but touches immediately upon the confession and the practice of the Church. For this practice was always claimed to be scriptural, and thus was attended with prayer and thanksgiving. Furthermore, the Church spoke of a special responsibility of baptized children before the God of the Covenant. All this explains why the controversy about whether infant baptism was or was not justifiable had its immediate effect in ecclesiastical life, for example, in the Netherlands, Switzerland, and France.[1] The lively discussion had bearing on the many connections in which infant baptism was seen, so that opposition against infant baptism implied opposition against those connections.

It has been generally agreed that this controversy, which flared up again with Karl Barth's criticism, could not be decided with an appeal to tradition as such. To be sure, there was a time-honored tradition, but the Reformed confession has never desired

---

1. Important in the case of France is *XLIVe Synode national* (Chambon-sur-Lignon, 1951), including an extensive report by Rev. P. Gagnier (pp. 62-81).

to establish its basis on that, especially when the criticism against infant baptism appealed to Scripture itself. When the Church is accused of misapprehending Scripture, one's duty is to reflect again on the validity of this complaint so that not traditionalism, but the gospel of God will dominate the practice of the Church. This is all the more necessary because the Church has admittedly sometimes practiced infant baptism merely because it was traditional, failing thereby to appreciate the richness and responsibility of baptism.

It is necessary to see clearly that the Church can continue with this practice of infant baptism only if it realizes fully that this is not a matter of an edifying institution and custom of the Church, but of a practice in which the children are responsibly involved. In this sacramental act there is mentioned not only an ecclesiastical act, but especially a divine act. That is why the controversy about infant baptism is so important: it involves that which God himself signifies and seals. Those who oppose infant baptism are therefore accusing the Church of exceeding its qualifications by speaking of what God does in the midst of the community.

That is why Calvin's remark is still of eminent importance when he spoke of infant baptism and said that the appeal to the authority of the Church should not be "a miserable place of refuge."[2] He did not mean thereby to neglect the authority and tradition of the Church, but to assert that this authority and tradition could never be the profoundest foundation for an act of the Church regarding children in which she confessed simultaneously an act of God with respect to the essence and the efficacy of baptism.[3] That is why we are called upon to reflect again on the justifiability of infant baptism in the light of Scripture.

Ever since Karl Barth began around 1940 to oppose the justifiability of infant baptism, the controversy has continued

---

2. Cf. *Inst.*, IV, VII.
3. It is clear that much depends on whether baptism is seen as an act of the Church or an act of God. In the latter case, the question about the justifiability of infant baptism is much more urgent. If infant baptism were a symbolic act on the part of the Church, as it is with many spiritualists, one could plead for infant baptism without arguing about the institution (by God) of infant baptism. But if it is seen as an act of God, the question is whether a basis for this act can be indicated in the institution of God.

unabated. Even though it cannot be said that Barth's criticism exerted great influence, his considerations nevertheless gave rise to new reflection and a tremendous number of publications. But one should not think that it was only Barth's criticism that evoked new reflection. In the Netherlands there is also a controversy about infant baptism in the Reformed churches — not, to be sure, about its justifiability, but about the background of infant baptism, involving such questions as the connection between baptism and regeneration, and the difference between infant baptism and adult baptism. When we see all these points, we understand that a very important question is involved, namely, whether the relation between baptism and faith still plays a role of significance in infant baptism. Almost all questions revolve about this problem of correlation, in the Anabaptist controversy of the sixteenth century as well as in the discussion of Barth's criticism.

This question of correlation is especially important because we have already seen that the relation between faith and sacrament plays such an important role in Reformed sacramental doctrine. Both Luther and Calvin emphasize repeatedly that the sacrament is nothing without faith and that we participate in the blessing of the sacrament only if we use it in faith (*usus sacramenti*). If something really essential is involved here, can we then still adhere to the justifiability of infant baptism? (For one cannot speak of a believing use of baptism on the part of children.) With adults there is a letting-oneself-be-baptized, but not with children. The infant does not let himself be baptized, but is baptized. Does it not follow then that infant baptism automatically becomes problematical? It seems to us that this question touches the core of the criticism against infant baptism and that the answer to this question is decisive for the correct practice of the Church in the administering of the sacrament to the children of believers.[4]

4. Literature on infant baptism: K. Barth, *Die kirchliche Lehre von der Taufe, TS*, XIV, 1943; Barth, *Die Christliche Lehre nach dem Heidelb. Katech.*, 1948, pp. 95ff.; O. Cullmann, *Die Tauflehre des N.T.*, 1948; F. J. Leenhardt, *Le baptême Chrétien, son origine, sa signification*, 1946; T. Preiss, "Die Kindertaufe und das N.T.," *TLZ*, LXXIII, 1948; H. Schlier, "Zur kirchlichen Lehre von der Taufe," *TLZ*, 1947; G. C. van Niftrik, "De Kinderdoop en Karl Barth," *NedTT*, II, 18ff.; Joh. Schneider, *Die Taufe im N.T.*, 1951. For further literature see my *Karl Barth en de kinderdoop*, 1947.

This question came sharply to the fore when Barth began to direct his criticism against infant baptism, for he posed the thesis that the correlation of baptism with faith made it impossible to baptize children. Baptism, as he put it, is a matter of a cognitive relation, not a causal working, and hence baptism without a confessing person to be baptized is like an execution without a convict. Elsewhere[5] I have argued that Barth's criticism is based fundamentally upon the correlation-motif, and I am still of the opinion that we are confronted here with a most important question involving the whole baptismal doctrine. It need not surprise us, therefore, that discussions about infant baptism are repeatedly concentrated upon the relation between faith and baptism, asking whether this relation is indeed so important that it can lead to a rejection of infant baptism.[6]

One could get the impression that the problem of faith and baptism is purely a dogmatic one, requiring mainly clear rational analysis. But this is not so. The only proper basis for infant baptism is the authority of Scripture, and as we look to Scripture we find ourselves involved in a set of complex relationships that require careful exegetical study. We must inquire, for example, about circumcision and baptism, Old and New Covenant, the Covenant and baptism. All these questions are profoundly related to infant baptism. We need to discover the total view of Scripture with respect to the children of believers and the covenant relation between God and these children, and the manner in which these children also share in the salvation of the Lord.

This is clearly revealed in the repeated appeal of the Church to baptism as taking the place of circumcision. This "replacement" has played a great and decisive role in the institution and defense of infant baptism, because one sees already in the Old Covenant a specific relation between believers and their children, which leads one to reflect on that relation in the New Covenant. Barth has directed his criticism against this very institution and foundation. To be sure, he accepts the idea that baptism has come in the place of this circumcision,[7] but he denies that therefore the sign of the Covenant may now be administered to the children of believers. This is because circumcision deals with the

5. Cf. my *Karl Barth en de kinderdoop,* 1947, ch. 7.
6. Cf., e.g., Cullmann's criticism of Barth, *op. cit.*
7. K. Barth, *Die kirchliche Lehre,* p. 31. See also K. Barth, *Die Christliche Lehre,* p. 96: "It is correct that baptism replaces circumcision."

natural, namely, the sacred lineage that was reaching its end with the coming of the Messiah.[8] Circumcision was pre-messianic, but for that reason a decisive turn came with the coming of Christ and the Kingdom of God, which requires faith in the Messiah rather than family lineage. Circumcision is the sign of the sacred lineage in Israel which ended with Christ; hence this sign has now lost its significance.

Barth's later considerations show how seriously he meant this. In his ethics he speaks of the redemptive-historical change which has come about in the relation between parents and children. In the Old Covenant, marriage and propagation were determined by their place in the history of redemption: before Christ came there was "a redemptive-historical necessity of propagation." But after Christ came this necessity ceased to exist because the sacred lineage had found its fulfilment and hence also its termination. "It could be continued, but it did not have to." Christ's coming also implied a re-evaluation of the relation between man and woman.[9]

Since the coming of the Messiah, salvation is no longer bound to the succession of generations. "It was now a matter of man being God's child in his spiritual communion with the one Son of God and Men. Of God's children it can henceforth be said with John 1:13 that they do not receive life by means of the will of man, but from God."[10] God's Kingdom has come, and for that reason regeneration is all that matters. To be sure, natural birth (and marriage) is still "a gift of God's goodness,"[11] but since Christ's birth the natural relation between parents and children no longer plays a constitutive role.[12] Now faith is the essential thing, and hence infant baptism is not legitimate within the Kingdom of God. In this practice the Church sets its clock back to the pre-messianic period, and thus travels a road that leads to theological Judaism, to a past which God himself has closed off because it has been fulfilled in the Kingdom of God. Our relation to God is now no longer determined by our belonging to a sacred line of descent, but by the grace of God.[13] And because this grace of God is at stake, only faith as an individual

---

8. *K.D.*, III, 4 (1951), 158.
9. *Ibid.*
10. *Ibid.*
11. *Ibid.*, p. 299.
12. *Ibid.*, p. 298.
13. Cf. also K. Barth, *Die Christliche Lehre*, pp. 96ff.

act can recognize and accept this grace of God. That is why in the New Testament Church only this order of events is mentioned: preaching of the Word, faith, and after that as the visible sign of this spiritual birth, baptism.[14] It is flagrantly contradictory to the Kingdom of God as it now exists to baptize someone who does not consciously desire this baptism.[15] One must come to baptism by an active deed, and without that deed baptism becomes an objective act of the Church in which the relation between faith and baptism is broken.

It turns out that the fundamental point of Barth's criticism against infant baptism lies in a contrast which he assumes between natural and spiritual birth. It need not surprise us that precisely at this point he has received serious criticism. For this contrast is completely unknown by Scripture. To contrast spiritual birth since the coming of the Messiah with natural birth in the lineage of Israel, is to misunderstand the spiritual significance of God's Covenant and of circumcision. One cannot say that under the Old Covenant natural birth was constitutive, while under the New Covenant spiritual birth is constitutive. It was never the case in the Old Testament that natural birth, apart from faith, placed a person automatically among the people of God. This was precisely the notion that the prophets criticized, as we also find in the New Testament when Christ turned against those who, without repentance or faith, appealed to their having Abraham as a father (John 8:33, 39). Christ did not deny natural descent (John 8:37, 56), but therein lies no guarantee or privilege of a good relation with God. In their unbelief they do what Abraham did not do; there is a contrast between Abraham and his children (John 8:40). That is why Christ speaks of a different father, namely, Satan, whose will they do. The line of the Covenant of God is understood in its richness and responsibility only in repentance and faith.

When Christ spoke with Nicodemus, he did not announce something so new that Nicodemus could have had no knowledge of it when He said: "Verily, verily, I say unto thee, except one be born of water and the Spirit, he cannot enter into the kingdom of God" (John 3:5). Christ speaks here of spiritual birth, and when Nicodemus then asks how these things can happen, Christ answers him: "Art thou a teacher in Israel, and under-

14. Barth, *Die kirchliche Lehre,* p. 8.
15. *Ibid.,* p. 30.

standest not these things?" (3:10). It is therefore incorrect to say that the Kingdom simply replaced natural birth with spiritual birth, for otherwise Nicodemus as a teacher in Israel could not have known of spiritual birth. And hence the foundation of Barth's criticism of infant baptism in the Kingdom of God is clearly refuted. As Paul says, "Know therefore that they that are of faith, the same are sons of Abraham" (Gal. 3:7). The blessing of Abraham has come upon the gentiles in Christ Jesus (Gal. 3:14).

The redemptive-historical fulfilment in the Messiah does not exclude faith from the Covenant with Abraham, and therefore no contrast can be made between natural and spiritual birth. Rather, we see a continuity which does not, to be sure, negate the decisive significance of the fulfilment, but which nevertheless points to the unity of God's work, in which believers from both Old and New Covenant are called to salvation in Christ.

All this corresponds fully with the Old Testament itself, in which prophetic criticism inveighs against unbelieving pretense on the basis of natural birth. It calls for circumcision of the heart. Natural birth is never detached from the calling, the admonition, and the comforting of God. Every appeal to this natural birth or to circumcision is nothing but a serious perversion of the Covenant of God, while the continuity becomes clearly visible in the connection between faith and the sign of the Covenant.

Cullmann is therefore correct when he writes: "According to Romans 4, continuity refers to faith."[16] For in Romans 4 we read that Abraham received the sign of circumcision as a seal of the righteousness of faith which he had possessed in his uncircumcised state (4:11). That is why he could be a father of believers, namely, of those who not only are of the circumcision, but those also who go in faith, the faith which our father Abraham possessed in his uncircumcised state (4:12). Without this faith, the meaning of circumcision is empty. It becomes a mere "natural" sign of the sacred line of descent, which in its "naturalness" no longer functions in the hands of the God who reveals himself. The mystery of circumcision lies precisely in the fact that the sign of the Covenant was not given objectivistically apart from faith and repentance. To be sure, the sacred lineage existed for the coming of the Messiah, but this purpose is not detached

---

16. Cullmann, *op. cit.*, p. 63. Cf. J. Koopmans, *De Ned. Geloofsbelijdenis*, p. 229.

from the Old Testament believers who are repeatedly called to seek and affirm this great mystery in the sacred lineage. The mystery of Abraham and the mystery of Israel do not lie in a natural preparation in the natural sphere for the coming Messiah, but it is the redemptive-historical prelude that cuts through the hearts and is involved with faith.

There is a divine perspective on the progress of the generations, which becomes clearly visible already in the Old Covenant. This progress was not just a matter of God going his way through the centuries and the generations, but of the acts of God in the midst of the changing generations, calling for belief in the coming of the Messiah. All of Israel's life was involved in that. Precisely this sign of the Covenant called for surrender of man's heart to this God of Israel. That is why it is understandable that we can read in the New Testament that Abraham had two sons and that thereby no distinction was made between natural and spiritual (Gal. 4:22-23), but rather the qualitatively different distinction between unbelief and faith in the promise of God. When Christ says: "Think not to say within yourselves, We have Abraham to our father: for I say unto you, that God is able of these stones to raise up children unto Abraham" (Matt. 3:9; Luke 3:8), he is not denying the sacred line or the natural descent from Abraham, but he is indicating that other contrast which, as God's judgment, cuts right through the natural line.

It is God's judgment that condemns the statistics of unbelief, and the failure to recognize the living God in his Covenant and the sign of the Covenant. This judgment is directed against abstracting a formula from the words of God: "You and your seed" (Gen. 17:7ff.; Acts 2:39; 7:6ff., etc.), and turning it into an arithmetic problem. These words were not given to be calculated with, but to be understood in faith.

It does not follow, then, that the relation between parents and children in the New Covenant no longer has significance because the Kingdom of God is at hand. Hence when the Reformed confessions declare that baptism has come in the place of circumcision, this must be seen not as a supplanting but as a fulfilling. Cullmann speaks correctly of the "redemptive-historical fulfilment of circumcision."[17] Paul's polemic against Judaism, which made the blood of circumcision still necessary, is based on this fact of fulfilment and on this "replacement" of circumcision by

17. Cullmann, *loc. cit.*

baptism. But that does not lead him to a contrast between the natural and the spiritual. To be sure, he can say with emphasis: "For he is not a Jew who is one outwardly; neither is that circumcision which is outward in the flesh: but he is a Jew who is one inwardly; and circumcision is that of the heart, in the spirit not in the letter" (Rom. 2:28f.). But this contrast between "in spirit" and "in the letter" indicates that he is not concerned with a contrast between natural and spiritual, but with understanding the divine sign of the Covenant. Besides, he speaks of a contrast that was already revealed in the Old Testament.

There is no devaluation here of circumcision. Paul allies himself with the criticism in the Old Testament against abstracting circumcision from its natural connections. In the Old Covenant, the call and the warning are spoken: "Circumcise therefore the foreskin of your heart, and be no more stiffnecked" (Deut. 10:16). This admonition goes to the "seed of the fathers" with whom the Lord had made a covenant (Deut. 10:15). So also we hear the word of promise about the sacred lineage: "Jehovah thy God will circumcise thy heart, and the heart of thy seed, to love Jehovah thy God with all thy heart, and with all thy soul, that thou mayest live" (Deut. 30:6).

We see here clearly the fact of natural circumcision, and along with it the critical function of this sign of the Covenant. Circumcision is not a self-evident and automatic guarantee of God's favor and grace. Rather, it is a sign that points to the salvation of the Messiah, which can be understood only in the circumcision of the heart.[18]

In opposition to the isolating of the natural sign in the flesh, Paul can write that the gentiles who do not know the law of Moses and who nevertheless do the things that are in the law, will judge the circumcised Jew who, with his ancestry in Abraham and with the law of Moses, does not know the circumcision of the heart (Rom. 2:24-29). His critical remarks have nothing to do with what later will be called spiritualism because he does not devaluate the outward sign but protests against making it an automatic guarantee of the inward sign. Dodd is correct when he calls Paul's words in Romans 2 "an echo of prophetic teaching."[19]

---

18. It seems merely speculative to find a symbol of circumcision in such words as Jeremiah 4:4 (L. Koehler, *Der hebräische Mensch*, 1953, p. 2).
19. C. H. Dodd, *The Epistle of Paul to the Romans*, 1949, p. 42.

This echo does not set forth a contrast between natural and spiritual, but presents an outlook on the fulfilment of circumcision in which the old is truly fulfilled in the new. When the question arises what the advantage is of the Jew, and what is the profit of circumcision, Paul's answer is: "Much every way... they were intrusted with the oracles of God" (Rom. 3:2), and — as he writes later — "[theirs] is the adoption, and the glory, and the covenants, and the giving of the law, and the service of God, and the promises" (Rom. 9:4). There is a sacred, purposeful continuation of the generations, but there is no such contrast with the New Testament situation as would supposedly find its core in the contrast between natural and spiritual birth.

In the light of what has been said above, it is understandable that the Reformation should state emphatically that baptism had come in the place of circumcision, not in a sense that makes infant baptism unlawful, but as one of the strongest arguments for the lawfulness of infant baptism.[20] This is because the contrast between the natural and the spiritual had no place in the Reformed redemptive-historical concept of "replacement." It was emphasized, rather, that Christ was the end of the law, that he had done away with circumcision, and that he had given in its place the sacrament of baptism.[21] Precisely for that reason baptism could also be given to children "who we believe ought to be baptized and sealed with the sign of the covenant, as the children in Israel formerly were circumcised upon the same promises which are made unto our children."[22]

This sameness of promise is something different from identity, for identity neglects the differences; what is referred to here is the promise of God of which the confession says, "what circumcision was to the Jews, baptism is to our children."[23]

Instead of introducing the contrast between natural and spiritual, one must think of the power of the divine promise. That explains why the Reformation saw the way opened to a full appreciation of the promise of the Covenant "for thee and thy seed." It was confessed that this connection should also have a full place in the New Testament fulfilment, no less richly than under the Old Covenant. This becomes clear in the words

20. On Col. 2, see my *K. Barth en de kinderdoop,* pp. 91ff.
21. Conf., Art. 34.
22. *Ibid.*
23. For the variations in the concept of "national Church" see my *Gevaren en perspectieven in ons kerkelijk leven,* 1946.

of Calvin, that Christ had the children come to him and that he rebuked the disciples because he wanted to give a proof "by which the world would understand that he came to enlarge rather than to limit the Father's mercy" (*Inst.*, IV, XVI, 7).

The word "enlarge" is striking here, especially when we remember that the enlargement of salvation has repeatedly been mentioned in connection with children and infant baptism. Much depends on how this enlargement is understood. Some have inferred that it implies some sort of "national Church," against which, for instance, Karl Barth has protested, saying that those who favored infant baptism wanted to "Christianize the nations" by the enlargement of baptism. It cannot be denied that some have left themselves open to such criticism, but it is also clear that the Reformation was not concerned with the construction of a *corpus Christianum* in this broad sense, neglecting the spiritual background, but only with that enlargement which is implied in the words "thee and thy seed." This does not automatically extend the Covenant over "the nations" or anticipate their Christianizing by universal baptism, but it is a respecting of the relation that was already incorporated into the Old Covenant by the acts of God.

Some have used the expression "physical categories" when this relation of parents to children was applied to the New Testament Church. But we must remember that the Church spoke so emphatically of this Covenant relation on the basis of the New Testament itself. For the New Testament shows us repeatedly that the relation between God and his people is not individualistic; already in Acts, the coming of the Spirit is accompanied by the promise: "for to you is the promise, and to your children" (2:39). As in the Old Covenant a certain enlargement became clearly visible, so also when the fulfilment came in the outpouring of the Holy Spirit.

This enlargement of salvation does not threaten the responsibility that always accompanies salvation. It is undoubtedly an anxiety for the arbitrary enlargement of salvation over a whole nation that often led to criticism of infant baptism. Remembering the evils that attended the family-line enlargement in the Old Covenant, they feared that a similar expansion in the New Covenant would secularize the Church, making it a national Church where belief in the remission of sins is unnecessary. But we do not encounter this problem in the Reformation, because it saw infant baptism in direct relation to the promise in Jesus Christ, and from that it concluded correctly that in the New Covenant the expansion of salvation was also maintained in the generations. The Reformers saw, in the Old as well as in the New Covenant, that God did not isolate man from the contexts of his earthly life, but went out toward him in the line of families. Therein was realized the mystery of the salvation of the Lord from generation to generation.

The words "thee and thy seed" are important in the discussion of infant baptism because herein the nature and structure of the work of God in this world are at stake. Already at the time of the Reformation, the Reformers appealed to these words of Peter against the Anabaptists. They found in them a principle of continuity with the Old Covenant, and inferred by the analogy of Scripture the justifiability of infant baptism on the basis of the divine promise. They were aware that the sign could be detached from the promise of God and looked upon as an automatic guarantee of God's blessing, bound to the natural bonds of flesh and blood, as had happened in Israel. But it is not permissible to deny the validity of infant baptism just because it can be misinterpreted. Baptism did not replace circumcision because circumcision could be corrupted into an unspiritual guarantee having nothing to do with the heart, but because the offering was fulfilled in Christ.

The work of God in the New Covenant is not antithetical to his work in the Old Covenant, and that is why the Church of Christ in the sacrament of incorporation into the Church also deals with its children. They do not stand apart from the grace of the Covenant. Not one a priori counterargument, based on the correlation between faith and baptism, can be brought against this revelation.

The words "thee and thy seed" play a much more important role in Reformed polemics than the appeal to ancient practices of the Church. The Reformers stressed the continuity of scriptural teaching about the relation of God with believers, who were not detached as abstract individuals from the connections in which God had placed them, but who were seen in the line of the generations. Not only Acts 2:39 was quoted, but also I Corinthians 7:14, which speaks of the purity of children because one partner in the marriage is a believer. Barth has occupied himself with this text, but it has not led him to a correction of his statements.

Barth sees in this and in other passages of the New Testament

an indication of the universality of the Kingdom of Christ, but he
does not see it as a basis for the argument that herein the promises of the Old Covenant are fulfilled. He can see "the seed"
as a spiritual category only, in contrast with the natural seed,
and therefore he can approach the relation between baptism
and faith only by way of this contrast. Belief then becomes the
spiritual, which stands over against the natural relation between
parents and children. This natural element cannot be taken up
into the grace of the Covenant. To be sure, the line of the succession of generations is continued, and marriage is seen as a
gift from God, but this structure belongs nonetheless to the
nature of the era that lies in the past, so that it cannot have a
constitutive significance for the Kingdom of God. It is really so
that the coming of the Kingdom of God abruptly ends the old
history. Grace comes to stand over against the structures of the
bygone age. Barth's argument against infant baptism, then, turns
out to be fundamentally eschatological.

But eschatology cannot furnish an argument against infant
baptism, for life is not threatened in the salvation of God in
Jesus Christ, but reconciled and blessed. The grace of Christ in
the Covenant of God does not destroy life, but resurrects it, as the
circumcision of the Old Covenant touched common life with
the seal of purification. When this Covenant is fulfilled, that
common life is also saved. Eschatology does not contrast with that
life but fills it with God's salvation. That is why God's speaking
in the New Covenant is not a speaking in individualistic style,
as if men were detached from the obligations of the "old" world,
but the Word of God comes to man in the full reality of his life,
as it did under the Old Covenant.

That is why we receive such a strong impression of continuity
between the Old and New Covenant concerning the place of
children in the Covenant of God. This place has nothing to do
with an automatic guarantee, any more than the Covenant gives
a guarantee to adults. But they do receive a place in the reality
of the acts of God. The "thee and thy seed" functions also in the
New Covenant, and places there in full light the richness and
the responsibility of children. It is not enough merely to speak,
as does Barth, of the universality of the Kingdom of Christ, for
then one cannot avoid the danger of contrasting this universality
with the fulness of the Covenant of God, and separating this
universality from the Church of Christ. Nowhere in the New
Testament can we find a trace of the idea that children have a

separate status outside the Covenant of God and therefore also beyond the grace of the Covenant. Those who start with the idea that children are a *tertium genus* along with believers and unbelievers cannot possibly explain how the New Testament starts from the light that falls over parents and children, and calls children to obey that command which is given in the Old Covenant as the command with a promise, the promise of the salvation of God in the midst of life (Eph. 6:1-3).

When therefore the Reformers maintained emphatically that the grace of the New Covenant was no less than that of the Old Covenant, and that therefore the "thee and thy seed" belonged essentially to the structure of the New Covenant, that did not imply an expansion of salvation to include "nature," as if something unspiritual had been incorporated into God's Covenant. Rather, it was their conviction that grace does not disrupt that natural life which is received from God's hand. As Bavinck says, Christian faith does not disrupt the natural order, but confirms and sanctifies it.[24] Of course it is possible to empty and devaluate baptism to a symbol without significance for the Kingdom of God, but this misuse of the relation between parents and children does not give one the right to assume that spiritual birth stands opposed to natural birth. That would be correct only if natural birth were surrounded by a self-evident grace, apart from faith, a grace which is bound to blood descent. But this is subject to the same prophetic criticism that was raised in the Old Covenant against boasting of one's circumcision. Such a view has nothing to do with the covenant for children; nor is it relevant to the sign of the Covenant in infant baptism.

Van Ruler is therefore correct when he writes that the Covenant of Grace does not mean that we as individuals are placed in the salvation of God, but that we *together* receive it. "Not man for man, each one by himself, and detached from one another; but us together. So much together that this communal aspect of grace is preferably expressed in the communion of nature: us and our seed."[25] He is not preaching "blood and soil" here, but only pointing out that grace does not pass beyond normal life but blesses it. Eschatology cannot separate us from our children, because eschatology is not "strange" in the sense that it destroys the work of God; on the contrary, it acknowledges that work of

24. H. Bavinck, *Geref. Dog.,* IV, 507.
25. A. A. van Ruler, *Religie en Politiek,* 1945, p. 83.

God and leads to full richness. Eschatology and reconciliation are intimately linked, and that is why a contrast between the old era and the new era can never support a critique of infant baptism as sign of the Covenant of God.

One can say, therefore, that every criticism of infant baptism runs the danger of falling back on the position of the Anabaptists, who always started from the contrast between nature and grace. They could not believe that "the natural" could have a place in the Covenant, because they thought that this threatened "the spiritual" of the Covenant. The Reformers, however, always maintained that the contrast was not between nature and grace, but between flesh and spirit, sin and grace, and that for that reason the richness of baptism could not be threatened by normal life, unless it be through superficiality. The position of the Reformers is inviolable here. It rests immediately upon Scripture. Against those who asked for a direct scriptural proof in which infant baptism was divinely commanded, the Reformers courageously pointed at the injustice of this question. In response, they asked their critics precisely where the Bible says that this fundamental Covenant relation is broken in the New Covenant.[26]

One can say without exaggeration that this view of the unity of the Old and New Covenants formed the essential and profoundest basis for the defense of infant baptism. There was no a priori dogmatic reason for the decision, and neither was there an explicit scriptural command. The intention, nevertheless, was to think and conclude on the basis of Scripture as a whole. Such an appeal to the totality of Scripture is not without danger. This totality can be constructed by the insertion of individual, "home-made" notions, and thus one can make errors; but the Reformers realized that when they pointed to the line of the Covenant in the Old and New Testaments they were not making up an insertion.

26. Cf. the question of Murray: "Has it been discontinued? Our answer to these questions must be, that we find no evidence of revocation. In view of the fact that the new covenant is based upon and is the unfolding of the Abrahamic covenant, in view of the basic identity of meaning attaching to circumcision and baptism, in view of the unity and continuity of the covenant grace administered in both dispensations, we can affirm with confidence, that evidence of revocation or repeal is mandatory if the practice or principle has been discontinued under the New Testament." John Murray, *Christian Baptism* (Philadelphia: 1952), pp. 52f.

That is why this Covenant was indicated as the basis for infant baptism, and why little was said about the idea that infant baptism presupposes a divine grace which has already been given to the children in the sign of the Covenant before they become aware of it. To be sure, this thought has been broached more than once since then, with special attention being drawn to the fact that divine grace precedes any human activity and hence also precedes the act of infant baptism. But this was not seen as the principal foundation for infant baptism. Indeed, if it were, less value would have to be attached to the baptism of adults, with whom baptism follows upon faith. Preiss says correctly that "with respect to baptism, the New Testament hardly ever speaks emphatically of prevenient grace."[27] To be sure, the New Testament speaks of baptism in connection with what has happened formerly, for example, in Romans 6, but there is no special connection with the baptism of children. Hence it is not permissible to base infant baptism on prevenient grace, but only on the scriptural preaching of the Covenant of God.[28] The prevenient aspect of the grace of God lies not in the temporal priority of the acts of God in baptism in comparison with the conscious acceptance of the divine promise, but in the temporal priority of the cross of Christ with respect to the baptized person, whether child or adult. Therein — and certainly not in infant baptism only — we see the predestinational motif which undoubtedly is of great significance in baptism. Infant baptism does not find its basis in the clarity of prevenient grace; it rests on the light of Scripture, which shows us clearly that God's Covenant does not touch man in abstraction from the fulness of his life relations, but in the totality of his existence and in the involvement of his seed in the calling, the blessing, and the comforting of the Covenant of God.

We have explained why the Reformers did not reject infant baptism even though they believed strongly that faith is essential to the sacraments. It is conceivable that they might have concluded, as did Barth, that there can be no infant baptism because the one pole of the correlation (i.e. faith) was not present here. The fact that they did not draw this "logical" conclusion shows that they were more interested in being guided by the Word of God than in being logically rigorous.

27. T. Preiss, *op. cit.*
28. Cf. *XLIVe Synode National* (Chambon-sur-Lignon, 1951), p. 79.

That does not mean, however, that we may now avoid the question of faith and sacrament in the doctrine of infant baptism. This question has, indeed, dominated almost all the discussion of baptismal doctrine. Does the correlation between faith and baptism have consequences for infant baptism? Is it not necessary — in order to keep baptismal doctrine pure — to assume somehow some form of "belief" in the child, so that the essential correlation remains intact? Various answers have been proposed. Some have assumed, for example, that the faith attached to infant baptism lay in the belief of the parents, that is to say, in a so-called *fides aliena*.[29] More often, however, reference is made to the child's belief, or perhaps to the capacity to believe, or to regeneration, from which, later on, faith would come in the active sense. This regeneration then became the necessary presupposition of baptism, since without it there can be no faith of any sort and infant baptism becomes "false baptism."

In this last interpretation especially, the problem of the nature of the correlation comes to the foreground sharply. It is in fact clear that a mutation has occurred here; the historic Reformation concept of the correlation between faith and baptism has gradually faded away. In its place came the notion that for a correct administration of baptism, inward grace had to be present in the heart beforehand. The Reformation had understood faith in the context of *usus sacramenti*, viewing it as an active faith directed toward the divine promise; this faith was in no sense a human "component" in the whole picture of baptism, a necessary subjective element. But this more recent view holds that belief, or whatever came in its place, is some sort of prerequisite of grace and baptism, a *habitus* which must be assumed so that baptism may be real baptism. Thus, too, one can still say that the sacraments were truly instituted only for believers.

This view distorts the true function of faith in the sacrament. The problem is not simply that faith was often indicated as a *habitus*, which could mean that faith is an act of man in his concrete human life. But it is substantially wrong to make regeneration as a human quality the necessary precondition of baptism even though this be a quality worked by the Holy Spirit.[30]

---

29. For the *fides aliena*, see *Geref. Dog.*, IV, 499, and my *Karl Barth en de kinderdoop*, 1947, p. 53.
30. Cf. Polman, *Onze Ned. Geloofsbelijdenis*, IV, p. 208.

It is good, therefore, to learn that Calvin did not hold that such a *habitus* must be present before baptism can be meaningfully administered. He did not infer from the correlation between faith and baptism that regeneration must precede baptism in order to make baptism a real baptism, even though he did not for a moment deny the relation his concept of faith, which does not contribute a human share to the works of God or to the promise, but acknowledges the mere grace of God. That is why the problem of the temporal priority of faith is never decisive with Calvin. This does not mean that Calvin constructed a *tertium genus* for children, or believed that the working of the Spirit in man's heart can begin only with the development of the intellectual functions and with the years of discretion. Calvin objected against setting limits beyond which the Spirit cannot be effective, but refused to make the validity of baptism dependent upon antecedent belief (or whatever takes its place). He who walks this way cannot turn back. He must walk it till the end and conclude that baptism can be "real" only if some form of faith precedes it.

Kramer's criticism, to the effect that if Calvin had not gone beyond the Consensus Tigurinus his baptismal doctrine would have to be regarded as a failure, is incorrect even though understandable.[31] Kramer starts from the biblical relation between baptism and regeneration, but he draws a wrong conclusion when he says that baptism is actually meaningful only if grace is present as "realized grace" in the heart of the person to be baptized. The real problem in this theory lies in the concept of "realized grace."[32] One can ask whether this concept does not do injustice to the full value of the biblical concept of "grace" as grace of God, and whether one can really speak of the justification of sinners as nonrealized grace. To be sure, one can speak without misunderstanding of *gratia interna,* but not of realized grace (when referring to this working of the Holy Spirit), because there never can be such a thing as nonrealized grace in contrast with it. The subjective pole is here detached from the Reformed context, and "realized grace" begins to function as the temporally prior reality in man's heart, the reality without which baptism loses its meaning.

It is clear that Calvin has also spoken emphatically of the

31.   G. Kramer, *Het verband van de doop en de wedergeboorte,* 1897, p. 133.
32.   *Ibid.*

working of the Spirit in men's hearts and of his dwelling in the Church, but this is a *directed* dwelling and working. The Spirit causes believers to rest in the faithfulness and the grace of God — not a "realized grace," but the reality of grace, the reality of the forgiveness of sins and the washing in the blood of Jesus Christ, which cleanses from all sin. That is why the working of the Spirit cannot for a moment be separated from the grace of forgiveness and justification by means of the concept of "realization." Forgiveness is not something that can or must be realized. It is too rich and too real for that, and it is therefore impossible to indicate the subjective pole of the correlation by referring to "realized grace" which must be present in man's heart. That is why Calvin's point of view (in which he does not want to fix the temporal moment) falls beyond the criticism based on the concept of "realized grace."[33]

Calvin did not start from a dogmatic construction but from the Covenant of God, in which he saw the basis for the Church's calling to infant baptism. Hence he did not worry about the temporal relation between the Holy Spirit's indwelling and the time at which the sacraments are received.[34] He acknowledges the free sovereignty of the Spirit and does not see faith as a *conditio sine qua non* in the sense that children require it before baptism. Calvin's correlation between baptism and faith does not require the joining of objective and subjective moments, but rather points to the faith which God commands in baptism and which is fulfilled throughout life.

Neither is Calvin guilty of Barth's reproach, according to which he cuts baptism in half, leaving the rest to be completed in a later confession of faith. Calvin sees confession, the acceptance of baptism, not as a complement of something incomplete, but as the answer of faith which, because of its nature, can never function as a complement of anything. For faith is precisely this complete acceptance of the baptismal promise, which is recognized in its full, gracious priority, and as the promise which is valid for all of man's life.

The question of correlation will always pose this dilemma: either one says that valid baptism must always be preceded by faith, capacity of faith, or regeneration, or one acknowledges

---

33. For Polman's interpretation of Calvin's view of infant baptism, see *op. cit.*, IV, 213.
34. Cf. The Genevan Catechism in Müller, *Bekenntnisschriften*, 1903, p. 149.

the sovereignty of the Spirit to establish the connection between sign and that which is signified in the fulness of life as a whole, but not necessarily at the very beginning of life. Those who think that God's revelation does not permit this latter view must adopt some theory of presumptive regeneration — a theory that seems to be logical because it shows the conjunction of sign and that which is signified at a definite point in time. But it does not acknowledge sufficiently that this conjunction is in the hands of God, and that we do not need this kind of definite conjunction in order to provide a basis for infant baptism.

The error of this view is not that it overemphasizes the connection between baptism and regeneration. Who would dare to speak of overemphasis in the light of the New Testament? But the doctrine of baptism on the basis of presumed regeneration goes beyond the limits of revelation here insofar as it implies a certain view of the foundation of baptism. While it opposes correctly all superficial theories that regard baptism as some kind of magic sign and seal that work from the outside only,[35] it can provide no defense against the subjectivism of the Anabaptists, who "honor" baptism fully on the condition that a person presently possesses certain qualities.

It is clear that the controversy about the declaration of Utrecht in 1905 involves the questions discussed here, especially because, then and later, the question was raised whether presumptive regeneration is a basis for infant baptism. The critics of this declaration realized, to be sure, that the doctrine of presumptive regeneration was not directly stated; but they believed that the declaration implied it, especially in view of its later interpretations. Though we cannot discuss the whole issue here, a number of points relevant to our argument should be brought out.

Even though the declaration of Utrecht 1905 no longer has validity in the Reformed churches (it has been replaced by the statement of 1946), the problem remains because some critics see the same fault in the substitute definition of 1946. The latter is not just an unimportant, historical interpretation of the statement of 1905; behind and in that interpretation lies a dogmatic problem that touches immediately upon the relation between baptism and regeneration. Unfortunately, an

35. See Kuyper's preface to Kramer's dissertation, which clearly shows Kuyper's own views.

incorrect interpretation of baptism has stood in the background
of all the discussions, an interpretation which holds that baptism can be meaningful (according to the judgment of the
disputed synod) only if it could be assumed that this baptism is
a sign and seal of what Kramer called "realized grace," *in concreto,* of regeneration. As we saw already, the synod's emphatic
statement against false baptism could not persuade the critics
that this view of the deepest backgrounds of the baptismal doctrine was not present in the Reformed churches. We do not
hesitate to declare that, if this representation of the Reformed
baptismal doctrine is correct, it is fundamentally nothing but
the old baptismal doctrine of the Anabaptists, which makes the
integrity of baptism dependent ultimately on subjectivity. But
in the light of history this interpretation simply cannot be
maintained.

It is therefore of great importance that the statement of 1905
explicitly discusses the matter of the temporal moment when
it mentions the sovereignty of the Spirit in his regenerating
work in the heart. The very accentuation of the sovereignty of
the Spirit in this connection indicates that the matter is more
complicated than a simple reference to presumed regeneration
can explain. On the basis of the facts, one can say with a good
deal of certainty that the statement of 1905 could be accepted
by many for a long time just because they did *not* find the doctrine of presumptive regeneration in it. It cannot be denied
that the peace of 1905 was based on these facts; later, however,
various factors began to operate which caused this impression
of 1905 to fade and which gave rise to the suspicion that actually
the statement of 1905 *favored* the doctrine of presumptive regeneration.

Nevertheless, it is precisely the thesis regarding the moment
of the regenerating work of the Spirit that excludes the doctrine
that regeneration must absolutely precede baptism.[36] To be sure,
1905 maintains the relation between baptism and regeneration,
but no one can maintain that its statement about the temporal
moment admits the view — even indirectly — that baptism depends for its validity on whether grace has been, or has not
been, "realized." The doctrine of presumptive regeneration is
designed to combat the phantom of false baptism; and precisely
in view of that phantom, emphatic reference was made by the

36. Cf. J. Ridderbos, "Begin en slot van 1905," *Geref. Weekblad,* I, No. 15.

synod to the responsibility of all baptized persons. But when the Synod of 1943 spoke of the connection between baptism and the Covenant of God, it did not thereby try to offer a rationally transparent solution. Rather, it sought to preserve the mystery of the Covenant and baptism when it fully acknowledged "that in the doctrine of the Covenant two things must receive due justice: on the one hand, God's sovereign election, the efficacious working of his grace and the unshakable stability of the Covenant of grace and reconciliation; on the other hand, the call to belief and repentance which in the Covenant is heard with emphatic urgency and which presents to all (!) the children of believers the richness of the privilege granted to them and also the greatness of their responsibility if they do not heed such great salvation."[37]

It is not difficult to recognize that this is not an attempt to interpret the Covenant and baptism subjectivistically, but rather to respect the connections between promise and demand and the connections between richness and responsibility against the background of the sovereignty of grace. In these and similar statements, it is therefore not the case that the election of God threatens the stability and trustworthiness of the Covenant and of the promise of baptism. It is of course possible to speak of election in such a manner that the promise of God does indeed lose its power and trustworthiness. But then one has not spoken of election in accordance with Scripture, but has substituted a deterministic interpretation of election which Calvin certainly would have rejected most emphatically. The remembrance of the sovereign election and the efficacious power of God's grace is certainly not such a deterministic threat, but is essential, not only for theological explanation, but also for pastoral practice, in which election is not opposed to the Covenant. The sovereign grace of God in the way of the Covenant is not at all just a "truth" to be committed to memory. Those who separate this message of the sovereignty of election and of the grace of God from the kerygma and the pastorate must then suppose that faith itself has some efficacy, which is completely contradictory to the essence of Christian faith.

This is why many have observed that the various Reformed statements about baptism and the Covenant are not disguised

---

37. This statement of November 23, 1943, was emphasized and maintained by the synod in a statement of December 16, 1943.

presentations of the doctrine of presumptive regeneration as a basis for baptism, but are contemplations of the Church with respect to the promise of the Covenant.[38] It is precisely in this connection that it is said that the moment of regeneration is completely left up to God, while at the same time it is acknowledged that the notion of the community does not imply an automatic guarantee of regeneration, for the promise of God is a promise that cannot be identified with such a guarantee.[39]

The connection between baptism and regeneration does not go beyond the *usus sacramenti,* and cannot be indicated as a transparent relation apart from faith. When viewed in the light of the Christian community, baptism cannot be seen as a legal relation possessing independent value in itself, as a sign apart from the reality and the offer of God in the sign. Such a violation of the mystery of conjunction has more than once threatened the Church and made baptismal practice an empty rite that no longer had an echo in faith. Baptism was then seen as a soothing guarantee no longer having anything to do with the sacred assurance of God's promise, accepted in faith.

This externalization of baptism, which is easier for infant baptism than for adult baptism, is no less fatal in the light of the New Testament and of Church history than the spiritualistic superficialization of the sacrament in which God's sign is devaluated. But even in the face of this latter danger, the conjunction of sign with the reality signified may not be used for a purpose other than that for which it is presented to us in calling, admonition, and comforting. And neither may it be used to set limits upon the time when the Spirit does his regenerating work, as though the integrity of the sacrament lies, after all, in subjectivity.

For that reason, our objection to such solutions as the *fides aliena,* or child-belief, or the doctrine of presumptive regeneration as a basis for infant baptism, is not that each insists on the connection between faith and baptism. That motive, in the light of the New Testament, is legitimate for baptismal doctrine. We object solely to the implications of these theories for the administration of baptism, because they do not

---

38. Cf. G. Bouwmeester, "Krachtens de belofte Gods," *Geref. Weekblad,* I, Nos. 9, 10.
39. Cf. K. Dijk's report on "te enge binding" in the Acts of the Synod of 1949 and 1950; p. 480.

give full weight to the institution of baptism by God. The way to false baptism is not consciously taken by them, but nevertheless it becomes inevitable.

Though men may continue to disagree regarding the interpretation of a historical, human text, the controversies will not be without hope as long as everyone takes seriously the statements about the richness and responsibility of the Covenant and its sign. God's promise is truly given — that is the meaning of the administration of baptism and of the words that are therewith spoken — in promise and calling, in consolation and admonition in unbreakable connection. Thus one is able to honor God's prior grace without making that thought the dogmatic foundation for infant baptism. This grace precedes all human activity, and one can certainly see in infant baptism that the Covenant is not a matter of God and man facing each other as equal parties. The efficacy and the certainty of the promise certainly do not issue from human activity. How then could this baptism and its content ever rest on human decision, or be an "outward" relation which is then later realized by ourselves? Can the human answer derive its richness from anything other than the acknowledgment that that richness cannot be found elsewhere, and are we not baptized into the death of Christ?

It is this sign which according to our confession is not only beneficial as long as the water is upon us, but for all of our lives.[40] This benefit can never be described in a theoretical solution, but can only be understood in that *usus sacramenti* toward which, according to God's ordinance, infant baptism is also directed. This is possibly only if we understand that we are dealing here with God's sign, whose significance transcends all human signs, and which God uses majestically and mercifully for promise and comfort, for admonition and calling.

On that basis one can confess that there is no fundamental difference between infant baptism and the baptism of adults. The remark has been made more than once that only the doctrine of presumptive regeneration makes this identity possible, since in both cases regeneration (or belief) necessarily precedes baptism. But neither in Calvin nor in Reformed theology do we notice any cardinal difference between the two. Both stand unshakable against the Anabaptist doctrine of correlation (the

40. Conf., Art. 34.

Anabaptists also had their correlation; it was essentially a subjectivistic one), and maintain nevertheless the involvement of infant baptism with faith. The identity between infant and adult baptism does not, however, presuppose that in both baptisms faith and regeneration necessarily precede baptism, but that there is one promise of God toward which faith must be directed.

To reflect on baptism administered to adults or infants always makes one aware of God's inscrutable acts. It is possible, of course, to rationalize the mystery of God's promises which are signified and sealed in the sacraments, by giving a solution in which those promises are either objectivized or subjectivized. But the mystery of the promise of God lies precisely in the fact that it is directed toward faith and can never be understood apart from faith. One understands the veracity of the promise only in this faith, and only in this faith can one know that faith does not form the basis for this veracity. It is therefore impossible to apply judicial categories to God's promise in infant baptism making it "objective" in the sense that it can be detached from that personal involvement of faith toward which it is oriented. For then one cannot avoid the real danger that faith acquires the function of making the general promise into a promise "for us." This theory of a "legal" relation affects the very essence of the promise, which then becomes abstract and loses its personal character. It becomes the gate through which one can enter, but this entering then automatically acquires a peculiar feature because faith adds something to the promise, namely, its realization. This theory threatens the assurance of salvation and the sealing by the Holy Spirit. Between this "general" promise and this subjective sealing there will always be required an additional something to support the assurance of salvation. Neither man's mind, nor faith as a human act, is capable of that. Faith can rest in the promise of God only if it acknowledges and rests in this promise as a veracious and personally oriented promise.

This is undoubtedly the point to which the statement of the Synod of 1946 was referring when it added to the new formulation that it rejected every interpretation which "lets the Covenant promise disappear in a conditional promise."[41]

It has been argued more than once concerning this and

41. Acts of Synod 1946, Art. 50.

similar statements that a straw man is being attacked, but in this statement the crux of the matter is something of great importance for the whole Covenant doctrine. For here, the full outlook on the correlation between Covenant and faith becomes visible. This statement does not at all mean to deny that one can speak of conditions with respect to the act and words of God, as was always done in Reformed theology. But it does deny that the nature of the promise of the Covenant — sealed and signified in baptism — could simplistically be made transparent by means of the concept of conditionality.[42]

The mystery of the Covenant cannot be described by saying that faith accepts this conditional promise and that it can do so through the working of the Holy Spirit. For then it must be asked *which* promise is accepted by this faith, and whether this faith does not — through the acceptance — realize a general promise instead of God's specific promise in all its comfort. That is why the Covenant problem cannot be solved by speaking here of a legal relation, as if that would shed some light upon that question which decides everything, namely, that promise of God to us. This question remains unsolved in the solution of the "conditional" promise, and that question cannot be solved afterward by appealing to the Holy Spirit.[43]

---

42. Cf. *TWNT*, II, 576ff.; E. D. Kraan, "Wat bedoelt het N.T. met het woord belofte?" *Geref. Weekblad*, I, 18ff. Cf. the Canons of Dordt, II, 5 and III-IV, 8.

43. We touch here upon Prof. Dr. K. Schilder's remarks in "Looze kalk," 1946, when he speaks of the reproach of remonstrantism, the way Greijdanus has often tried to waylay this objection by pointing out that the faith that accepts the conditional promise does not issue from flesh and blood, but from the power of the Holy Spirit. But it is clear, especially in the defense against the reproach of remonstrantism (Schilder's pamphlet), that he did not see sharply enough that the actual problem of remonstrantism did not lie in the question about the origin of faith, but in the one about the function of faith in connection with conditionality. It is clear that Schilder rejects the "condition" in the remonstrant sense (p. 57), but when he describes this condition as a theory which gives the honor to man, rather than to God, we think that the problem of the remonstrants is much more complicated because it is primarily based, not on a doctrine of man's merit, but in the misappreciation of the function of faith, which is also found in the remonstrant doctrine of election (election on the basis of *praevisa fides*). Schilder comes much closer to the remonstrant problem when he speaks of the remonstrant view, not on the reality, but on the "possibility" of the New Covenant. Remonstrantism touches here upon the discussion of the conditional promise. When Schilder emphatically rejects this "doctrine of possibility"

This way is dangerous because one gives the impression unjustifiably that justice is thus done to the calling and the demand of the Covenant of God. But the danger must be recognized for what it is, and one can do that by never making the demand of the Covenant independent of the promise of the Covenant, and by understanding that faith, which understands and acknowledges the sign of God, never places promise and demand alongside of each other in simple dualism. The great Giver of salvation calls us in the way of his promise to the fulfilment of his demand. From that, it can be understood that the real mystery of the Covenant and of baptism does not lie in the fact that faith is conscious that it answers to the Covenant and its treasures by fulfilling the demand, but that in the fulfilling of this demand of the Covenant the confession is heard that God's promise is unconditional and that one can rest in it for time and eternity. He who sees this as a misappreciation of the calling of the Covenant misjudges the profoundness of the divine promise, which comes toward us in the way of the calling of God, but which realizes itself precisely in that way, and which is experienced in faith as his trustworthy Word and as the Word of his Covenant which is unshakable.

---

he should — consequently — have had to come to a review of his interpretation of the nature of the conditionality of the promise of God. In that light, a renewed reflection on the promise of the Covenant in baptism would have been possible and would have, perhaps, cleared up some misunderstandings. See also the valuable criticism of L. van der Zanden, *De kinderdoop. Sacrament der gelovigen,* 1947, pp. 46ff.

CHAPTER NINE

THE INSTITUTION OF THE LORD'S SUPPER

FOR THE SACRAMENTS in general as well as for baptism in particular, we were confronted with the importance of the institution of the sacraments. This turns out to be of significance with respect to the Lord's Supper as well, for this sacrament is also more than a humanly originated edifying and symbolic rite of the Church. It is rather a divinely ordained act in which God strengthens our faith, and of which the Reformed formulary for the Lord's Supper says that the Lord Jesus Christ at his last evening meal broke the bread and took the cup ... so that we should firmly believe that we belong to this Covenant of Grace. Precisely because the Lord's Supper provides assurance of faith in dependence upon Christ's complete offering, the institution of the Lord's Supper is of great significance for the Church.

Throughout the centuries the Church has spoken unanimously about this institution. That this should be so, amidst all the contention about the meaning of the Lord's Supper, is undoubtedly to be explained by the great clarity with which Scripture speaks of this institution. That is true in Paul as well as in the synoptic Gospels, where the image of the Redeemer Jesus Christ rises before our eyes as he gave to his disciples the signs of his suffering and dying in the night of his betrayal, and called for remembrance. These institutional words became the Church's point of departure for its reflection on the significance of the Lord's Supper.

Only later, with the rise of historical criticism, was this institution of the Supper by Christ himself surrounded with all sorts of critical reservations or even completely obscured. That happened not only to the Gospels, but also to Paul, and if one studies the relevant critical considerations there seems to be very little left of the positiveness with which the form calls us to celebrate the Lord's Supper with the words: "as delivered unto us by the apostle Paul." It is clear, especially because of the relation between the celebration of the Lord's Supper and the certainty and stability of faith, that the Church noticed this criticism with great disquiet and that there has been (and still is) much contention regarding this point. When the biblical account of the institution seemed to become untenable, speculation began about what had actually happened and had been said during that last supper of Christ with the disciples. The results of those endeavors have been very contradictory, and the Church — one could say — has generally held on to the trustworthiness of the words of Scripture regarding the institution of the Lord's Supper.

In doing so, the Church in effect repudiated the critical distinction between history and the New Testament apostolic kerygma, for in the institution of the Lord's Supper the Church saw something that was both historical fact and the source of the authority and significance of the Lord's Supper. And even though the Church — because it adhered to the authority of these biblical words — was suspected of not recognizing fully the significance of historical criticism, there was nevertheless a strong conviction in the Church that the critical challenge to the validity of the institutional words came not from a responsible approach to Scripture, but from "presuppositions" that failed to recognize the authority of Scripture. One can speak in this connection of the kerygma which has authority for us, but if the kerygma has no ties with what happened in history, nothing of significance is gained. For the message in question is not only something handed on in specific forms through the tradition of the Church or from the theology of the community, but a message that underlies the authority of the Lord's Supper in the Church of Jesus Christ.

The tension between kerygma and history becomes very acute when we consider the institution of the Supper. Even in those circles where historical criticism was accepted as a legitimate approach to Scripture in its human aspects, people continued nevertheless to attach great value to the historical trustworthiness of the words of Scripture regarding the institution of the Lord's Supper. But this acknowledgment cannot rest merely upon a postulate because one is interested in the Lord's Supper, nor upon a quiet traditionalism; the decision here will always depend upon the significance that one ascribes to the authority of Scripture. For if this authority is regarded as a debatable point, one can still speak of the tradition of the Lord's Supper, but it will be difficult to continue ascribing to the Supper that significance by which it gives us assurance of faith. It is once for all impossible to find a basis in human institutions that is stable in the midst of the temptations of life. Only if the Lord's Supper has been instituted by the Lord of the Church himself, can one say that the practice of the Lord's Supper in the Church has not been a great aberration, but a way of obedience and faith.

We read of this institution of the Supper in the Gospels of Matthew, Mark, and Luke, and in the chapter of Paul's epistle to the Corinthians in which he harks back to this institution in the night of betrayal. The Gospel accounts are not identical in details, but together they portray a decisive event, namely, the institution of the Lord's Supper. It is not a normal meal of which we read at various occasions, but a meal in which a special call is given to eat and to drink, simultaneously with the indication of the meaning of this eating and drinking, the meaning of these acts: "this is my body" and "this is my blood of the covenant, which is poured out for many unto remission of sins" (Matt. 26:26-28), or "this is my body which is given for you" and "this cup is the new covenant in my blood, even that which is poured out for you" (Luke 22:19-20), while we read in Luke also — as in I Corinthians 11 — the call to remember: "this do in remembrance of me" (Luke 22:19; I Cor. 11:25).

All these passages have decisively determined the practice and confession of the Church regarding the Lord's Supper.[1] They have been heard as the direction-giving word of the Lord of the Church; and the Church lived from the first times onward in the awareness that this Supper had been given as a gift and as a command which would last until the return of Jesus Christ, when he would be present in the midst of his Church in a new manner. The Church saw in these passages

---

1. Works that discuss the institution of the Lord's Supper: W. Goossens, *Les origines de l'Eucharistie. Sacrament et Sacrifice,* 1931; K. G. Goetz, *Das Abendmahl ein Diatheke Jesu oder sein letztes Gleichnis?,* 1920; Goetz, *Der Ursprung des kirchlichen Abendmahls. Blosse Mahlgemeinschaft von Jesus und seinen Jüngern oder eine besondere Handlung und Worte von Jesus?* 1929; H. Huber, *Das Herrenmahl im Neuen Testament,* 1929; W. von Loewenich, *Vom Abendmahl Christi,* 1938; E. Gaugler, *Das Abendmahl im N. T.,* 1943.

the care of this Lord for the period in which he would no longer be with them, and in which he would not leave them as orphans, but would send his Spirit, and in which this Spirit would lead them in all truth. The Church has confessed in connection with the Lord's Supper a presence of the Lord in his Supper, but this presence was differently understood than the presence during his earthly life, and hence many have attempted to express the significance of his presence in the time between the ascension and the parousia.

The Church has placed the Lord's Supper in direct relation to his return at the end of time because the accounts of the Lord's Supper in Scripture stress this relation. In the synoptic Gospels as well as in Paul, this eschatological connection between the Lord's Supper and the future is clearly revealed to us. In the Gospels the Supper is linked specifically with the eschatological perspective of the Kingdom of God, as we see, for example, in two passages of Luke: In the first, Christ expresses his desire to celebrate the passover with his disciples and then adds that he will no more eat it until it will be fulfilled in the Kingdom of God (22:16), while in the second, Christ, after taking the cup and after the prayer, states: "For I say unto you, I shall not drink from henceforth of the fruit of the vine, until the kingdom of God shall come" (22:18). In Matthew and Mark we find this eschatological perspective in the same manner, but at a different place (Matt. 26:29; Luke 22:29).

All this shows that these passages refer to the future, and are connected with Christ's words of farewell.[2] The Lord's Supper is given to the Church in its going through the world. To be sure, the bond of communion between the Church and Christ will not be broken and he will be with it until the end of the world (Matt. 28:20), but this will be full Messianic reality only through the farewell, and for that reason it does not eliminate the present distance. One day, he will drink the wine new — with you (Matt. 26:29) — in the Kingdom of his Father.

The celebration of the Lord's Supper will always stand in this eschatological light, in the sign of this urgent "not yet," in the sign of expectation and prospect. The Lord's Supper and the "with you" comprised in that Supper are oriented toward a different "with you" in a new presence (parousia),

2. H. N. Ridderbos, *De komst van het Koninkrijk,* p. 351.

toward the ultimate fulfilment in the Kingdom of God. When Paul writes that in the Lord's Supper we proclaim the Lord's death "till he come," he is not only setting a temporal limit to the celebration of the Supper but is also indicating its eschatological orientation now. Precisely in the proclamation of Christ's death, the celebration extends toward the fulfilment in the Kingdom. In the Lord's Supper, the Church stands between the death of Christ and his new presence. "The glory of this event that puts all others in the shadow (what Jesus has done through his death), makes it the duty of the Church to proclaim his death. . . . But at that time there was not yet a song of praise to the crucified One which at the same time glorified the coming One."[3]

In this eschatological relation between the Supper and the return of Christ the significance of the Lord's Supper for the Church is decisively determined. The moment of distantiation (I shall no more eat the passover) points to the fulfilment: before it is fulfilled in the Kingdom of God. This orientation of the Supper is not contrasted in any sense with the celebration of the Supper as directed toward the strengthening of faith of the Church. For that strengthening does not mean an event in the individualistic sense, or a strengthening of our subjectivity in itself. Faith is not an arbitrary subjectivity which is found in us and which experiences strengthening, but the faith that is filled by the promise of God and its fulfilment. That is the very reason why there is such a profound interrelation between the earthly Lord's Supper and the eschatological perspective which is inseparably linked with the institution of the Lord's Supper. The slightest neglect of the Supper must therefore be condemned, for therein the community of believers loses its connection with the past (the death of Christ) as well as its outlook on the fulfilment. Furthermore, therein the "calling of the Church" is affected, and in the neglect of the Supper its whole historical life is at stake.

The celebration of the Lord's Supper takes place until he comes, in time, in which the tension and the longing of the Church is directed toward the future. Only in that celebration

---

3. A. Schlatter, *Paulus der Bote Jesu. Eine Deutung seiner Briefe an die Korinther,* 1934, p. 325. Cf. O. Cullmann, "La signification de la Sainte-Cène dans le Christianisme primitif," *Revue d'Histoire et de Philos. Religieuses,* 1936, pp. 1ff.

of the Lord's Supper which has truly eschatological orientation, will one be able to discover the contours of the true institution of the Supper by Christ.

This eschatological perspective, which comprises the profound responsibility of the Church, stands in full harmony with the call to remembrance of which we read in Luke and Paul. For it is not a matter of an outlook on vague distances in the future whereby the remembrance of the past fades, but the outlook is essentially and completely connected with what has occurred in the past, in the historical act of reconciliation. This harmony becomes clearly visible in Paul's words about the proclaiming of the Lord's death (I Cor. 11:26). There is a question whether Paul means to say: proclaim the Lord's death (imperative), or: so you proclaim . . . (indicative); but he refers in any case to the celebration of the Lord's Supper as announcement, as a proclaiming act wherein the community in faith gives expression to the glorious and decisive significance of the death of Christ. The call to remembrance harks back to the historical actuality of the reconciling suffering and dying of Christ. The eschatological orientation of the Supper does not make our attention to this past fade. On the contrary: only on the basis of this past, of this reconciliation, can the life of the believer be eschatologically directed. The fact that another call to remembrance occurs apart from Scripture, "the institution of ancient commemorative rites,"[4] is no indication against the trustworthiness of the word of Scripture, or against its unique significance in the institution of the Lord's Supper. For the latter is not just a general "remembering" or a pious "thinking" of someone dead, but a remembrance of this incomparably significant suffering and dying, of the ransom for many (Mark 10:45), of his obedience until death (cf. Phil. 2:8), of the life which he gives for the life of the world (John 6:51), of his fulfilling the command of his Father (John 10:18).

In the center of this remembrance stands the dying and the bearing fruit of the wheat (John 12:24), and this remembrance can therefore not be understood through merely historical and psychological categories. No matter how much it is connected with history and with the heart of man, this is the remembrance of faith; it is oriented toward the death of the Lord, which is proclaimed to us in the message of salvation.

4. Jeremias, *Die Abendmahlsworte Jesu,* 1949, p. 115.

The remembrance is more than a remembering of a contingent historical event which has some significance for us; this is also revealed in the fact that the Church remembers an event of which it itself has not been a witness. We think of the other remembrance to which Paul calls Timothy: "Remember Jesus Christ, risen from the dead" (II Tim. 2:8). In the preaching of salvation, the reference to what has happened in the past in the acts of God is incorporated as essential. This remembrance stands squarely opposed to the forgetting mentioned in Scripture, which cannot be approached with psychological categories either. Scripture speaks warningly about the "forgetting" of what God in his grace and mercy has done (cf. Ps. 103:1), but this forgetting is not a psychic defect of man's memory, but an act of neglect, of unbelief and ungratefulness in which the heart allows to be superseded what should never be superseded.

Christ's call is directed against this forgetting. It is the call to the continuous remembering of the Covenant that has now been established, of the blood that was shed, of the remission of sins, of the sacred ransom. The call to remembrance until he comes is not the setting of a relatively arbitrary temporal limit, but a reference to the short time between his suffering, dying, and resurrection and his return,[5] the short time during which believers are called upon to resist the temptation of which Christ speaks after the institution of the Lord's Supper, as the New Covenant becomes historical reality in the *passio magna*: "Watch and pray, that ye enter not into temptation: the spirit is indeed willing, but the flesh is weak" (Mark 14:38).

Jeremias has suggested that the call, "do this in remembrance of me" does not apply to the disciples.[6] "Does Jesus fear that the disciples might forget him? But this interpretation is not the only one possible; it is not even the most possible; it is not even the most obvious one." He reminds us in this context of Acts 10:4, where the angel says to Cornelius that his prayers and alms have gone up for a memorial before God, where God is the One who remembers; and he refers also to Mark 14:9, where it is said of the woman in Simon's house that the whole

5. Cf. L. D. Poot, *Het oudchristelijke avondmaal en zijn historische perspectieven*, 1936, p. 192. Poot quotes Bengel's word: "hoc mysterium duo tempora extrema conjugit."
6. He calls this "the normal exegesis" (Jeremias, *op. cit.*, p. 117).

world shall speak of her. On that basis Jeremias wants to think of God as remembering, making the passage read: "so that God will remember me."[7]

This seems a weak argument, for the question is not whether Jesus fears that his disciples will forget him psychologically. It is the meaning and the significance of the dying of Christ which can be forgotten and neglected, as Judas was full of remembrance of Jesus Christ and knew the place of Gethsemane, "for Jesus oft-times resorted thither with his disciples" (John 18:2), but nevertheless became a traitor without true "remembrance."[8]

In the light of this biblical sense of true remembrance[9] we must also reject the dilemma of Jeremias, namely, that in the Lord's Supper the death of the Lord is proclaimed "not as an event in the past but as an eschatological event."[10] This dilemma fails to appreciate the essence of Christ's reconciling work, which is not *either* past *or* eschatological, but eschatological *because* of the significance of the acts of God in history. The biblical remembrance thus reaches far beyond this dilemma; being historically determined, it is simultaneously oriented fully toward the future. In this connection lies the harmony of the New Testament proclamation of the Lord's Supper for the Church of all times.

The remembrance also plays an important role already in the Old Testament, being focused mainly on the passover, in which Israel must contemplate what God has done in the history of the people. The day of the passover will be a day of remembrance for Israel: "ye shall keep it a feast to Jehovah: throughout your generations ye shall keep it a feast by an ordinance for ever" (Exod. 12:14). The deliverance out of Egypt may not disappear into a gray past, but must dominate all of Israel's life. It is the day of remembrance, but at the same

---

7. Dr. Y. Feenstra, in his dissertation *Het apostolicum in de 20ste eeuw*, has stated: "There are good reasons to understand the words: 'Do this in remembrance of me' (I Cor. 11:24) in the causative sense" (Thesis VIII).

8. That Mark 14:9 speaks of the "remembering" of this woman does not say anything regarding the significance of the remembrance in the institution of the Lord's Supper. Everything depends on how and in which context mention is made of remembrance. Jeremias' explanation gives a meaning to the remembrance of the institution of the Lord's Supper which cannot be connected with the N. T.

9. On the "in remembrance of me" cf. Nils A. Dahl, "Anamnesis," *Studia Theologica*, II, 84f.

10. Jeremias, *op. cit.*, p. 118.

time also a feast of joy in which the people of God start on their way to the future in the remembrance of the past. Historically, the Lord's Supper has always been associated with this passover, until this relation was criticized in more recent times.[11] Still later, however, under the influence of various motives, it has again been maintained that there was really a connection. The scriptural basis of the connection is found in the Gospels, where we read that Christ was desirous to celebrate the passover with his disciples and then comes to institute the Supper (Luke 22: 15; cf. Mark 14:12-16; Matt. 26:17ff.). The passover and the Lord's Supper may not be identified with each other. There is a historical progress from the passover to the Lord's Supper, and it has been emphasized correctly that the Lord's Supper is not just a fulfilment of the passover alone but of the whole Old Testament sacrificial worship.

It has been asked why Christ instituted the Lord's Supper at that particular time, and even whether it would not have been more "natural" if he had first effected salvation through his death and resurrection, so that baptism and Supper would have both been instituted between his death and ascension. Odo Casel thinks that there is a "profound divine reason" for this manner of acting, namely, that the Church which lives by faith, not by sight, still needed the veils in which the sacred reality lies hidden. Hence the Church received the gift of Supper from the hand of him who was still a "pilgrim" on earth, and not yet the glorified One.[12]

But this explanation will not do, because, as Casel says, the veils also belong to the signs of the eucharist. Hence it cannot be the case that Christ instituted the Lord's Supper for that reason before his death. Rather, we shall have to be content with the fact that Christ — before the *passio magna* and in the approaching crisis of faith of his disciples — wanted to speak to them at that time of the meaning of his suffering and dying. Already at that time he wanted to shed the light of victory over what at first still seemed to be an obscure and misunderstood reality.

11. Concerning this criticism, cf. *op. cit.*, pp. 354-58; H. Ridderbos and Jeremias, *op. cit.*, *passim*. Against the relationship the chief critics are: H. Lietzmann, *Messe und Herrenmahl*, 1926; R. Otto, *Reich Gottes und Menschensohn*, 1940, pp. 220ff.; G. v.d. Leeuw, *Sacramentstheologie*, p. 52.
12. O. Casel, *Heilige Bronnen*, 1947, p. 55.

And so Jesus called the disciples to the marvelous light that issues from his death. That is why the Supper was not a sad repast to bid farewell, but a meal full of Messianic joy. Christ preaches in his word of farewell that the New Covenant now has become reality, and that the blood is poured that implies the remission of man's sins. The prophecy of Jeremiah is fulfilled when the covenant of forgiveness is constituted in the Messiah (Jer. 31:31-34), the Messiah in whom God no longer remembers our sins. The remembrance of the disciples and of the Church in later times is oriented toward this no-longer-remembering of God. There is no tension between the joy-motif of the Supper and its content, the remembrance of Christ's death. For the Messianic joy is completely based on the death of Christ.

This relationship, which points out the richness and the fruit of the Lord's Supper, is so clear in the Gospels and in Paul that this harmony can be threatened only by means of arbitrary hypotheses. That is evidently the case with Lietzmann, who distinguishes two types of the Lord's Supper in the New Testament, namely, the one of Jerusalem and the one of Paul.[13]

The original Supper was, he thinks, nothing but a *chaborah*, a communal repast of everyday type held by the disciples with their Teacher. This was also continued after Christ's death as if he himself were present, a gathering of disciples waiting for his return.[14] It was a joyful repast with an eschatological perspective. But there was another type of Supper called the Pauline which was no longer the old communal repast but rather "a meal commemorating the death of Christ" (p. 251). This latter type of Supper is joined to one specific meal, the last, and is repeated by the community. Lietzmann thinks that the usual meaning of "this is my body" does not belong to the archetype of the Supper. There is a rupture between the first and the second type. The simple table-communion completely changes in nature and character, for in the Pauline type the Supper becomes an analogy to Hellenistic meals commemorative of the dead. Heavenly efficacy comes to lie in the elements; it is hence-

---

13. H. Lietzmann, *Messe und Herrenmahl*, 1926. For comment see Ridderbos, *op. cit.*, and R. Otto, *Reich Gottes und Menschensohn*, 1940, p. 222. See also K. G. Kuhn, "Über den ursprunglichen Sinn des Abendmahls und sein Verhältnis zu den Gemeinschaftsmahlen der Sektenschrift," *EvT*, 1950-51, pp. 508ff.
14. Lietzmann, *op. cit.*, p. 250.

forth not just a matter of the simple meal but of an "enjoying"
of the body of Christ and of the communion with the Lord:
"thus originates the *corpus mysticum* of the Church. The simple
table-communion of the first period becomes mystical *koinonia*"
(p. 252). The only connection between the two types is the
eschatological perspective, which occupies an important place
in both of them. But the rupture cannot be denied. The two
types cannot go together, and the result has been that the
Pauline type "has carried the victory" (p. 254).

It is clear, however, that Paul gives no indication whatsoever
that he was altering the original type.[15] Rather, he introduces
his exposition with the words: "For I received of the Lord that
which also I delivered unto you, that the Lord Jesus in the
night in which he was betrayed..." (I Cor. 11:23). Paul was
fully aware of the nonoriginality of his "interpretation."[16]

At this point Lietzmann must choose: Did Paul simply follow a tradition or did he originate? Lietzmann acknowledges that
Paul knows of the last supper from the communal tradition as
we find it, notably, in Mark. But Paul declares that he has
received the correct insight into this repast: it is a commemorative meal and in that sense the Supper must be held repeatedly. "The liturgical words which are characteristic of the
text of Luke but which are lacking in Mark [namely, "do this
in remembrance of me"] formulate the decisive revelation which
lifted the new type of the Lord's Supper above the first type."[17]
Thus Paul and no one else became the instituter of the second
type of Supper. While Lietzmann had first believed that Paul
followed another communal tradition for his interpretation, he
abandoned this view later because of the great gap between the
two types. "If it was not Paul who instituted this type, where
then is the strong man who, against the authority of the first
Church of Jerusalem gave a new and profounder meaning to
their sacred meal?" In this manner, says Lietzmann, Paul's awareness of continuity (I have received it from the Lord) is given
a "very enlightening meaning."

Everything depends, however, on whether Paul has good
reason for disclaiming any sort of originality. Is Paul's awareness

15. Cf. G. Sevenster, *Christologie*, p. 122.
16. That is especially clear when Paul speaks of "tradition." Cf. Sevenster,
    op. cit., p. 122, and Grosheide, *Commentaar, ad loc.*
17. Lietzmann, *op. cit.*, p. 255.

of continuity adequately explained by Lietzmann's commentary
on I Corinthians 11: "But Paul adds a new trait when he lets
the Lord himself say that this celebration must be repeated
as a 'commemorative meal' "?[18] No, for Lietzmann alters quite
arbitrarily the significance of the words spoken at the Lord's
Supper. The "do this in remembrance of me" is actually no more
than "an addition grown out of liturgical need" (p. 223). With
that, the Supper of the Christian Church loses its essential connection with the institution of the Supper by Christ. It becomes
an illegitimate commemorative meal "and thus becomes part
of a quite specific type of religious repast which was customary
everywhere in the Greco-Roman world" (ibid.). But at the same
time the Supper of the Christian Church also loses its eschatological perspective. For Lietzmann, the original eschatological
motive has nothing to do with the reconciling suffering and
dying of Christ, while in the later Supper the eschatological is
linked with the death of Christ. At any rate, the Lord's Supper
of the Church becomes an illegitimate construction in which
there is no mention at all of "fulfilment."

If arbitrary theories are needed to devaluate the unity of
the Supper accounts and the institution of the Supper by
Christ, one cannot doubt the importance of this institution,
which harks back to the past as well as points toward the
future. No matter how great the differences in interpretation of
the meaning of the words of the Supper and how great the
results of these differences for the dividedness of the Church
concerning this "testament" of Jesus Christ "in the night of
his betrayal," that does not alter the fact that differences of
opinion must always go back to the words that were spoken
when the Lord's Supper was instituted, for only in that manner
can the light shine upon the profound significance of this sacrament of the Church.

In connection with these diverse interpretations, we may ask
whether this institution by Christ is then so obscure that it
accounts for the great diversity. Does not the acceptance of the
institution of the Lord's Supper by Christ himself threaten to
become a merely formal belief that no longer has binding
power for the unity of the Church and the celebration of the
Lord's Supper? How is it possible that there is no great agreement regarding the actual gift of the Lord's Supper in the

18. Lietzmann, An die Korinther, I-II, 1949, p. 57.

Church of Christ, while there is agreement regarding its institution?

In this connection many have pointed to the original Christian community, which *was* one, not only in the teachings of the apostles, in fellowship and in prayer, but also in the breaking of the bread (Acts 2:42). It is also said of that community that it was united in the temple and broke the bread at home and ate the meal with "gladness and singleness of heart" (Acts 2:46). This jubilant joy of the first Church has been seen as a sharp judgment upon the later controversies about the Lord's Supper, and all this has been deduced from an elementary lack of simplicity in man's heart.

In the confusion, people harked back to this evangelical simplicity and saw the most basic cause of the confusion in the many distinctions that were made. All sorts of attempts were made to find a way out of the impasse of these discords, and to recover the jubilation of the Church which was on its way toward the future of Christ. Was there not a common doxology and a common eucharist? We now know the word "eucharist" practically only as the designation of a specifically Roman Catholic sacrament, but is it not a basic word of the New Testament and therefore of the "catholic" Church? That is precisely why there is such an urgent call for continued reflection on this eucharist, for this gratefulness is, after all, central to the celebration of the Lord's Supper.

But the impasse certainly cannot be overcome by means of the contrast between simplicity of heart and theological reflection. The simplicity of heart in the first Church did not stand in tension with the teaching of the apostles and the fellowship and the prayers. Precisely because the Lord's Supper is a sacred institution by Jesus Christ himself and therein pertains to his salvation of the world, people may never turn away haughtily from the controversies about the Lord's Supper. To be sure, it is easy for theological self-righteousness to penetrate into these controversies, but that does not eliminate the fact that the Church is called to confession, not least on this subject, and to the proclaiming of Christ's death. Moreover, we see in the history of the Church that impure reflection on the Lord's Supper has often led to a serious devaluation of the Supper.

The controversies about the Supper have focused repeatedly on the dilemma of *symbol* or *reality*. It is of decisive significance to pose the question whether this dilemma issues from the institution of the Lord's Supper itself.

CHAPTER TEN

SYMBOL OR REALITY?

THIS IS NOT the first time that we encounter the dilemma of symbol or reality. We saw already how this dilemma has played an important role in the history of the baptismal doctrine and in the struggle among various interpretations of baptism. And now we find a clear parallel with respect to the doctrine of the Lord's Supper. Here, too, we must insist that the dilemma of symbol or reality can never give us clear insight into the fierce dispute that has raged concerning the Lord's Supper, and is still going on. As we saw in the case of baptism, it is impossible to define the Reformed sacramental doctrine as a "symbolic" doctrine where baptism is only an outward sign — of illustrative value and significance to be sure, but nevertheless other than a "reality" because as a sign it only points to a "reality." The same is true of the Lord's Supper, as is clearly indicated by the Reformed confessions and by Reformed theology.

In spite of this unmistakable fact, however, both Lutherans and Roman Catholics have persisted in calling the Reformed doctrine "symbolic." They allege that Calvin did not really get beyond the Zwinglian symbolistic interpretation of the Lord's Supper, and neither does the later Reformed doctrine.[1] In spite of all attempts by the Reformers to attach "reality value" to the Lord's Supper, the critics maintained that they appreciated the

---

1. We think of Lutheran criticism in former centuries, e.g., by Wilmar. Hohler has pointed out that, to be sure, it has been said by the Reformed that, in order to pose the problem correctly, one should not stop at the contrasts of Marburg 1529, nor with the contrast between *"est"* and *"significat,"* because not Zwingli but Calvin decisively influenced the Reformed doctrine of the Lord's Supper; but ... "the conversation stagnates at this point." H. Hohler, "Das Abendmahl ist kein konfessioneles Problem," *EvT*, X (1950-51), 452. See also P. Althaus, *Die Christliche Wahrheit*, II (1948), 383; W. Elert, *Der Christliche Glaube*, 1940.

Supper only as a sign, a symbol, a reference to the reality of the salvation in Jesus Christ. Roman Catholics, especially, have interpreted this as a radical misappreciation of the actual mystery and of the profound sacramental reality. Actually, they say, the eucharist is the main sacrament of the Christian Church. To be sure, the other sacraments also involve reality, the reality of supernatural grace; but the eucharist is still different: in this sacrament it is not a case simply of applying Christ's work, but of his personal presence in grace and power.[2] As far as Rome is concerned, any other affirmation of the reality of the sacraments fades in comparison with this reality.

This confession of Christ's inscrutable presence belongs to the essence of Rome's interpretation of the Lord's Supper. It is seen as the absolutely necessary "plus" which separates Rome from the Reformation. It is the plus of the sacramental and personal presence of Christ — the *totus Christus* — who in the eucharist gives himself as food and drink. This reality supposedly corresponds to the profoundest longings of man's heart. "Catholicism, which attaches such an eminent significance to the real, eucharistic presence of Christ for the spiritual union with Christ, confirms thereby the reality of God's coming to man in Christ's humanity."[3]

Nevertheless, Rome also wishes to acknowledge the signifying character of the eucharist. The Council of Trent declared that the eucharist has in common with the other sacraments that it is a "symbol" of a sacred matter and a visible form of invisible grace.[4] But the sacrament is more than sign and symbol; this is especially clear in the eucharist because in it "is contained not only the divine grace, but the prime cause of grace himself."[5]

That is why Roman Catholics pose the symbol-reality contrast for baptism, but especially for the eucharist, and speak the anathema against those who deny that Christ's body and blood are really present and who teach that it is only a matter of a "figure."[6] The dilemma is posed: image or reality?[7] Es-

---

2. Denz. 876.
3. G. P. Kreling, in *Antwoord op het herderlijk schrijven,* 1950, p. 35.
4. "symbolum esse rei sacrae et invisibilis gratiae formam visibilem" (Denz. 876).
5. Bartmann, *Dogm.,* II, 289.
6. Denz. 883.
7. Cf. G. T. Liesting, *De zin van het laatste avondmaal volgens de N. T. ische teksten. Beeld of werkelijkheid?,* 1948.

pecially in the Reformation, Rome sees fundamentally only sign, figure, representation, sign and seal, and thus misses the full and complete reality aspect which is primary and essential for the eucharist.

The question has been asked whether Trent's varied designations *(in signo, vel figure aut virtute)* indicate three different Protestant heresies, and whether *aut virtute* is aimed especially at Calvin's "dynamic" doctrine of the Lord's Supper, as distinguished from Zwingli's.[8] Whatever may have been the exact intention of Trent, it is clear in any case that it wanted to reject every "symbolical" interpretation of the Supper[9] and to maintain that the signs or symbols indicate the true and real, substantial presence of Christ as the only One who corresponds to the gospel's integral presence[10] in the *"admirabile sacramentum,"*[11] which can hardly be expressed with words.[12] It is a real, sacramental presence and reality of him who at the same time sits at the right hand of God.[13] Against this twofold manner of existence, human reason rises in opposition "because it is completely submerged in the darkness of the mystery."[14] But the believer is not shocked by this riddle. He is rather comforted and gladdened by this extreme form of the coming of God to man.[15]

One can meet the real Christ only in adoration, not in rational analysis. This reality is not at all a speculative invention but is unshakably based on the institution of the eucharist. That is why the struggle of "realism" against "symbolism" is always concentrated upon the words of institution of the Lord's Supper. The literal sense of the words, says Rome, implies the reality of Christ's body and blood.[16] This is the most obvious meaning, and refers us to the mystery of transubstantiation. Through the priest's words of consecration, the indescribable miracle enters the reality of our earthly existence, as it was

8. Bartmann, *op. cit.,* II, 293.
9. *DTC,* V, 1344.
10. Denz. 874.
11. *Ibid.*
12. "quam verbis exprimere vix possumus."
13. Denz. 874.
14. Kreling, *op. cit.,* p. 36.
15. *Ibid.*
16. Grossouw, in *Antwoord,* p. 57.

already indicated at the Fourth Lateran Council in 1215.[17] In instituting the Lord's Supper, Christ has given us his body in the form of bread,[18] and now through the consecration in every eucharist there occurs the marvelous and mysterious *conversio* which is so fittingly called transubstantiation.[19] This consecration[20] is the act of the priests through which "the corporeal gifts of bread and wine are dedicated to God in the most strict sense through their change into the body and blood of Christ"[21] in an "act of change."[22]

The words of consecration hark back to the institution of the eucharist, and the question how the "change" can now take place is answered in this manner: "Over the gifts of bread and wine the proclamation of the sacred meal of the Lord is spoken. The proclamation has a mysterious power which is able to change the bread and the wine over which it is spoken."[23]

The heart of Roman Catholic liturgy beats in the reality that thus came about: the eucharistic Christ. To be sure, all one sees are the "accidents" (form, color, taste) of bread and wine that have remained,[24] but hidden under these signs Christ himself is present. Because the consecration of the priest brings about the mysterious change, Christ is immediately and really present, already before the use of the elements as he is present after their use.[25] The sacrament is thus a matter of the "continuation of the presence of Christ,"[26] of the *reservatio* in connection with the honor that must be brought to the Christ who is present in the eucharist.[27]

17. This council treats of Jesus Christ as priest and as offering "cuius corpus et sanguis in sacramento altaris sub speciebus panis et vini veraciter continentur, transsubstantis pane in corpus et vino in sanguinem potestate divina" (Denz. 430).
18. Denz. 877.
19. Denz. 884 (*mirabilis et singularis conversio*).
20. "peracta consecratione" (Denz. 886).
21. *Theol. Woordenboek* (Dr. H. Brink), p. 3.
22. J. Braun, *Handlexikon der kath. Dogm.: Konsekration*. Cf. my *Conflict met Rome*, 1949, pp. 289ff.
23. Schmaus, *Kath. Dogm.*, IV, 1, 236.
24. "manentibus dumtaxat speciebus panis et vini" (Denz. 884).
25. Therein, according to Trent, lies the unique aspect of the eucharist in distinction from the other sacraments, that Christ is here already before the use. Cf. Trent Sess. XIII, 3.
26. Schmaus, *op. cit.*, pp. 286ff.
27. This is seen very clearly in Canons 6-8 of Trent, Sess. XIII (Denz. 888-890).

Because of this doctrine of the presence of Christ in transubstantiation, the Reformed Church was seen as lacking the plus of the sacramental reality, and its doctrine was seen as "symbolic." On the other hand, however, the Reformation rejected this doctrine of transubstantiation as a theory having no foundation in Scripture and which could be maintained only in terms of the philosophical view on the relation between substance and accidents. The Reformed criticism of this "reality" was similar to that advanced later by the "Old Catholics." Van Rinkel, for example, speaks of the unhappy theory of the real presence.[28] "In the history of the Church this theory has become quite dangerous, since it has been made into a dogma which links the doctrine of real presence with the theory of transubstantiation."[29] Van Rinkel thinks that the Reformed side has also more than once identified the doctrine of transubstantiation with that of the real presence; moreover, he points out that the doctrine of transubstantiation is twelve years more recent than the one of Christ's real presence, and that its scholastic distinctions surround the dogma with many subtle and insoluble problems.

With respect to Van Rinkel's valuable criticism, one must only remark that Luther and Calvin certainly did not identify transubstantiation with the real presence of Christ. While rejecting the doctrine of transubstantiation, they both, albeit in a different manner, confessed the real presence of Christ in the Lord's Supper, as we shall see in the following chapter. But it is already clear here that the contrast "symbol or reality" is a completely unsatisfactory dilemma that cannot do justice to the real contrasts. If the Roman Catholic doctrine of the Lord's Supper can with good reason be called "realistic" because of the specific manner in which it speaks of the real body and blood of the Lord, one cannot correspondingly speak of a "symbolic" Reformed doctrine of the Lord's Supper (Zwingli excluded), if this is taken to mean a denial of the real presence.

It is clear that the Roman Catholic doctrine of the Lord's Supper requires a very special kind of "reality." As we saw,

28. A. van Rinkel, *Die heilige Eucharistie*, 1952, p. 87; cf. pp. 57ff.
29. *Ibid.*, p. 87.

Rome appeals repeatedly for support to the words of institution. "When the Lord, pointing at the bread in his hand, said 'This is my body,' not bread but the body of the Lord had to be there as soon as he had spoken those words; otherwise, the word he spoke could not have been true."[30] Transubstantiation must then occur between the "this" and "my body." If these words of Christ are true, "the body of Christ must come into existence where the bread first was."[31] Because of this exegesis, many violent controversies have raged concerning "this is my body." While some saw transubstantiation clearly implied by the *"est,"* the Reformers replied that this view was based on the prejudice of the bodily presence of Christ in the eucharist. This struggle is usually described in terms of the distinction between the *est* (is) and the *significat* (signifies), and also repeatedly in terms of realism and symbolism.

Rome thought it could discern in the *significat* the symbolistic interpretation, even though Rome itself is unwilling to deny the signifying character of the eucharist. Furthermore, Rome thought the *significat* to be completely contradictory to the simple meaning of the words of institution. To be sure, it has been shown more than once that the Roman Catholic exegesis simply introduces transubstantiation, whereas a truly "literal" exegesis would lead one rather to a consubstantiation doctrine ("this" is connected with "my body"). But Rome has rejected this interpretation, and has held that the only literal interpretation is to be found in its ecclesiastical doctrine of the change of essence. That makes it clear that this doctrine is fundamentally not based on exegetic obedience, but on a trend of thought that introduces an extrinsic element into the text.

In reply to the argument that Rome emphasizes the little word "is" too much, although that word is not found in the Aramaic text,[32] Grossouw says that this argument means nothing because "is" is always omitted in Aramaic and Hebrew.[33] But that does not prove at all that "is" may now be interpreted as implying a change of essence. In excluding all appeals to reason

30. J. B. Heinrich, *Dogm. Theol.,* IX (1901), 578.
31. *Ibid.,* p. 583.
32. Grossouw, in *Antwoord,* p. 26.
33. *Ibid.,* p. 57.

with respect to this miracle of miracles,[34] Rome has simply cut off all debate with its opponents.[35]

For Rome, the doctrine of transubstantiation is a new element introduced to explain the real presence. "Although the texts do not emphatically speak of this change, they confront us nevertheless with the fact that that which at first was normal bread, is now the body of Jesus."[36] Leaving aside the fact that the official Roman Catholic distinction between the changed substance and the remaining accidents has no shred of support in Scripture, we want here simply to deny that this doctrine is the legitimate, literal exegesis of the sacred institutional words.[37] Rather, a peculiar theory of change is introduced here whereby all difficulties come to rest under the rubric of the mystery: the real Christ. In the history of the doctrine, the "is" became increasingly the answer to every objection. To be sure, Rome admits that Christ in Luke 22 says of the cup that it "is" the New Covenant in his blood and that this is an "unreal mode of speaking," but this acknowledgment does not extend to the "is" of the other institutional words. Here in Luke, they say, it is evidently the *content* of the cup that is meant, while in the other passages this is not so clear; hence the latter must be understood as implying a change of essence.

This interpretation of the words of Christ is often supported with the thesis that it is impossible to understand these institutional words in a signifying way because of the very relation between the bread and Christ's body. If it were a matter of signifying, the bread would represent Christ's body as a picture represents something else by similarity, or as something out of human life or from nature (as in the parables) is compared with the Kingdom of God. There is then always some common feature which by analogy gives basis to the comparison and

---

34. Cf. Liesting, *op. cit.*, p. 120: "And if it is Jesus' body, it is no longer bread." Liesting even calls this "the foundation" for transubstantialism (p. 120). Compare the defense of the Roman Catholic theologians against the argument that Jesus himself was still in their midst, for instance with Grossouw (*Antwoord*, p. 58), where he points out that this argument will not do because we are confronted here with a "great and incomprehensible mystery of faith."

35. The problem regarding the relation between transubstantialism and consubstantialism is very intriguing. The latter doctrine was developed by the disciples of Berengarius.

36. Cf. Liesting, *op. cit.*, p. 122.

37. As we find already said by Calvin (*Inst.*, IV, XVII, 20).

makes it possible. Now Rome does acknowledge that "is" in Scripture often means "signifies," but in all these cases the common basis of comparison is clear. This is not true, however, of the eucharist, and this settles the issue for many persons. "Does Jesus present bread and wine as the symbols of his suffering, or does he intend to give his real body and blood to the apostles, albeit in a mystical manner?"[38] The answer is clear, for this is not a matter of clear figurative speech, but of a definite act which is accompanied by the words of institution. This "is" is completely incomparable with other figures of speech. Liesting remarks that the eucharist lacks what is present in other figures of speech, namely, the natural relation between bread as such and Jesus' body. If this were figurative discourse, it would have been "senseless language."[39] "For a figure of speech which in no wise reveals what is presented by it and which can be interpreted in many ways, is without meaning," so that the conclusion is "that bread and wine cannot be signs of Jesus' body and blood."[40]

It is clear that this argumentation is entirely insufficient in the light of the preaching of Jesus Christ. With the institution of the Lord's Supper, we must start by seeking the meaning toward which these signs point us. And in the light of Christ's preaching it is not at all strange that he speaks in this manner. First of all, we think of his designation of himself as the bread of life (John 6:35). He is the true bread which the Father gives, which has descended from heaven and which gives life to the world (John 6:32-33). Therein we see already a clear connection between the bread and the fruit and blessing of the work of Jesus Christ which dominates and pervades all of John 6. It is clear that, unlike Liesting, we may not take away the signifying relation from the institution, especially not because "this is my body" is connected with "take, eat."

Precisely because Christ speaks of the meaning of his reconciling suffering and dying, and because he calls for the remembrance of reconciliation, there is reason to ask whether one can speak of the signifying connection between the bread and the body of Christ. Because the concern lies with the meaning of Christ's reconciling offering, Christ can speak of his surrender

38. W. Goossens, *Les origines de l'eucharistie*, p. 187.
39. *Ibid.*, p. 189.
40. Liesting, *op. cit.*, pp. 96-98.

for those who are his, of his flesh which he gives for the life
of the world and of his blood which is poured out for many.
This is not a matter of ontology, taken by itself, which as such
must draw our attention. We see that clearly already in John
6, where the words about the decisive significance of Christ's
offering unmistakably pervade all of this chapter; but no less
clearly do we see it in the institution of the Lord's Supper,
which also speaks of his surrender in death and of the salvation
that is therein implied. One can understand the institutional
words only if this relationship is fully respected and if one
does not begin to speak of the "substance" of Christ's body
and blood in itself, as if such a substantialistic interpretation
were the crux of the matter.

The meaning of this institution can be understood if one
does not insert the "becomes" of transubstantiation between the
"this is" and "my body." Christ commands the bread to be
eaten, and in this way bread and wine receive sacramental significance by way of the qualification of these earthly elements.
It is the blood of the Covenant which is poured out for many.
Christ's "body" and "blood" may not for a moment be detached
from his surrender unto death. It is not the blood as such that
is the point of the matter, but the pouring of the blood in personal surrender (Matt. 26:28). The Lord's Supper is indeed a
matter of the bread of life, and even though we do not find in
John 6 an institution of the Supper, one will nevertheless have
to acknowledge the profound connection established there between Christ's self-surrender of body and blood and the blessing
of his dying. It is the bread of God which gives life eternal.

In the institution of the Lord's Supper the important thing
is the indication of Christ's significant self-surrender. He who
begins to think of body and blood as substances that can be put
on display, unwittingly fails to appreciate the personal character
of Christ in his surrender and the manner in which Christ continuously speaks of this. His blood is the purifying blood, and
the important thing is our communion with the blood of Christ
(I Cor. 10:16), which purifies us of all sins (I John 1:7), and
which makes the gentiles draw nigh (Eph. 2:13). The New
Covenant is realized in this blood. "The interest of the New
Testament does not stand still at the blood of Christ as corporeal
material, but at his poured blood, at the life that forcedly

was taken from him."[41] "The blood of Christ, like the cross of
Christ, is another graphic expression for the death of Christ in
its saving significance." To acknowledge this has nothing to
do with spiritualization. On the contrary: this is the "realism"
of Christ's sorrowful way to Golgotha, the pouring of his blood,
which stands in the light of his surrender for reconciliation,
of the personal giving of his flesh for the life of the world.

We are far removed here from all substantialistic thinking
about the offering of Christ which thinks of body and blood as
substances with which we are united.[42] In the pouring out of
Christ's blood, his death becomes historical reality. That is
why the signs refer to participation by faith in the blessing
and the fruit of his dying for reconciliation.

All this becomes very evident in the manner of the institution of the Lord's Supper. The bread is not just distributed
without words, but the call is given: take, eat. The disciples
are thereby involved in a manner unusual for the passover:
they must take and eat.[43] This eating at the command of Christ
points toward the nourishing with the bread of life. It is the
joy of Christ's work in which the disciples are involved. Is not
the cup of gratitude a communion with the blood of Christ (I
Cor. 10:16)? This is not just a symbolization of Christ's way
to his death, but the reality of his fruitful dying. Our form
speaks of that when it says that Christ has confirmed the Covenant of Grace and of reconciliation with his death and with his
blood, when he said: "It is finished." In the sign, we are oriented
toward this reconciliation.

In this connection we cannot escape the question whether
the breaking of the bread and the pouring of the wine must
be incorporated into the symbolism of the Supper. This is not
at all a secondary liturgical question, but a matter that has
immediate bearing on the "sign language" of the Lord's Supper.
The breaking of the bread often occurs purposely in such a
manner that it is clear that the breaking of Christ's body is
indicated and symbolized. On the Reformed side a different
interpretation has found defense. We think, for instance, of
the thesis of Meuleman: "It is incorrect to involve symbolism in

41. *TWNT*, I, 173.
42. Cf. H. Ridderbos, "Woord en Sacrament," in *Het avondmaal, VT*, 1949,
p. 35.
43. Cf. H. Ridderbos, *Korte Verklaring*, Matt., II, 188. Cf. also Leenhardt,
Le sainte cène, p. 29.

the rite of the Lord's Supper in the breaking of the bread and
the pouring of the wine."[44] This thesis evidently harks back
to the view of Jeremias and Herman Ridderbos, who defend
the same position. "The view has become very common that
Jesus signifies with *touto* [this] the act of the breaking of the
bread and the act of the pouring of the wine. This interpretation (which shipwrecks already on the term *touto estin* [this is])
would be possible only if the acts mentioned would temporally
coincide with the explanatory word of Christ. This, however,
is not the case."[45]

The arguments against this "symbolism" of breaking and
pouring indicate that the breaking of the bread was simply a
customary act with every meal, and that this breaking does not
evoke association "of forcibly tearing a body apart."[46] Moreover, we read nothing about a symbolical "pouring" of the
wine,[47] and the wine — says Ridderbos — stood for some time
already poured on the table when Jesus applied to it the para-
ble of his blood.[48] Jeremias comes to the conclusion: "Jesus does
not refer to the act of the breaking of the bread and the pouring
of the wine; rather, he refers to bread and wine as such."[49] When
Ridderbos writes: "What is symbolized is therefore not Christ's
surrender proper but the fruit of it for the lives of those who
are his,"[50] he does not intend to separate the one from the
other but to indicate that we are concerned here with "the death
of Christ in its redemptive significance."[51] What is symbolized
is not the manner of Christ's self-surrender (breaking and pouring), but the salvation and the blessing of the reconciling
offering of Jesus Christ.[52]

Polman points out regarding this matter of symbolism in the
Lord's Supper that there were formerly differences of opinion
among the Reformed, and he adds: "We do not need to decide
here about this centuries-old difference because all are agreed
that the Supper is not an offering, but, like the passover, an

---

44. G. E. Meuleman, *De ontwikkeling van het dogma in de R. K. theologie,*
    1951 (thesis).
45. Jeremias, *Die Abendmahlsworte,* p. 104.
46. H. Ridderbos, *Komst van het Koninkrijk,* p. 364.
47. *Ibid.*
48. *Ibid.*
49. Jeremias, *op. cit.,* p. 105.
50. Ridderbos, *loc. cit.*
51. Behm in *TWNT,* as quoted by Ridderbos, *loc. cit.*
52. Ridderbos, *loc. cit.*

offering-meal."[53] The question can be asked whether one has not already decided for the interpretation of Jeremias and Ridderbos if one speaks of an offering-meal. For then the breaking of bread and the pouring of the wine have already been taken out of the symbolism, and one has already oriented the symbolism toward the fruit of the suffering and dying of Christ. Polman says correctly that the symbolism of breaking and pouring is not found in the Confession of Faith.[54] The same can be said of the form for the Lord's Supper, except that at one point it reminds us of the breaking of the bread, though — interestingly — not of the pouring of the wine.[55]

Furthermore, in the same context, the fruit of the Lord's Supper is mentioned "that it nourish and refresh your hungry and thirsty souls with my crucified body and shed blood."[56] This blessing of the dying is signified and sealed in the Lord's Supper. That is why Polman and Ridderbos speak of a "sacrificial banquet," which has nothing to do with the idea that in the Lord's Supper an "offering" takes place, as in the Roman Catholic doctrine of the mass.

The sacrificial banquet is completely separated from any repetition of the offering; it excludes this repetition once for all and definitely. In the Lord's Supper the concern lies with the food which Christ has ordained for his believers, with the heavenly food and drink. In the Lord's Supper, our trust and faith are directed toward Christ's offering as the only basis of our salvation. So the prayer before the Supper has the petition: "that our burdened . . . hearts . . . may be nourished and refreshed. . . ."[57]

The important thing in the Lord's Supper is that blessing, and in the symbolism of the Supper we are directed toward this blessing by Christ himself when he speaks of his body and of the blood of the Covenant which is poured for many unto a remission of sins. That is why he has those who belong to him share in his surrender of body and blood in his reconciling work, and that is why he gives us in the bread and in the wine

53. Polman, *Onze Ned. Geloofsbelijdenis,* IV, 260.
54. *Ibid.,* p. 259.
55. Cf. also H.C., Q. 75.
56. *Ibid.*
57. Cf. Ridderbos, *op. cit.,* pp. 366ff., and his article "Woord en Sacrament," *VT,* 1949. Also: Markus Barth, "Das Abendmahl, Passamahl, Bundesmahl, und Messiasmahl," *TS,* 1945, pp. 25ff.

the nourishment for life eternal and the joy of his redeeming work.

Markus Barth has made the remark that "the Reformed doctrine, which would see in the symbolical breaking of bread a representation of the fact and manner of Jesus' death, stands much closer to the Roman Catholic doctrine of the representation of the sacrifice than it is aware of, and closer than it would like to be."[58] This judgment is most unjust, for it is precisely the Reformed interpretation of the Lord's Supper that emphasizes the absolute significance of the offering of Jesus Christ (which happened only once), and whose polemics were especially directed against every element of repetition. But we shall have to ask ourselves continually whether we really do look upon the Lord's Supper as a "representation" of the suffering of Christ himself in the sense of a passion play which is performed before our eyes. Markus Barth maintains correctly — and Ridderbos agrees — that the Lord's Supper must not become "the passion play of the breaking," because, as Golterman says, the drama proper becomes *praesens*. It is certainly not the intention of form and confession to refer to a passion play.[59]

The danger of the passion play is certainly not imaginary in the celebration of the Lord's Supper, because this accent upon symbolism can dilute the profound meaning of the communion of the Supper. The Supper should not be made into a commemoration of the terrible seriousness of the suffering of Christ in itself, even though this seriousness has an important place in the form for the Lord's Supper.[60] Everything depends on how one speaks and thinks of this suffering. He who loses himself in the bitterness of this suffering and dying can easily drift into an aesthetic contemplation of Christ in which the beauty is somehow closely linked with the cross ("Oh, flame of passion on this somber hill") and forget that all this belongs exclusively to Good Friday. But Good Friday cannot be under-

---

58. M. Barth, *op. cit.*, p. 28. Cf. Bultmann's interpretation of Paul's sacramental doctrine (*Theol. des N. T.*, p. 147). Bultmann sees I Cor. 11:26 as a sort of mystery-drama.

59. M. Barth says correctly that the table at the Supper is not something outward only (*ibid.*, p. 61).

60. We find this especially in the passage that confesses: "Jesus Christ... was sent of the Father into this world... assumed our flesh and blood... has borne for us the wrath of God," etc. But all this occurs not in isolation, but in a profoundly evangelical context, as is revealed already in the prefatory passage.

stood without paying attention to the essential goodness of this day, and therein we find the joy of the Lord's Supper.

The Lord's Supper is no place for veils of romanticism which shroud the real mystery of the eating of the bread and the drinking of the wine. This is Good Friday, but the joy does not do away with the remembrance of the death of Christ. On the contrary, this celebration includes this death. This death has been incorporated into the kerygma in all its appalling reality, as the carrying of the curse. This is the way Paul portrayed it so vividly to the Galatians, as the Christ crucified. But the cross and the death have received a place in the message, in the apostolic kerygma, and there it becomes a message of joy and peace; and the Lord's Supper becomes a repast which looks toward the new repast in the Kingdom of God. The Supper is therefore a matter of peace and joy, of nourishment and of salvation and communion. The shadows of Christ's death have their place here, but only in connection with the preaching of salvation, in which we are taught that the shadows of death are changed into the morning dawn and that the dying wheat will bear fruit. Only when the Church understands this symbolism, which comes forth from Christ's command to eat and drink, will it be able to participate joyfully in the communion with Christ.

In this way the Church understands the preaching of the Lord's Supper and the blessing of the body and the blood therein of the bread of life. For the Supper signifies and seals the Word of promise: "I am the bread of life: he that cometh to me shall not hunger, and he that believeth on me shall never thirst" (John 6:35).

We can now return to the question posed at the beginning of this chapter, namely, whether the dilemma between symbol and reality is indeed responsible and justified. This question can be answered only if we do not interpret the symbolism in the Reformed doctrine of the Lord's Supper simplistically. That has often been done (also with baptism), and this leads easily to the contrast between "symbolism" and "realism." Realism was then that interpretation of the Supper in which somehow there is concern for the real Christ in the Supper, while symbolism stands for mere illustration, an image, a symbol of the suffering and dying of Christ which reminds us of the historical actuality of his death and of its significance. This latter view led to the interpretation of the Lord's Supper as a *nudum signum,* bereft of all reality, except for the reality of the sign and the psychological reality of the remembrance.

But this empties the Reformed doctrine of the Lord's Supper in a way diametrically opposed to its intents and formulations. We shall discuss the doctrine of the real presence below, but we want to point out at this time that when a doctrine of the Lord's Supper sees the signs of the Supper as "symbols" of salvation, which imply the reconciling death of Christ, it cannot be called merely symbolic. That could be the case only if these signs were nothing more than rites instituted by the Church for the psychological or pedagogical benefit of the believers. The sacrament would then belong — in its symbolism — to a pastoral work which the Church had itself devised. But the Reformed doctrine of the Lord's Supper differs altogether from this symbolistic one; for it appeals not to man-made signs, but to the institution of Christ and to his power in and over the signs. These signs can now no longer be detached from him who instituted the Lord's Supper.

That is why the Supper has not yet been described fully and sufficiently if it is understood as "symbol." On the one hand, there is no need to be distressed about the name "symbol" just because there are many considerations and interpretations of "symbol" that do not contribute to the understanding of the Lord's Supper. Any word used to designate the Supper can be misinterpreted, including "sign," "seal," "symbol," and "sacrament." And one certainly cannot flee from the word "symbol" and its context because of a certain fear for "symbolism," for in the Lord's Supper the crux of the matter is indeed a sign, a symbol, an indication which is given to us for our salvation. But in that case it must be made clear that this sign is not an arbitrary human illustration, but a sign which is given to us by Christ and which therefore can never be detached from Christ. It is a repast, but in the bread and wine we come into contact with those signs which Christ himself uses with a very specific purpose: the strengthening and assurance of our faith. "The certainty that with the bread we also eat and drink the body of Christ lies not in the eating and drinking as such, nor in faith, but in the receiving of these qualified signs from the hand of Christ."[61] This implies that the signs can no longer be detached from Christ, for he instituted the signs and gave

---

61. H. N. Ridderbos, "Woord en Sacrament," p. 2.

them to his Church as signs of his reconciliation and peace. Therein lies the basis for the Lord's Supper and also the inviolable comfort for faith.

There is then no longer a contrast between symbol and reality for him who knows that through these signs communion is experienced and salvation is represented and given. He who sees this profound meaning in the institution of the Supper by Christ himself will understand the sacramental manner of speaking, which is not a meaningless and exaggerated phraseology but which indicates the conjunction between the believing eating of the bread and the drinking of the wine and the blessing and efficacy of Christ's reconciling suffering and dying. This celebration is threatened by symbolization if the signs are detached from this context of the institution by Christ and of the involvement with faith, but this symbolization does not belong to the essence of this interpretation of the Supper; rather, it is radically excluded. For the signifying and sealing are not matters of subjective psychology, but of the acts of Christ himself, who in an inscrutable manner connects what only he can connect: the taking of the earthly sign with the receiving of the gift of the Supper.

The confessions and forms of the Church speak against a symbolism which is fundamentally nothing but abstraction. This abstraction, which carries with it the spiritualization of the Lord's Supper, has always had appalling results for the practice of the Church. Unwittingly, people concluded repeatedly that the Supper could have some psychological value but that one could not speak of its necessity. In our discussion of baptism we pointed out already that in the full sense one can speak of the necessity of baptism because of its institution by Christ and the weakness of our faith. The same can be said with respect to the Lord's Supper, and therein lies the defense against all spiritualism. He who holds correctly that the Lord's Supper is necessary comes to that view, not because of some sacramentalistic overestimation of the sacrament, but because of its sacred value which was conferred upon it at its institution. The Church rests here in its celebration of the Lord's Supper; when it consecrates the elements it does not annihilate them but indicates their significance in the hands of Christ, who speaks here of his reconciliation and of being nourished unto life eternal. Thus, the Church of Christ stands with this sacrament of peace and reconciliation between cross and resurrection and the return of Christ.

In this Supper the Church does not receive a special brand

of ontological salvation in distinction from the salvation received through faith. Those who make the Lord's Supper a matter of "ontology," which would eliminate in principle the blessing of believing,[62] are able temporarily to give the Supper the appearance of very special worth. On this basis they can criticize the Church of the Lord which does not live sufficiently in the light of this "ontology." But if this ontology of the Lord's Supper breaks through the limits of belief, the bond of the Supper to the Word will inevitably weaken, and consequently the certainty of these ontological experiences runs the danger of becoming uncertainty or irrational mystical experience. There seems to be almost a law for the celebration of the Lord's Supper. The signs of the Supper can keep their value and significance only if they are not detached from the word of promise. If they are so detached, everything becomes illusory and the signs lose the value that they originally possessed. They come to stand apart from the hands of Christ, and become unrecognizable.

The correct appreciation of the Lord's Supper is not a matter of theology. Theology can ponder the meaning of the words and the meaning of the Supper as instituted by Christ. Only the believing use of it, however, will lead to the true fruit of the Lord's Supper. And when we reflect on this fruit in churchly confessions and forms we encounter a question which is connected with every celebration of the Supper, namely, the question about the communion with Christ. It need not surprise us that historically this question often came to the foreground. The Reformed doctrine of the Lord's Supper, which does not intend to be symbolistic because it sees the symbol in the light of its institution, through which signs have "become" sacraments, is also greatly interested in the reality of this communion.

This is the question that has been repeatedly directed toward the Reformed doctrine of the Lord's Supper: can one still speak justifiedly of the "mystery" in the Supper, namely, the real presence of Christ in the Lord's Supper?

---

62. Cf. Ridderbos' defense, *ibid.*, p. 33. Cf. also J. G. Woelderink, *Pastoraat rond het avondmaal*, 1942, pp. 87f.

CHAPTER ELEVEN

THE REAL PRESENCE

WE HAVE pointed out emphatically that the dilemma between symbol and reality must be considered unacceptable. Nevertheless, the reproach of symbolism continues to play a role. While it is often acknowledged that Calvin, for instance, cannot be interpreted in the categories of Zwinglian sacramental doctrine, many nevertheless claim that neither Calvin nor Reformed sacramental doctrine in general really allows for the presence of Christ in the Lord's Supper.

This presence of Christ has come to be a central issue of late. From all sides there is pressure to admit the real presence of Christ in the Supper and to give this truth fitting emphasis. Protestants, especially in their polemics with Rome, urge that they will have nothing to do with *nuda signa*. In addition, there are new discussions between Lutherans and Reformed, who had differed already in the sixteenth century about the presence of Christ in the Lord's Supper and who now wonder whether the old dispute should be kept alive. The Reformed, in particular, declare that they, too, adhere to a *praesentia realis,* and differ with the Lutherans only about the manner of Christ's presence.

In spite of many such statements, the reproach continues to be heard from the Roman Catholic as well as from the Lutheran side that the Reformed doctrine of the Lord's Supper reveals a dearth of "sacramental reality," especially with regard to the comforting and saving real presence of Jesus Christ in the Lord's Supper. The Reformed, they say, do speak of this presence, but at the same time they reject the notion of a separate sacramental grace. Hence, they conclude, for Reformed theology the sacrament is nothing but a strengthening of subjective faith.

The question before us is very real and important, and has direct bearing on the meaning and significance of the Lord's Supper, for the presence of Christ in the Supper is such a profound matter that one can only speak of it with great seriousness. Our reflections must touch the deepest reality of the sacrament, so it is fitting that we should speak of the presence of Christ only with the greatest care. What is meant by that *praesentia realis?* Is it more than a reference to the promise of Christ before his ascension: "Lo, I am with you always, even unto the end of the world" (Matt. 28:20), or to that other word: "Where two or three are gathered together in my name, there am I in the midst of them" (Matt. 18:20)? It seems to me that especially in a time when the sacramental reality is at stake, one must speak with great clarity of Christ's presence in the Lord's Supper, so that the declaration that the Reformed sacramental doctrine also knows of such a "reality" may be free of all vagueness and the seriousness of the controversy about the presence of Christ in the Supper may be understood.[1]

It is important that the Reformed, when speaking of the reality of Christ in the Lord's Supper, have made it clear that they were not agreeing with the Roman doctrine of transubstantiation. Yet they also differed from the Lutherans, who confessed in a well-known formula that Christ is present in the Lord's Supper in, with, and under the signs of bread and wine. In opposition to the symbolization of the Supper by Zwingli and others, Luther pointed to the words of institution and declared that, although bread and wine are not transubstantiated, Christ nevertheless is present in the Supper.

There has been much ado about this doctrine, especially about the question how Luther and the Lutherans themselves imagined this presence; and it is not easy to give a clear presentation of the Lutheran view. The discussions are especially concerned with the relation between Luther's doctrine of ubiquity and his doctrine of the Supper. We may leave these discussions for what

---

1. See regarding the questions about Christ's presence in the Lord's Supper: H. Berkhof, *De hervatting van een confessioneel gesprek. Onder eigen vaandel,* III (1938), 114ff.; H. Gollwitzer, "Die Abendmahlsfrage als Aufgabe kirchlicher Lehre," *Theol. Aufsätze für Karl Barth,* 1936; Gollwitzer, *Coena Domini,* 1937; H. C. von Hase, *Die Gegenwart Christi in der Kirche,* 1934; M. H. Bolkestein, *Het heilig avondmaal,* 1947; W. F. Dankbaar, *De sacramentsleer van Calvijn,* 1941, pp. 180ff.; "De tegenwoordigheid van Christus in het H. Avondmal," *VT,* 1952, pp. 33ff.; Vilmos Vajta, *Die Theologie des Gottesdienstes bei Luther,* 1952, pp. 157-195; A. F. N. Lekkerkerker, *De Reformatie in de crisis,* 1949; "Woord en werkelijkheidsopenbaring," *Kerk en Theologie,* I, 35ff.

they are, since it is at least clear that the two doctrines are coherent[2] and that Luther advanced his doctrine of ubiquity in order to show how Christ's bodily presence is possible and actual. It certainly was not Luther's intention to involve himself in all sorts of spatial speculations. He was concerned with the real, comforting, and gracious presence of Christ. Even so, one can clearly discern the coherence with his doctrine of ubiquity when, with the help of this doctrine, he advances many refinements of the *praesentia realis.* Luther, and the Lutherans with him, deny that it is impossible that Christ's body is really present because he is sitting at the right hand of God in heaven. They reply that the possibility of the *praesentia realis* is essential for the veracious comforting of the presence of Christ in the Supper, for our benefit and to encourage us in all temptations.[3]

These connections evoke all sorts of questions, because in the Lutheran doctrine of "communicatio idiomatum" Christ's human nature participates in the attributes of divine nature, especially in the ubiquity. This, however, does not yet prove the specific presence of Christ in the Lord's Supper. Grass remarks correctly that "this argumentation on the basis of hypostatic union leads to the ubiquity of Christ as man since the beginning of his life on earth."[4] He then asks whether this line of thinking does not prove too much, namely, Christ's omnipresence not only in the Lord's Supper but everywhere. "What advantages then could the Supper elements still have?"[5] But for Luther there is a way to pass from ubiquity to the *praesentia realis* to the *hic et nunc* of the *praesentia realis in coena.* The latter is a gracious presence, limited for us to this encounter, in which he wants to be close to us in a specific manner. Straight through the infinity of omnipresence breaks the light of this comforting *hic et nunc* in Luther's doctrine of the Lord's Supper. Luther is concerned with a "redemptive interest, with the presence of grace." Thus the ubiquity becomes, after all, a device which is hurriedly counterbalanced by the line of nonubiquity, the line of the presence of Christ in the Lord's Supper. Precisely because this religious motif

---

2. H. Grass, *Die Abendmahlslehre bei Luther und Calvin,* 1940, p. 51.
3. P. Schempp, "Das Abendmahl bei Luther," *EvT,* 1935, p. 292.
4. Grass, *op. cit.,* p. 55.
5. *Ibid.* "The decisive question for Luther was not the How, but the Why of the presence of Christ," namely, for us, unto our salvation (V. Vajta, *op. cit.,* p. 178).

in the Lutheran doctrine is essential to it,[6] it raises questions directly related to the Reformed doctrine of the Lord's Supper.

Nevertheless, it is impossible for the Lutherans to separate the religious motif from the form in which it is elaborated. The religious motif becomes visible in the emphasis with which this real, bodily presence is taught as the comfort of salvation. It is a matter of the true body and blood of Christ as they are present before us in the form of bread and wine, as Augustine teaches. We hear in the Apology that Christ's body and blood are "truly and substantially" present "with the visible things, bread and wine."[7]

The "true" and "veracious" returns repeatedly in connection with this presence, for instance, in the Smalkald articles,[8] while in the Formula Concordiae the doctrine of the Lord's Supper is summarized when the question is affirmatively answered: "whether in the Lord's Supper the true blood and body of our Lord Jesus Christ is truly and essentially present, distributed with bread and wine, and received with the mouth by all those who use this sacrament...."[9]

It is striking that two sorts of interpretations can be given here: the one clearly declares that in the Lord's Supper only bread and wine are present, and the other — the most dangerous — partly agrees with the words of the Lutherans by holding to the "veracious presence of the true, essential, living body and blood of Christ in the Lord's Supper, but that happens spiritually, through faith."[10] The Lutheran protest is especially directed against this second view, against the "spiritual" understanding of the presence of Christ, which is also clearly an attack against the core of the Reformed doctrine of the Lord's Supper. In response, the Lutherans pose that the "in, with, and under"[11] refers not merely to the efficacy of Christ's body and blood, but to himself, to his own presence, even though "we do not know — and we should not know — how that happens or how it is in the

6. "Truly present under the form of bread and wine in the Lord's Supper" (Art. X). Cf. the Latin text: "vere adsint et distribuantur vescentibus." The *Variata* of 1540 reads: "cum pane et vino." Cf. O. Fricke, *Die Christologie des Joh. Brenz*, 1927, p. 258; O. Ritschl, *Dogmengesch. des Prot.*, IV (1927), chs. LVI, LVIII.
7. *Apologie* (Müller, *Bekenntnisschriften*, p. 164).
8. *Ibid.*, p. 320.
9. *Ibid.*, p. 538.
10. *Ibid.*, p. 539.
11. "Under the bread, with the bread, in the bread" (*ibid.*, p. 654).

bread."[12] The real presence is in this sense "the true heart of the Lutheran doctrine of the Lord's Supper."[13]

It was inevitable that attempts were made repeatedly to find the real difference between Lutherans and Reformed. Was there a truly religious difference or only a difference in the theological formulation of a common motif, namely, that of the comforting presence of Christ? This question has once again come to the fore, especially in the form that perhaps now — after more than four centuries — it is possible to take the controversy between the two confessions to a higher level. Especially Gollwitzer has occupied himself with this question. He acknowledges the great importance of Christ's presence in the Lord's Supper and emphasizes that the Reformed also taught such a real presence of Christ and that they would not consider making the Lord's Supper only an act of believing subjectivity.[14] Has there still remained an essentially religious difference when — as it is often expressed — the crux of the matter is not a difference between *praesentia realis* or not, but a difference regarding the *mode* of this presence?[15]

How must this be understood: a difference in the mode, the manner of presence? Is that difference so important as long as both confessions are concerned with Christ's comforting, real presence? And is not Gollwitzer's remark understandable: "One is tempted to ask whether the differences were really so great as they were thought to be."[16] Or does the sharp Lutheran rejection point to a deeper difference which goes beyond theological formulations and touches upon the comfort of this presence? And does this sharpness then perhaps correspond to Calvin's defense, when he continues to deny the *praesentia invisibilis* and the ubiquity of the body of Christ in spite of all attempts at reconciliation?[17]

There are some who answer these last questions affirmatively and who continue to speak emphatically of the great gap between

12. Cf. Grass, *op. cit.*, p. 116.
13. Gollwitzer, *Coena Domini*, p. 133.
14. Gollwitzer, in *Theol. Aufsätze*, p. 281.
15. Cf. also G. C. van Niftrik, "Het avondmaal," *VT*, 1949, p. 54.
16. Gollwitzer, *Coena Domini*, p. 153.
17. Cf. Van Niftrik, "Luther en Calvijn over het Avondmaal," *VT*, 1949, p. 63. Cf. Polman, *Onze Ned. Geloofsbelijdenis*, IV, 237, regarding Calvin's acknowledging the "religious motives" of the Roman Catholic and Lutheran Churches and their doctrines of the *praesentia realis*.

Lutherans and Reformed. Werner Elert, for instance, sees the core of the conflict in the so-called "myth of localization," that is to say, in the thought that according to the Reformed, Christ's body is in a certain place in heaven. He thinks this to be a myth, which he finds in Augustine, Zwingli, and Calvin. This myth makes the *hic et nunc* of the presence of Christ in the Lord's Supper impossible.[18] "All strenuous efforts to minimize the difference between Calvin and Luther regarding the question of the 'how' of the real presence of Christ's body are for that reason doomed to fail." Given the myth of localization, he says, one can hold only to a "quasi-presence," and this is therefore not a matter of minor importance, but of "two theologies, two beliefs," between which no compromise is possible, not even in the light of the new exegetic situation. For the Reformed cannot possibly speak of real presence, since the Spirit comes in place of the spatially distant body of Christ. Christ can be near us and fulfill his promise only if he is really present in the body. "He who understands this differently, speaks falsely when he speaks of presence" (p. 470). Elert says that the aim of the Lord's Supper cannot be "to lift our hearts up to heaven, for if he comes to us, he does not expect that we lift ourselves up to heaven." "If he gives us his body, we have no business seeking him in distant spaces. That is the way we understand his real presence."

The Reformed doctrine of the presence of Christ in the Lord's Supper is here clearly marked as a lie. It is no more than false appearance. Elert points to the "clear and decisive" statement of Calvin: "as if he were present in the body," in which, according to Elert (p. 468), the whole structure of Calvin's teaching on the Lord's Supper is revealed, up to the last edition of his *Institutes* of 1559. There he writes that Christ proves his power from heaven wherever he wills and that "He shows his presence in power and strength, is always among his own people, and breathes his life upon them, and lives in them, sustaining them, strengthening, quickening, keeping them unharmed, as if he were present in the body" (*Inst.*, IV, XVII, 18).

Elert, and others with him, know, of course, that Reformed theology speaks of the real presence of Christ in the Lord's Supper; but they do not see how this presence can be taken quite seriously, and they wonder why we do not prefer to speak of the presence of the Holy Spirit instead of the presence of Christ.

18. W. Elert, *Der Christliche Glaube*, 1940, pp. 468ff.

The big question is whether this presence is indeed to be interpreted as a "quasi-presence" only. Are Calvin's statements regarding the presence of Christ perhaps not to be taken so seriously, or do they really express a basic motif of his doctrine of the Lord's Supper? And has perhaps his emphasis on this real presence something to do with his rejection of Zwingli? When Gregory Dix discusses the statements in Calvin's *Institutes* regarding this presence[19] and reminds us especially of the fact that according to Calvin the true and real communion with the body and blood of the Lord is given to us under the signs of the Lord's Supper, and that believers receive the body and the blood, not "solely by imagination or understanding of mind, but to enjoy the thing itself as nourishment of eternal life" (*Inst.*, IV, XVII, 19), Dix adds, "But such traditional language must not mislead us as to his real meaning" (p. 633). With all his appreciation for the warmth and the awareness of reality of Calvin, Dix is nevertheless of the opinion that Calvin has not seen the difficulty, that Christ did not give us his Spirit, but his body. "The last supper is not Pentecost, even if one leads to the other. The real eucharistic action is for Calvin individual and internal, not corporate" *(ibid.)*. This criticism, which runs parallel to that of the Lutherans in former and later times,[20] stands diametrically opposed to the seriousness with which Calvin spoke of the communion with Christ's body and blood.[21]

Already in 1887 Bavinck pointed to the characteristic element of Calvin's doctrine of the Supper, when he said that he was struck by Calvin's emphasis on the real presence. "He can hardly find words powerful enough to show that he adheres to the real, essential, veracious presence of Christ's body and blood in the Lord's Supper." Bavinck, too, declares that the difference between Calvin and his Lutheran and Roman Catholic opponents lies in the manner of that presence.[22] To be sure, Calvin calls the physical, spatial presence "spiritual," but his opponents interpret this incorrectly as unreal and imaginary (p. 172), as a presence

19. E.g., Gregory Dix, *The Shape of the Liturgy*, 1949, p. 363: "Nevertheless Calvin will not agree with Zwingli, that communion is merely a 'bare sign.' There is a presence of Christ at the eucharist — he does hesitate to call it a 'Real Presence.' "

20. Cf. E. Mersch, *Le corps mystique du Christ*, II (1951), 422, where we find the same criticism.

21. Cf. Niesel, *Calvins Lehre vom Abendmahl*, p. 91.

22. H. Bavinck, "Calvijns leer over het avondmaal," in *Kennis en leven*, 1922, p. 171.

that exists only in the believing subject or in man's imagination. Calvin was not satisfied with Zwingli's view that the Lord's Supper provides no other communion with Christ than the benefits obtained for us at the cross (p. 173). According to Calvin, says Bavinck, there was a still deeper communion, "a communion not only of the benefits, but with the person of Christ himself, with his own flesh and blood." It is thereby not just a matter of the power that flows from the crucified body to the believers, as Calvin's opponents have it (p. 176), but a matter of the communion with Christ's person, a hidden but very real communion. It is not a matter of his power, but of himself (p. 177). Calvin rejects the dilemma between physical-spatial presence (Lutherans) and presence in the "spirit" (Zwingli). He rejects both Roman Catholic realism and Zwinglian spiritualism and reaches far beyond these two. It is a communion with Christ through the efficacy of the Holy Spirit (p. 178). This communion is not something new, as if it was not given until the Lord's Supper; but it is signified, confirmed and strengthened in the Lord's Supper. And thus, says Bavinck, this doctrine has also entered the Reformed confessions.

The exact character of this doctrine is "often not clearly realized" (p. 181); and in contrast with any superficializing interpretation of the Lord's Supper it must be maintained that "the Reformed also adhere to a real, veracious presence of Christ, yes, also of his own natural flesh and blood" (ibid.). The spiritual presence is "no less, but all the more true and essential" (p. 182).

We come close to the core of the controversy here, for we find the same emphasis in the confessions and the forms. We read in the Heidelberg Catechism that "with His crucified body and shed blood He Himself feeds and nourishes to everlasting life" (Q. 75), and that "His crucified body and shed blood are the true food and drink of our souls unto eternal life," and that we are "really partakers of His true body and blood, through the working of the Holy Spirit" (Q. 79).

We find the same emphases also in the Confession of Faith, where it is confessed that we receive the true body and blood of Christ our only Savior in our souls, for the support of our spiritual life" (Art. 35). The Lord's Supper is a spiritual table "at which Christ communicates Himself with all His benefits... nourishing, strengthening, and comforting our poor comfortless souls by the eating of His flesh and refreshing them by the drinking of His blood" (Art. 35). The form for the Lord's Supper speaks in the same spirit: "in order that our burdened and contrite hearts, through the power of the Holy Spirit, may be nourished and refreshed with His true body and blood, yea with Him, true God and man, the only heavenly bread." And when an objection was raised at the Synod of La Rochelle against the phrasing of the Confessio Gallicana, which confesses that Christ feeds us and makes us alive through his Spirit with the "substance" of his body and blood,[23] this phrasing was deliberately maintained. The synod stated that this word "substance" did not mean a blending or change, but served to express that spiritual relation by which we become his and he becomes ours. It was furthermore said that we not only have communion in his merits and his gifts, but with himself.[24]

It becomes evident here, as in Calvin and the Reformed confessions in general, that special emphasis is laid upon the unbreakable relation between the communion with Christ's benefits and with himself in the one communion of salvation. The concern is focused on personal communion with Christ, not on an impersonal gift, for the gift comes from the Giver.[25] The gift in itself is nothing but an abstraction, having no reality. Christ gives himself, so that faith has communion in his gifts with himself. Only thus can one understand Calvin's doctrine of the Lord's Supper and the nature of the controversy between Lutherans and Reformed.

It has become clear that in the Reformed view there is no completely new gift given in the Supper which is never present apart from the Supper. Calvin's view is in the spirit of Article 22 of the Confession of Faith, which says that through faith (as an instrument) we embrace Christ and that faith "keeps us in communion with Him in all His benefits." The communion of the Lord's Supper stands in direct relation to this. For Calvin the reality of this communion is a matter of the consolation of salvation, of that which is not far away, but close at hand. This is what bears decisive significance for Calvin.[26] Calvin's rejection of transubstantiation and consubstantiation does not mean a dilution of Christ's presence and communion. The "reality" of

23. Conf. Gallicana, Art. 36, in Müller, *op. cit.*
24. Cf. Müller, *op. cit.,* pp. 230f.
25. Cf. Dankbaar, *op. cit.,* p. 187.
26. *Ibid.,* p. 190: "Calvin wanted to maintain the reality of the joy of the Lord's Supper."

which he spoke was not simply a concession to Rome and the Lutherans, but the real, personal presence of the living Lord. It is noteworthy that Calvin, while maintaining the ascension of Christ, speaks continually of our communion with the true body and blood of the Lord.[27] But this is not dissimulation or inconsistency, as so many Lutherans and Anglicans (e.g., Dix) think; it is possible for Calvin to speak in this way because he never considered the body and blood abstractly, as something "substantial" by itself, in the first place.

If Calvin had spoken in such an abstract sense of the communion with the true body and blood of the Lord, he could not have criticized the Lutherans so regularly. But Calvin continues to speak of this communion with Christ's body because he is certain that the body and blood of Christ pertain to the act of Christ's self-offering, of his personal self-surrender.[28] This has nothing to do with spiritualization; he is hereby thinking of the reference to the death of Christ and the salvation of reconciliation that is contained in it. Calvin thinks always of that offer of Christ which is his personal, reconciling self-surrender, not behind, but in the surrender of his body and blood in death. His criticism against Rome and the Lutherans — one could say — is directed against the "depersonalization" which is undeniably present both in transubstantiation and in the doctrine of consubstantiation. "Body" and "blood" are here placed by themselves as "substances" that form the point of departure of true communion. When La Rochelle maintained the word "substance" in the Confessio Gallicana, his concern lay with substance in a different sense. It was a matter of Christ himself in his gift, and this personal insight Calvin thinks was lost with Rome and also with the Lutherans. It is not at all a playing with words to say that it was precisely the communion with "substantial physicality" in the Lutheran doctrine of the Lord's Supper that threatened the *praesentia Christi realis* in the Supper.

The Lutheran motif of the proximity and comfort of Christ is rightly to be respected; yet this does not guarantee that Christ's presence is discussed by the Lutherans in a responsibly scriptural manner. The Lutherans place a great emphasis on "physicality," on the body and blood of the Lord, as the only way in which he could be present. For Calvin, however, the simple and clear

27. *Ibid.*
28. *Ibid.*, p. 191.

words of Scripture about the ascension of Christ, about his no longer being with us in his bodily presence, were decisive. Therein lay a determinative factor for his view of the Lord's Supper. Calvin was not at all concerned with spiritualizing or subjectivizing, but with the *praesentia realis* according to the mode of its elevation.

Repeated attempts have been made to compel Calvin to acknowledge that in this mode Christ is present in the Supper in his power, the power of his Spirit, and not by his own presence. Would it not be better for Calvin to be silent about Christ's presence? Should he not rather speak of the presence of the Spirit? Calvin refused to follow this advice, which can be explained only by his remarkably sound intuition. In many respects Calvin was ahead of his time; he saw that the crux of the matter lay with the presence of Christ and with our communion with his true body and blood, but that the "body" and "blood" are to be understood in terms of Christ's act of reconciliation, not in themselves.

One can oppose Calvin by saying that his concern is not with the presence of Christ himself in the Supper, but with his power. This dilemma, however, simply did not exist for Calvin. He did not seek a relation between some distant source of power and the effect of that power, but the living presence of Jesus Christ in his flesh and blood, in the reality and forever valid power of reconciliation and blessing of his sacred offering. That is why Calvin is not affected by such as Gregory Dix, who reminds us that Christ promised not only his Spirit, but also his body. To speak thus of Christ's "body" is to misunderstand the fundamental fact about the body and the blood, namely, the act of reconciliation. That is why the emphasis of the Reformed confessions and theology was not a confession or a desire to "outbid" in declarations of reality, but a responsible manner of speaking which is understandable only in the light of the rejection of all substantializing and depersonalizing of the gift of the Lord's Supper.

In thus making such strong statements about the *communio,* the reality of the true body and blood of the Lord, the Reformed Church and theology has rendered a service to reflection which later was also accepted by many Lutherans — often without emphatic vindication of Calvin — in a different, more biblical manner of understanding the significance of the body and blood of Christ. The issue involved did not lie in what Elert called the "myth of localization," but in the outlook on the personal presence of Christ's saving work in his ascension as well, and therein of himself with his comforting proximity.

In the discussion above we raised the fundamental question regarding the real presence of Christ in the Lord's Supper. This becomes further evident from the fact that in the Lutheran interpretation of the Lord's Supper the real mystery is displaced, just as it is displaced even more in transubstantiation. We see nowhere more clearly than here that reference to the mystery does not guarantee a correct interpretation of the Supper, for everything depends on *where* this mystery is acknowledged and confessed. This appears already in the doctrine of transubstantiation, where the mystery undergoes duplication in the sacrament in the transition from the mystery to the sacrament; here it is no longer understood that the mystery of the sacrament can be nothing other than the New Testament mystery.[29] It appears also in the Lutheran doctrine, however, when the union with Christ's body and blood comes to the fore in a very special way.[30] The objection of the Reformed is not of a "logical" nature, but is directed against the *locale inclusio* which went together with an abstract interest in the "body" and "blood" as substances.

In this light, the whole issue becomes clear. Because the Lutherans understood "body" and "blood" differently than Calvin, they missed what the Reformed meant by the real presence and saw there only "a presence of the workings and powers of this body and not the presence of the body itself as it was understood to have been promised in the words that instituted the Lord's Supper."[31] But Calvin himself indicated the way out of this impasse when he criticized those who are not able "to conceive any other partaking of flesh and blood except that which consists in either local conjunction and contact or some gross form of enclosing" (*Inst.*, IV, XVII, 16). Calvin himself thought that he understood some such "other partaking" and he therefore rejected the dilemma between Zwingli and Luther. He was keenly aware of the impure elements in Zwingli's view, especially of his

---

29. Cf. H. de Lubac, *Corpus mysticum. L'eucharistie et l'Eglise au moyen age*, 1948, pp. 51ff.
30. Cf. especially H. Sasse, *Vom Sakrament des Altars, passim,* in his opposition to the Reformed.
31. Cf. Gollwitzer, *Coena Domini,* pp. 145ff., especially p. 148.

neglect of the real presence of Christ;[32] but in spite of that he did not want to accept the *locale inclusio*. Bavinck thinks Calvin's view of the Lord's Supper is unclear. He says that Calvin teaches that Christ, although not physically and locally present in the Supper, is nevertheless verily and essentially present with his person, also with his body and blood.[33] But Bavinck wonders what Calvin means by this communion with Christ's own flesh and blood.

We think, however, that Calvin is not at all unclear. He thought of a participation in which body and blood did not occur as isolated substances, but wherein communion was held with Christ himself in his true body and blood, with Christ in his offering. Here lay the difference with the Lutherans. To be sure, Gollwitzer declares that "Luther and his disciples had no interest in the physical presence as such," but he adds: "Over against certain statements of Luther and his disciples, it is often not easy to overcome the suspicion of a narrow, substantial concept of reality."[34] One can indeed say that the Lutherans were not interested in the physicality of Christ's body for its own sake, but they did believe that the communion of the Supper could be purely maintained only if one had communion with Christ's body and blood in corporeal presence. In polemics, the Lutheran religious motif of proximity and consolation obtained the form that Christ's presence could not be represented other than as the substantial presence of his "body" and "blood." Consubstantiation was not primarily intended as a parallel to transsubstantiation, because Luther was not concerned with the distinction between substance and accidents, so that one wonders whether the term consubstantiation is of any value for the definition of the Lutheran doctrine of the Lord's Supper. But bodily presence was indeed of the essence. Gollwitzer thinks that the actual tendencies of the Lutheran doctrine of the Lord's Supper have often been misunderstood, but then he gives this representation: "For this doctrine it is unrelinquishable that the Lord's Supper is not only a matter of the real presence of Christ, but of the distribution of the true, natural blood of

32. Cf. J. Beckmann, *Vom Sakrament bei Calvin*, p. 105, and Bavinck, *Kennis en leven*, p. 533.
33. Bavinck, *op. cit.*, p. 534.
34. Gollwitzer, *Coena Domini*, pp. 149f.

Christ in his own — it cannot be put differently — corporeal (albeit transfigured) substance."[35]

Gollwitzer also agrees with the representation by Vilmar, according to which it is not a matter of "it" but of "you" in the Lutheran Supper. He therefore rejects emphatically the new Lutheran interpretations which see body and blood as "man" or as a reference to the cross. No, "the whole struggle of the Lutherans in the sixteenth century was meaningful only as long as body and blood were quite literally meant as *externae res; as soon* as it is said that they are not to be understood 'as things,' . . . the way is open for the personalizing of the doctrine of the Lord's Supper, and closed for what was really meant in the older Lutheran doctrine of the Supper by *unio sacramentalis, manducatio oralis et indignorum*."[36] That is the only way, says Gollwitzer, that one can understand the vexation of the Reformed (p. 285).

These representations of the Lutheran doctrine are, I think, quite correct. But they are also full of consequences for our estimate of the controversy of the sixteenth century, and for our understanding of the struggle about the real presence. Gollwitzer asks whether it can be taken ill of the Reformed that they rejected the Lutheran doctrine in that form, which "no Lutheran today is able to hold in its original meaning without weakening re-interpretation" *(ibid.)*. He points to the contemporary exegetical situation *(ibid.)* and asks who would be willing to go back to the original understanding of "body" and "blood" as material things. He thinks therefore that the Lutherans have arrived at a "mutuality of question" with the Reformed, and that, he says, has great consequences (p. 290).

The question arises here whether perhaps such profound changes are also necessary in the Reformed doctrine of the Lord's Supper. This question is of more than historical importance because the Supper of the Christ himself is at stake. Gollwitzer thinks that the Reformed doctrine of the Lord's Supper was indeed faulty. To be sure, he holds that it often was misappreciated and that it often was subjectivistically understood (p. 295), and that Calvin's rejection of the *manducatio indignorum* was not intended to affect the objectivity of the Lord's Supper (p. 296); but that does not mean that he thinks it to be a matter of a choice between Luther and Calvin. He speaks very carefully of

35. Gollwitzer, in *Theol. Aufsätze für K. Barth*, p. 284.
36. *Ibid.*

Calvin when he writes that Barth has overcome the rationalism, subjectivism, and spiritualism of which the Reformed were accused, "insofar as it actually was present" (pp. 294-96). Evidently, the dangers of the Reformed doctrine of the Lord's Supper lie with spiritualism. Reformed theology is inclined — "and it is also present in Calvin — to let man's *spiritus* come to the foreground because of its name-relation to the *Spiritus Sanctus*, and to minimize the corporeal" (p. 296).

Gollwitzer apparently means that the Reformed have not always clearly distinguished the spiritual (the human spirit) from the Holy Spirit, as if the human spirit, in distinction from the corporeal, would be a suitable organ for the receiving of revelation (p. 287). However, this is more a warning in the Reformed direction than an indication of a real error in their doctrine of the Lord's Supper and their criticism of the Lutheran doctrine of the Supper. There is no doubt that spiritualism always remains a serious danger, which entails the further danger of subjectivizing the sacrament if everything is oriented toward the human "spirit" as the receptor of the revelation. But such spiritualism is not at all found in the Reformed doctrine of the Lord's Supper. Rather, spiritualism, which devaluates corporeality and sees in the sacraments nothing but fundamentally useless signs, is emphatically rejected. It is reasonable, therefore, to ask whether in Reformed circles there exists indeed a preference for such concepts as *spiritus* with regard to the gift of the Lord's Supper. We do not find such a preference in Calvin, and we read in Article 35 of the Confession that Christ is the living bread which is eaten and which is received through faith in the spirit. The Lord's Supper has been instituted to represent the spiritual and heavenly bread.

This is apparently not a matter of an anthropological distinction regarding a more suitable organ to receive the divine benefaction in Christ, and not a matter of preference for the spirit or soul in distinction to the body; for this article continues that the sacraments are not given to us without meaning and in vain, but that they are ordained and that God works in us all that he presents before our eyes in these sacred signs, even though the manner goes beyond our comprehension, as the working of the Spirit is hidden and incomprehensible. There is also later mention of the human spirit; but then, too, there is not a trace of spiritualism, but it turns out to be a matter of the faithful receiving of Christ's body and blood. The decision regarding spiritualism always falls here: do the signs become vain, empty, and inferior, unproportioned to the grace of God? At this point, Reformed theology has followed Calvin and from the very beginning has drawn the line of demarcation which Gollwitzer now — correctly — wants to draw over against the threat of the real presence of Christ in the Lord's Supper.

We have seen that the Reformed doctrine of the Lord's Supper has often been accused of speaking of communion with the true body and blood of Christ without meaning those words seriously, because the bodily presence of Christ in bread and wine was denied. It is curious that the newer Lutherans, who do not accept the older Lutheran substantialistic interpretation without modifications, continue to voice this reproach of inconsistency. Althaus, for example, starts from the point of view that according to Calvin the gift of the Lord's Supper consists of "Christ's glorified body and blood" and that he therefore should come to the conclusion that Christ is also bodily present in the Supper.

Calvin's inconsistency would lie in the fact that he teaches the presence of Christ's true body and blood in the Lord's Supper, but that he rejects his bodily presence.[37] The Holy Spirit must then bridge the gap and connect the believers with Christ's true body and blood. "This doctrine asks the impossible of us. Presence of the body and blood of Christ through the Holy Spirit in faith — that is an impossible thought. The corporeal can only be corporeally present, can only be corporeally understood. That is its essence."[38] That, according to Althaus, is why Westphal's criticism of Calvin was correct. Calvin supposedly tried to connect what cannot be connected. If one speaks of communion with the glorified body and blood of Christ, one must also speak of the corporeal presence in the Lord's Supper. That is why, in the light of the basic assumption of the early Reformers, the Lutheran solution is unavoidable. But it was Luther's and Calvin's mistake "that the Lord's Supper was supposed to be a matter of Christ's heavenly [corporeal] presence," a view that has become untenable.

Althaus' view is based on the assumption that Calvin and the Reformed interpretation of the Lord's Supper wanted to establish

37. P. Althaus, *Die lutherische Abendmahlslehre in der Gegenwart*, 1931, p. 35.
38. *Ibid.*, p. 36.

a substantial relation with the body and blood of Christ. Dank-baar, however, correctly denied this with respect to Calvin when he said that Calvin's concern lay with the humiliated and cruci-fied body of Christ.[39] This does not contradict the idea that be-lievers have communion in the Lord's Supper with the glorified Christ, and that he is present in the Supper, for such a contrast between the glorified Christ and the Christ who offered himself is nothing but an abstraction. Christ's surrender of his body and blood is not an event that can be detached from his person, but it is his act, and in the reality and power of that act Christ him-self is in the full sense present in the Lord's Supper. In the Lord's Supper, the believer has communion with the glorified Christ because he has communion with his body and blood. This com-munion is not a communion with Christ's glorified "body" and "blood" as a substantial, isolated reality, but a communion with him in his offering and in his true body and blood, with him "who has become flesh and was crucified in history and whose flesh is now in heaven."[40]

In precisely this way Calvin has overcome the substantial mode of thinking, which always has had the unintended character of impersonality; and therein Calvin's doctrine of the Lord's Supper becomes clear and pure, even though Calvin realized that he could only speak stammeringly of this real presence (cf. *Inst.,* IV, XVII, 32). Our communion with Christ in the Supper is not an isolated "ontological" communion, in contrast with the com-munion which believers possess with him in faith, but it is the communion with the crucified Lord who is now glorified. Herein we encounter in the time of the Reformation — and in contrast to the accusation of spiritualism — a pure intuition which issues from Scripture itself and in which future reference is made already to what later would be more generally acknowledged, namely, that one can never speak meaningfully of the body and blood of Christ without remembering his surrender unto death and the giving of his "flesh" for the life of the world.

The confession of the presence of Christ in the Lord's Supper is therefore not a matter of spiritualization, of which the Re-formed doctrine of the Supper has so often been accused. At the same time, this doctrine does full justice to the limit imposed on the manner of Christ's presence by the reality of his ascension.

39. Dankbaar, *De sacramentsleer van Calvijn*, p. 185.
40. Dankbaar, *De tegenwoordigheid van Christus in het avondmaal*, p. 36.

The Reformers were aware that this presence could not be identical with that of Christ's second coming, whereas this difference never became clear in Lutheran theology. The issue was linked with the significance that is laid on faith in the celebration of the Lord's Supper. By pointing at this faith (as distinguished from contemplation), the Reformers did not intend to minimize the reality of Christ's presence, but to indicate its nature. "The 'already' of the promised present and the 'not yet' of the future still to come should not outbalance each other, but should come together and together render the true and full comfort of faith."[41] That is also why Elert's criticism of the self-elevation of man's heart in the *sursum corda* is very unjust and impure, because this *sursum corda* to which we are also called by the form of the Lord's Supper is not at all to be separated from the reality of the cross and from Christ's true body and blood — the crucified body and the shed blood — but finds its direction and orientation in that. Christ's ascension is not a devaluation, but the acknowledgment of the full significance of the historical cross and its saving significance and therefore also of the meaning of the remembrance and the *sursum corda* contained in that.

It cannot be denied that a vacuum becomes visible in the Lutheran doctrine of the Lord's Supper rather than in the Reformed doctrine, because there is the permanent danger that the eschatological expectation — the new presence — is obscured by this presence already realized (as in the Roman Catholic doctrine of the eucharist). It is no exaggeration to say that the controversy about the real presence of Christ in the Lord's Supper ultimately comes down to a different insight into the significance of the return of Christ and the significance of the eschatological orientation of faith. This does not mean that speaking of the presence of Christ in the Lord's Supper automatically implies a danger to eschatological expectation, to the "not yet." If that were the case, Roman Catholics, Lutherans, and Reformed would agree on this point, for they all speak of a presence of Christ in the Lord's Supper. Hence everything depends on the manner of Christ's presence in the Supper.

The confession of Christ's presence does not mean that the difference between this presence and the *parousia* is not clearly seen, for we also speak of the reality of Christ in the Church

41. Gollwitzer, *Coena Domini*, p. 147.

apart from the Lord's Supper, and this presence does not disagree with the preaching of his future coming. The confession
of his presence in the Church is the answer to Christ's promise
that he would not leave us orphans and that he would be in our
midst until the end of the world. Now we see, however, that in
specific reflections about this presence it is sometimes assumed
that this presence goes beyond Christ's presence through the
Holy Spirit and through faith. This is clear from the fact that,
as happens often with Lutheran theologians, mention is made
of such a presence in the light of the incarnation, while it does
not become clear what the ascension means. Since it is the
physical presence that is emphatically defended against other
forms of presence, it is understandable that from the Lutheran
side[42] as well as from the Roman Catholic side there is repeated
mention of this relation between *praesentia in coena* and
parousia.[43]

This latter is not mere theologizing, but a reflection that had
to arise from the New Testament in the light of its longing anticipation of the return of Christ. The question is whether Christ's
supposed physical presence now does not automatically place in
the shadow the expectation of his future physical return.[44] When
one identifies the Church as body of Christ with the Kingdom of
God, or when one speaks of the physical presence of Christ in the
Supper or eucharist, he may not consciously be anticipating the
second coming of Christ, but in the light of this view it nevertheless becomes unclear what the basis is for the expectation of
Christ's ultimate coming when he will appear on the clouds of
heaven (Luke 21:27), and in which is fulfilled what John says
to the disciples: "we shall see him even as he is" (I John 3:2).

The New Testament message regarding the return of Christ
cannot be approached exclusively by way of the anthropological
category of "seeing," in the sense that Christ really is already
present now, but that in the future he will be revealed without

42. Cf. especially Gollwitzer's discussion on the relation between Supper
and eschatology, *Coena Domini*, pp. 147ff.
43. Also on the Roman Catholic side the attempt is made to show that
Christ's presence in the eucharist does not mean an "irresponsible anticipation of the future glory of Jesus' return." Cf. H. J. H. M. Fortmann,
*Bijdrage tot het gesprek over de tegenwoordigheid van Christus in de
Eucharistie* (Bundel Kreling, 1953), p. 105.
44. Barth calls the Roman Catholic Church "the exemplary form of this
eschatological Christianity" (*K.D.*, III, 2 [1948], p. 615).

the veils, including the veils of the eucharist. The concept of
seeing, which plays such a great role in the New Testament (cf.
Acts 1:11), is immediately linked with the present Covenant,
in which we do not live in contemplation, but in faith, in the
"not yet" of his ultimate appearance. One cannot "overestimate"
the significance and the value of Christ's presence in his Church
and in the Supper, but one can speak of it in such a manner
that the reason for expecting his future appearance is no longer
clear. That is why one can say that the idea of the "hiddenness"
of Christ's presence can never wholly answer the problematics of
Supper and eschatology. In the Covenant between Pentecost
and *parousia,* the provisionality of this time is not removed by a
presence more direct than is possible in the Word and through
faith.

Our reflection on the presence of Christ in the Lord's Supper
finds its sharp directive here. The unsatisfactory answer of
Lutheran and Roman Catholic theology to the objections against
the *praesentia realis* in these churches points to the critical
function of eschatology in the doctrine of the Lord's Supper.[45]
Those who seek more comfort and assurance here than what is
offered by the gospel, do not really honor the *praesentia Christi*
more than the others. The thesis that this presence is not a matter
of a *sursum corda,* but of an actual coming to us in the sphere
of the physical and in the sphere of the incarnation, is nothing
but a failure to understand the expectation of the New Testament Church, the community of the last days, as the celebration
of the Lord's Supper occurs in that community under the urgency
of this expectation: until he comes.

It is thus clear that the real presence of Christ in the Lord's
Supper is a matter of communion with the glorified Lord, but
that this communion can also be described as communion with
his true body and blood. For the reality of the glorified Lord
cannot be detached from the humiliation of Christ, and can
never be understood as glorification by itself without the meaning
of this glorification in the light of the gospel of reconciliation.

The Reformed doctrine of the *praesentia realis* was not, therefore, a belated accentuating of this presence in response to the
reproaches of the Lutherans and Roman Catholics with their
accentuation of the physical presence of the Lord. The Reformers

45. Cf. T. F. Torrance, "Eschatology and the Eucharist," in *Intercommunion,*
    ed. Baillie and Marsch, 1952, pp. 303-350.

rejected the suggestion that they speak only of the presence of the Holy Spirit and not of the presence of Christ. For although they emphasized that the presence of Christ was a reality for us in the Lord's Supper through the Holy Spirit, they did not thereby intend to replace Christ with the Holy Spirit. The Lutherans have repeatedly misunderstood this "with the Holy Spirit," as if it had been Calvin's intention to teach such a "replacement" and as if the crux of the matter was the attempt to overcome the "unconnectability" between Christ's "heavenly" body and believers on earth by some kind of "bridging" accomplished through the working of the Holy Spirit.[46] This attempt they rejected as unsuccessful and as an underestimation of the significance of the presence of Christ. This interpretation does not reveal the core of the problem that occupied Reformed confession and theology when it spoke of the presence of Christ through the Holy Spirit, for the Reformers did not think in terms of a simple "replacement," but rather in terms of the work of the Trinity in the history of redemption. Thus Christ's promise to send another "Comforter" does not mean a "replacement," but must be understood in the light of the progress of Christ's work (John 14:16). Just as the pneumatological never functions as a threat to Christology in the confession of the Church, so the presence of Christ through the Holy Spirit is no threat to the confession of his real presence.

The presence of Christ is fully presence, as it is a true communion with him and with his reconciling offering. The Reformers did not refuse the suggestion of the Lutherans, to speak only of the presence of the Spirit, because they were stubborn, nor was their speaking of the *praesentia Christi* only an appearance; rather they wanted to continue speaking in this way because their true concern lay with the communion with this Lord. Therein they desired to respect fully the truth of Paul's urgent word which was at the same time full of comfort: "The cup of blessing which we bless, is it not a communion of the blood of Christ? The bread which we break, is it not a communion of the body of Christ?" (I Cor. 10:16).

Paul is so aware of the reality of this communion that he can speak the words: "Ye cannot drink the cup of the Lord, and the cup of demons: ye cannot partake of the table of the

46. For this definition, appeals were made to Calvin, *Inst.*, IV, XVII, 12 and 24.

Lord, and of the table of demons" (I Cor. 10:21). The context — a warning against idolatry (10:14) — shows clearly that Paul wants to point to two sorts of communion that cannot coexist. He is not just prohibiting this twofold communion, but pointing to the impossibility of doing so. One cannot "exercise communion with Christ through the Lord's Supper and simultaneously [commune] with the powers of darkness through the sacrificial repast."[47] The cup of blessing is a true communion with Christ, as is the bread. The reality of this communion is beyond doubt for Paul. The pagan sacrificial repasts were also matters of "communion": "Spirits that work destruction draw them into their communion,"[48] and it is this communion which arouses the jealousy of the Lord (I Cor. 10:22). The communion with Christ is such a penetrating and profound reality that the other communion is made impossible by it.

It is therefore understandable that the Reformed have been unwilling to admit that the reality aspect of the *praesentia realis* could be satisfied by speaking of a communion with the fruits of Christ's work but not with Christ himself. Such a separation was deemed impossible because of the unity of Christ's person and work; and in spite of all accusations that they could not speak concretely of a real presence, the Reformed continued to speak of this presence, the real presence of Christ in the Lord's Supper, because they did not for a moment want to detach the fruits of Christ's reconciliation from his person. One therefore seeks for language (as did Calvin) that expresses this presence, as the Synod of La Rochelle did when it refused to give up the word "substance" in order not to separate Christ from his gifts, or our communion with him from the communion with the power of his offering.

The question arises whether one can speak of a special presence of Christ in the Lord's Supper. Is there a separate, special presence of Christ in the Supper which cannot be enjoyed apart from that Supper? The New Testament makes it clear that believers do not stand in true communion with Christ only in the Lord's Supper. We hear of his promise to be with us until the end of the world, and of his being in the midst of us even though only two or three are gathered together in his name. Furthermore, many references are made to our

---

47. Grosheide, *Commentaar*, p. 351; cf. the impossibility in I Cor. 6:15.
48. Schlatter, *op. cit.*, p. 299.

communion with Christ. To be sure, it is a communion with Christ through the Holy Spirit, but this does not at all minimize the reality of our communion with Christ of which we read that Christ dwells in the hearts of men through faith (Eph. 3:17) and that nothing can separate the believers from the love of Christ (Rom. 8:35).

This communion is represented as something so rich and full of blessing that it cannot be called inferior to the communion with Christ in the Lord's Supper. The latter is not like an interruption of the "desert life" of the community, as if only at certain high moments of life — in the breaking of the bread — as in an oasis of communion, there would be mention of him. Those who think in this way should ask themselves whether the accentuation of this real presence and of this communion does not issue from an awareness of poverty, as if there could be mention of such a communion only at special times. Normal life then becomes, so to speak, a desert, and the Lord's Supper becomes the oasis, an image that does not at all conform to the teaching of the New Testament. Rather, the celebration of the Lord's Supper is a matter of the strengthening of faith through the signs of bread and wine, and every Supper is precisely oriented toward continuous communion with the living Lord, the crucified, resurrected, and glorified Redeemer.

The Lord's Supper does not stand as a meeting isolated from normal life, separated from it by sharp boundaries such as fulfilment and enjoyment versus poverty and privation. The contrary is the case: the Lord's Supper is oriented toward that normal life and toward the communion which Christ promised to us all the days until the end of the world. The crux of the matter is, as Paul says: so that Christ may dwell in our hearts through faith. That is clearly indicated in the form for the Lord's Supper: "that through the operation of Thy Holy Spirit the remembrance of our Lord Jesus Christ and the proclamation of His death may tend to our daily increase in true faith and in blessed fellowship with Christ." We do not see the Lord's Supper as an interruption which stands without relations as a strange mystical rapture, but as a communion exercise in the light of the act and institution of Christ which is oriented toward the fulness of everyday life. We shall see later that this communion of the Lord's Supper also stands in direct relation to our mutual communion, but it is also directed toward daily faith, toward the increase of communion with Christ. The Lord's Supper is not therefore something specifically religious which is distinguished from normal communion with Christ. The call to joy that we hear in connection with the remembrance of the Lord's Supper is a commandment for every day, and for all of life under the new law.

That is why the problem regarding the frequency of the Lord's Supper can be solved only in the light of the meaning of the Supper. What, ultimately, is the reason for this frequency? It is possible that it is sought because of an incorrect interpretation of the Lord's Supper, if the Supper is seen as an actual communion with Christ which interrupts the life of the pilgrim, making it bearable by providing an oasis of remembrance of the Supper celebrated already, and expectation of the Supper yet to be celebrated. In such a desire for frequency, the blessing of communion with the Lord is devaluated. The desire for frequency then begins to cast shadows which are caused by aridity of faith. Frequency can never be a blessing for the Church if the celebration of the Lord's Supper remains an interruption of spiritless life in which the purpose and the consequences of the Lord's Supper are not understood or experienced. There lurks here a form of mysticism which can only be harmful for the life of Christ's Church.

But it is also possible to speak in a different manner of the frequency of the Lord's Supper. Calvin did so when he said that the Lord's Supper has not been instituted to be celebrated once a year, but "to be frequently used among all Christians in order that they might frequently return in memory to Christ's Passion, by such remembrance to sustain and strengthen their faith, and urge themselves to sing thanksgiving to God and to proclaim his goodness; finally, by it to nourish mutual love, and among themselves give witness to this love, and discern its bond in the unity of Christ's body" (*Inst.*, IV, XVII, 44). Here the seeking of frequency is not based on the contrast between desert and oasis, but on the significance of the Lord's Supper for the weakness of faith and for the communion of the Church and for the continual song of praise in normal life.[49] The decision concerning what Calvin calls "the frequent use" of the Lord's Supper lies in the *nature* of the seeking.

49. For the connection between preaching of the Word and the Lord's Supper, cf. G. Delling, *Der Gottesdienst im N.T.*, 1952, pp. 132ff.

Another danger occurs when people are not at all interested in the question of frequency, or in practice even begin to neglect the Lord's Supper. It can then happen that under the influence of a superficial interpretation of the Lord's Supper, one comes to the practical conclusion that the Supper cannot be called "necessary." It has always been true in the Church of Christ that one can try to be wise beyond what is given to us in such a sacred matter only if he is willing to suffer the damage.[50]

The confession of the *praesentia realis* is a profound matter for the Church of Christ. The divergencies and the confusion pertaining to this confession may not keep the community from reflecting on this presence. For the motif which the Lutherans and the Roman Catholics have repeatedly advanced for their doctrine, namely, of the comforting proximity of Christ in the signs, may not be neglected by anyone, even though his intention be to keep this proximity from being connected with considerations that threaten rather than conform to this comfort. Only those who agree with the confession of this communion with the really present Christ, with his body and blood, will be able to understand the connections in which Christ placed the Lord's Supper, the connection with the past, the past of remembrance, the *communio sanctorum,* the daily increase in faith, and the expectation of the blessed future of Jesus Christ in his new presence. These connections are contained in the acts of those who approach the table of the Lord. The Church speaks here already of the blessed communion with Christ in this earthly life,[51] but it does not forget the "not yet" in this blessedness, as Peter is called blessed (Matt. 16:17) and the believer is blessed in hope (Rom. 8:24). The bond of unity that comprises everything is the proclamation of Christ's death with the signs of bread and wine. This proclamation, as an act of the believer, does not compete with the act of Christ and his real presence. Rather, it is also taken up indissolubly until Christ will come in his new presence and faith becomes contemplation.

50. Much has been said about the frequency of the Lord's Supper. See, e.g., Dankbaar, *De sacramentsleer van Calvijn,* pp. 204ff.; Reitsma-van der Veen, *Acta,* VI, 98; H. Bouwman, *Geref. Kerkrecht,* II, p. 441ff.; Van der Leeuw, *Sacramentstheologie,* p. 75.
51. Cf. the form for the Lord's Supper.

CHAPTER TWELVE

UNWORTHY PARTAKERS

NOW THAT WE have spoken of the presence of Christ in the Lord's Supper, we want to discuss a dogmatic point that has played an exceedingly important role in the relation between Rome, the Reformed, and the Lutherans. We mean the celebration of the Lord's Supper by the *indigni,* the so-called *manducatio indignorum.* To be sure, we read in the form for the Lord's Supper — in accordance with the New Testament — that Christ has instituted his Supper only for believers, but since the Church cannot judge the hearts of the communicants in administering the sacrament, the problem always arises about which there has been so much discussion, namely, the relation of the Lord's Supper to those who are not worthy of it.

Manducatio indignorum means that the "unworthy" also participate in the true body and blood of the Lord, albeit that this participation contributes to their perdition. When the Reformed denied this *manducatio indignorum* in their doctrine of the Lord's Supper, the Lutherans and Roman Catholics accused them of violating the objectivity of the sacrament. No matter how much the Lutherans emphasized the correlation between faith and Supper and urged a believing celebration of the Lord's Supper, they nevertheless held that the unworthy also received the true body and blood of the Lord. To deny this, they said, leads to a detachment of the gift of the Lord's Supper from faith, that is to say, to a serious subjectivizing of the Supper. That is why this point of debate became a decisive crossroads. With an eye to the history of the Church one can even say that precisely at this point important decisions were made.

The struggle may not be dismissed as only a speculative discussion about *theologoumena.* When Otto Fricke writes: "... finally it became such a ridiculous matter that before the

Lutheran courts a theologian had to prove his orthodoxy on the basis of the question about unworthy partakers,"[1] this judgment is much too harsh because it neglects the background of the problem that arises here. For the problem regarding the partaking by the unworthy does not stand by itself, but is connected with one's insight into the *essence* of the Supper gift and thus becomes an important part of the discussion of the Lord's Supper.

We are confronted with the problem of the *manducatio indignorum* in the case of Judas Iscariot, who for many became the "prototype of the *Indignus.*"[2] Judas is also mentioned in the Confession of Faith — with Simon the Sorcerer — in a specific sacramental context. We read in Article 35 that the sacraments have been united with the reality signified but that not all people receive this reality. The wicked person receives the sacrament but not its truth, as Judas and Simon received the sacrament but not Christ who is signified by the sacrament, which is administered only to believers.

To be sure, there is no agreement as to whether Judas participated in the Lord's Supper or whether he had left before its institution. But this question is unimportant here, for the Confession of Faith is unwilling to make an exegetic statement regarding the celebration of the Lord's Supper by Judas; it evidently starts from the assumption that this is indeed the case and in connection with that it wants to say something definite about the relation of the unworthy to the Lord's Supper. The question, then, concerns the relation brought about when the unworthy receives the signs of the Lord's Supper. This was an important point of the controversy for the Lutherans.

The *manducatio indignorum* which they accepted was firmly linked with their doctrine about the real, bodily presence of Christ in the Supper. Nevertheless, it is not enough to point out that this is only a matter of a logical conclusion from the Lutheran doctrine of the Lord's Supper. The Lutherans themselves point out that their concern does not lie with a theological or logical conclusion from a certain doctrine, but with obedience to Scripture. "If there was a reason to formulate the statement

1. O. Fricke, *Die Sakramente in der prot. Kirchen,* 1929, p. 13; cf. M. A. Goossen, *De Heidelb. Catechismus en het boekje van de breking des broods,* 1893.
2. H. Gollwitzer, *Coena Domini,* p. 222.

of the *manducatio indignorum* and to repeat it in all Lutheran confessional writings with increasing exclusiveness, it was — as with the whole doctrine of the Lord's Supper — the serious desire obediently and faithfully to interpret and apply the Word of Scripture. It all turns upon the exegesis of I Corinthians 11:27-29."[3]

This appeal to Scripture, however, does not rule out the close relation between the doctrine of the *manducatio indignorum* and the whole doctrine of the Lord's Supper, in particular that of the Roman Catholic Church and of the Lutheran Church in connection with their interpretations of the presence of Christ in the Supper. One can say that for Rome as well as for the Lutheran Churches a special interpretation of the *modus praesentiae* formed the basis for the doctrine of the *manducatio indignorum,* which latter is an evident and necessary conclusion from the doctrine of this presence. But in this connection, attention is also drawn to the results of denying the *manducatio indignorum,* namely, that the great responsibility of the unworthy is abolished. The *manducatio indignorum* is designed to preserve the objectivity of the Lord's Supper and of the gift of the Supper for all those who in the circle of the Church have received and still receive the Lord's Supper. This responsibility of having really come into contact with the present Christ can only be maintained, it is thought, against the background of the reality of the *manducatio indignorum,* with which the judgment corresponds. The Lutherans held that it was impossible to maintain the radical seriousness of the "judgment" in I Corinthians 11 if the *manducatio indignorum* is denied.

The Lord's Supper can become a curse only if the *manducatio indignorum* is real. That is the judging function of the Lord's Supper when the unworthy partake. The *manducatio indignorum* is maintained in Lutheran confessions and theology with this meaning.[4] The Formula Concordiae in particular

---

3. F. W. Hopf, "Die Abendmahlslehre der ev. Kirche," in *Abendmahlsgemeinschaft?*, 1937, p. 157.

4. It is not surprising that also in the Roman Catholic doctrine of the *manducatio indignorum* a consistent appeal is made to I Corinthians 11 with the same tendency as in the appeal of the Lutherans. The eating and drinking of Christ's true body and blood (present through transubstantiation) becomes the assumption and the basis for the judgment, so that the parallel in the argumentation between Lutherans and Roman Catholics is here practically complete.

teaches that the body and blood of Christ are "really and essentially present in the Lord's Supper, that they are distributed with bread and wine, and that they are received by all those who use this sacrament, be they worthy or unworthy, pious or wicked, believing or unbelieving, a comfort for the faithful, a judgment unto the wicked."[5]

It is emphatically taught that not only believers and those who come to the Lord's Supper worthily truly receive the body and blood of the Lord, but also the *"indigni et infideles"* and then *"ad judicium et damnationem"* unless they repent.[6] Schlink says correctly that the *manducatio indignorum* is an "illuminating doctrine" of the Lutheran confessions;[7] even where it is not explicitly mentioned, it is "already implied if the words 'under the form of, in and with' are fixed in meaning, as happens in the confessional writings."[8]

There is not only a *manducatio spiritualis,* for the *manducatio* is twofold, namely, spiritual and "oral."[9] And in this oral way, the true body and blood of Christ are received by all — also the unworthy — who are guests of the Lord's Supper.[10] There is therefore in any case the matter of a *manducatio oralis.*[11] This is precisely why there is a judgment of the unworthy, because they thus become guilty of the body and blood of the Lord.[12] We find the effect of this thought throughout Lutheran theology.[13]

As the dominating motif of the *manducatio indignorum,* we see repeatedly the theme of judgment coming to the fore. Sin is based on the real *manducatio.*[14] The judgment is linked with the responsibility of having really received the gift of the Lord's Supper in this way.[15]

Not only the Lutherans, but also the Reformed have emphatically spoken of the responsibility implied in the use of the Lord's Supper. The solemn notes of judgment are sounded

---

5. Formula Conc., I (Müller, *op. cit.,* p. 538).
6. *Ibid.,* pp. 540-41.
7. E. Schlink, *Theol. der lutherischen Bekenntnisschriften,* p. 245.
8. See also the Formula Conc. (Müller, *op. cit.,* p. 661).
9. *Ibid.*
10. "indigni conviviae" (*ibid.,* p. 662).
11. "oralis et indignorum manducatio" (*ibid.*).
12. "et corporis atque sanguinis Christi rei fiunt" (*ibid.*).
13. Cf. Johannis Gerhardi, *Loci Theol.,* 1885, V, XXII, 224.
14. Gollwitzer, *Coena Domini,* p. 241.
15. *Ibid.*

in Article 35 of the Confession and in the form for the Supper. This accent is so strong in the confessions and in Calvin that it led Gollwitzer to warn against failing to appreciate the seriousness of the Reformed doctrine of the Lord's Supper.[16] His judgment corresponds to that of the Reformed themselves, who strongly emphasize the motif of judgment in the unworthy use of the Lord's Supper, but who deny that this motif must lead to the doctrine of the *manducatio indignorum*. The core of the question is therefore whether this seriousness regarding the unbelieving and unworthy use of the Lord's Supper can be called legitimate, or whether it is nothing but a happy inconsequence in the whole of the Reformed doctrine of the Supper. Can the *manducatio indignorum* be rejected while the seriousness of the judgment is maintained? These questions focus the controversy about the *manducatio indignorum,* and it is understandable that this struggle was especially concentrated upon Paul's words in I Corinthians 11.

In this passage we are indeed confronted with the question about the relation between the Lord's Supper and those who do not participate in the Supper in the correct manner. One could say that Paul speaks here of the critical, condemning attitude of the Lord's Supper against those who make themselves guilty with respect to the body and blood of Christ. Already in verse 17, Paul says that the gatherings of the Corinthian Church are not for the better but for the worse, evidently because their factionalism was so serious that the communion of the agape was seriously endangered and even eliminated. This factionalism acquired a special form precisely in the celebration of the Lord's Supper: each person takes care only of himself when the feast is held communally. Social differences are carried into the celebration of the Lord's Supper: the one brings much and is drunk, the other little and is hungry. Abundance and need become visible in the Lord's Supper. There is a disregard for the community in that the needy are put to shame (11:22).

In order to give a foundation to his criticism, Paul then speaks of the institution of the Lord's Supper in the night of the betrayal. He sees the Supper in the only frame in which it can correctly be understood, namely, of the death of the Lord and of the fruits of his work, of the remembrance and

---

16. *Ibid.,* p. 239; cf. also W. v. Loewenich, *Vom Abendmahl Christi,* p. 95.

the proclamation through which communion with him becomes possible and real by virtue of the blessing power of the "for you." "Here Paul says that the account of Jesus' deeds in this last night is the valid norm for all thoughts, desires, and acts of the Church when it celebrates the Lord's Supper."[17] The celebration of the Supper is a common proclamation, a feast of proclamation which will be repeated until the return of Christ in the unity of the Church. And what then follows is of special importance. "Wherefore whosoever shall eat the bread or drink the cup of the Lord in an unworthy manner, shall be guilty of the body and the blood of the Lord. But let a man prove himself, and so let him eat of the bread, and drink of the cup. For he that eateth and drinketh, eateth and drinketh judgment unto himself, if he discern not the body" (11:26-29).

This is the passage toward which the controversy about the *manducatio indignorum* is repeatedly oriented. For here, in direct connection with the Lord's Supper, the motif of judgment comes to the fore. The whole passage is evidently in a mood of great seriousness. It is possible to celebrate the Lord's Supper in an unworthy manner, namely, in a manner of eating and drinking that does not correspond with the "worthiness," the worth of the bread and the cup. That can happen in many ways. In Corinth, Church members turned the Lord's Supper into a feast from which all perspective and all depth had been taken. It is therefore necessary — before going to this Supper — to search and prove oneself. That self-proving tests the true worthiness that must become revealed if one is to respect the meaning of the Lord's Supper.

On the basis of the significance of the Lord's Supper, all superficiality is radically excluded here. Paul's words contain an urgent command which harks back to the sacred institution of the Lord's Supper.[18] If people harden themselves in their sins and do not see the depth of the Lord's Supper for the whole community, they become guilty of the body and blood of the Lord and eat and drink to their own judgment.

Paul speaks, then, of sin if unworthy use is made of the Lord's Supper. This is the text from which it is argued that the true body and blood of the Lord are eaten and drunk, and

17. A. Schlatter, *Paulus der Bote Jesu*, 1934, p. 320.
18. Cf. Kittel, *TWNT*, II, 263.

hence also the *manducatio indignorum*. But can this sin and
this judgment be interpreted differently? Both the Lutheran
and the Roman Catholic reproaches against the Reformed doctrine of the Lord's Supper can be summarized in this question:
the relation between the judgment-motif and *manducatio indignorum*.

It is clear that the *manducatio indignorum* does not have
to be deduced from the judgment on the unworthy use of the
Lord's Supper, for even if one does not accept the Lutheran
supposition (presence of the substantial, true body and blood
of Christ), the seriousness of Paul's warning is fully understandable. This seriousness is an extension of the seriousness
with which the New Testament always speaks about unbelief.
It has been said, however, that I Corinthians 11 is a special
situation because it concerns becoming guilty of the body and
blood of the Lord, and that would not be possible if body
and blood are not truly present in the full sense of the word.

This is not just a matter of disobedience or unbelief, but
of guilt with respect to the body and blood. This argument has
played a very important role in the controversy of the sixteenth century. Calvin discussed this question extensively when
he exegeted I Corinthians 11:27, namely, whether the unworthy
really eat the body of Christ. He speaks of those who believe
that Peter did not receive more than Judas in the Lord's Supper,
and he poses against the doctrine of the *manducatio indignorum*
that Christ cannot be detached from the Spirit.[19] It is impossible to receive the body of Christ apart from his Spirit
and power. According to Calvin, without faith one receives
only the sign. Whereas the Lutherans believed that this view
destroyed the foundation of responsibility and guilt, Calvin
saw it only as the beginning of closer reflection on the nature
of the sacrament. The significance of the sacrament of the
Lord's Supper is, as far as Calvin is concerned, not weakened
for a moment. Here, too, it is evident that he does not start
from a substantial interpretation of Christ's body and blood,
but that he looks at the meaning of these words. According to
Calvin, the body of Christ is offered to both the good and the
bad. He uses the word *offerre,* which plays an important role
throughout his sacramental doctrine. This word is completely

19. Calvin, *Comm.* on I Corinthians 11:27: "Christum non posse a Spiritu
    suo divelli."

unsatisfactory for the Lutherans to indicate the essence of the Lord's Supper if it does not at the same time comprise the *recipere*.

We see that Calvin more than once uses strong expressions to define the Lord's Supper and to maintain its objectivity. He says, for instance, that this is the truth regarding the sacrament which the world cannot possibly take away, namely, "that the flesh and blood of Christ are no less truly given to the unworthy than to God's elect believers" (*Inst.*, IV, XVII, 33); and he declares that "this spiritual food, if it enters a soul corrupted by malice and wickedness, casts it down with a greater ruin." He even says that they who do not distinguish the body of Christ, rob it of all its worthiness and profane and contaminate it by receiving it (IV, XVII, 40). The *offerre* seems here to be firmly linked with the *recipere*. But this is not really the case, for Calvin distinguishes at the same time between offering and receiving (IV, XVII, 33). Insofar as Calvin speaks of "giving" and "receiving," he evidently always means to emphasize the seriousness of *offerre*. *Offerre* expresses Calvin's conviction that one must distinguish between the sacrament and the truth of the sacrament. To be sure, *figura* and *veritas* are connected in the sacrament, but they are not linked in such a manner that they cannot be detached. Diametrically opposed to every objectivism in sacramental doctrine, Calvin maintains the relation between faith and sacrament. Christ as the truth of the sacrament must be accepted in faith. Against those who closely connect sign and that which is signified, Calvin says that the sacrament is separated from its truth in such a manner (because of the unworthiness of the receiver) that nothing is left but a vain and useless *figura* (IV, XVII, 33). In order not to receive the sign without the truth of the sacrament, it is necessary that faith make use of the gift of the Lord's Supper.

All this has led to the opinion that for Calvin the Lord's Supper is of no significance whatsoever for the unworthy, that it is only an empty sign. But this is a wrong interpretation, which fails to see that Calvin wanted to show by strong antithetical expressions that without faith the sacrament means nothing for salvation, and that salvation is not connected with the signs in an objectivistic manner. In the light of the true *usus sacramenti* Calvin speaks of useless and vain signs. Calvin speaks warningly and urgently of this "useless" without in the least minimizing the institution of God. He asks whether the wicked accomplish this uselessness of the ordinance of God, and he answers in the negative. But he maintains the relation between faith and sacrament; and he holds that the sign is sanctified through the Spirit and thus retains its power, but that it is nevertheless useless for a wicked and godless man (IV, XIV, 16). Calvin is not concerned to affect the nature of the sacrament, but to stress the blessing of the true body and blood of Christ which is connected with faith, the faith that is oriented toward the benefactions of Christ. This relation between faith and sacrament sheds a clear light on Calvin's rejection of the *manducatio indignorum*.

Calvin sees everything in the light of the relation between faith and sacrament, and between sacrament and Word.[20] The sacrament may never be detached from the Word. That is why for Calvin the relation between the "unworthy" and the Lord's Supper was an altogether different one than that held by the Roman Catholics and the Lutherans, while nevertheless the *offerre* creates a no less serious situation, and the judgment-motif is fully accepted. Calvin has spoken with great earnestness of the bad fruit of the unworthy use of the Lord's Supper. He says that misuse of the Supper entails perdition, and that the sacrament changes into harmful poison for the unbeliever (*Inst.*, 1536 ed.). That does not mean that for Calvin the signs themselves become poisonous; he speaks that way only when he thinks of the relation between unbelief and the Lord's Supper. And therein he knows of the guilt with respect to the body and blood of Christ. This is not the *manducatio oralis indignorum,* but the guilt versus that which is signified and sealed in the Lord's Supper under the divine sovereignty and institution of Christ. Here Calvin stands diametrically opposed to all forms of spiritualism in the doctrine of the Lord's Supper. The judgment-motif is not neglected when he rejects the substantialistic interpretation of the Lord's Supper, for in the sacrament the sacred act is seen whereby God causes the purifying blood of Christ to signify and seal for believers. That is why Reformed theology has always spoken of this earnestness, as we also find in the form for the Lord's Supper.

The judgment is not based on the fact that the unworthy communicant himself has eaten the "body" and "blood" of

20. Cf. also Polman, *Onze Ned. Geloofsbelijdenis,* IV, on the twofold integrity.

the Lord, but on the fact that he has desecrated the sacrament of Christ's body and blood by not discerning the body of the Lord.[21]

It is fully understandable that Calvin does not just speak here of unbelief and disobedience in general, for this Supper is full of that body and blood and therein of Christ's surrender unto death. Its meaning lies only in that, and only in that is it the gift of the Lord to his people. Unworthiness can penetrate into this Supper, and the nature of this sacred sacrament can be misappreciated. Man thus becomes guilty of the body and blood of the Lord, and eats and drinks to his own judgment.[22]

This guilt is based on the relationship established by God, and for that reason can never be seen as guilt with respect to the sign as such. This sign as such does not exist, except in the imagination of him who does not see this sacrament in its true significance.

Guilt is correlated with the relation established by God. This relation is unbreakable, and its blessed fruit is out of reach for the unworthy. The confrontation is therefore real and threatening. The offer is reality, and the institution of the Lord's Supper, which rests on that offer, is founded in this involvement: the body and blood of the Lord for us. In the unworthy use of the Supper, man sins against the body and blood of the Lord. The judgment follows upon this guilt, this qualified guilt. That is very clearly indicated when Paul adds: "if he discern not the body" (I Cor. 11:29).

Because Paul speaks here of "the body" *(to sōma)*, many have thought that it was not Paul's intention to say: "that he does not discern the body of the Lord," that is to say, that one does not distinguish the signs from normal bread in a normal meal.[23] They prefer, like Ehrhardt, to read first what Paul says, namely, "the body," and not immediately to join those who "think they must improve on Paul." Ehrhardt adds that the intention of the interpolator has been so successful "that the exegetes are still following in his wake."[24] He thinks that it was not Paul's intention to distinguish between Christ's body and something

21. Niesel, *op. cit.*, p. 80.
22. Grosheide, *Commentaar*, p. 396.
23. See, e.g., Lietzmann, *An die Korinther I, II*, 1949, p. 59.
24. Ehrhardt, *op. cit.*, p. 102. Cf. E. Käsemann, "Anliegen und Eigenart der paulin. Abendmahlslehre," *EvT*, 1947, p. 276; and Kittel, *TWNT*, IV, 948.

else, and that verse 29 is an admonition with a different thrust
from that of verse 27 (unworthiness). He thinks that verse 29
involves our participation in the suffering of the Lord rather
than secluding oneself, so that Paul means that the communicant should not isolate himself,[25] but that he should take upon
himself the suffering that speaks of the condemnation of Christ.

This is a highly speculative exegesis. The relation between
verses 27 and 29 is broken, and the acceptability of the connection with guilt is replaced with a connection between sacrament and suffering. But there is reason to maintain the connection between verses 27 and 29, and to read that guilt has
bearing on the failure to distinguish the body of the Lord.
The unworthiness is revealed precisely in the fact that the
worth of "the body" is not discerned. The eye is obscured and
all things mingle. There is a lack of understanding of what our
form for the Lord's Supper says about the sacred food and
drink, or, as Reformed theology expressed it at various occasions, ·the consecrated element. Bread becomes bread and
nothing more . . . for him who is unworthy. We recall that the
Reformed held (against transubstantiation) that the bread
was not annhiliated, but that it remained bread. This thesis,
however, does not do away with the warning against not distinguishing, for one who fails to discern knows not of "consecration," not even in the Reformed sense of the word.[26] The
bread is submerged in the triviality of the common; it is not
seen as part of the divine signifying word. It becomes nonsacred
bread, detached from the sacramental context. The correlation
between faith and sacrament is broken, with all the complica-
tions and dangers which that entails for a divided Church.

How serious this unworthiness and this nondiscernment of
the body of the Lord is with respect to the judgment, becomes
evident in what follows. "For this cause many among you are
weak and sickly, and not a few sleep" (I Cor. 11:30). Ehrhardt
denies the judgment that is here seen in traditional exegesis. He
thinks that this verse is a matter of the *suffering*. Therein lies
the kerygma of Paul's doctrine of the Lord's Supper.[27] It is
not the case "that Paul meant to hurl, as it were, an invective

25. Ehrhardt, *op. cit.*, p. 108.
26. Cf. regarding the use of the term by Luther: Vajta, *Die Theol. des
    Gottesdienstes bei Luther,* 1952, pp. 183ff.
27. Ehrhardt, *op. cit.*, p. 109.

at the deceased Christians from Corinth, even into their grave."
Rather, it is a word of comfort and admonition in the midst
of sickness, weakness, and death, that in suffering for Christ's
sake they will glorify God.[28] This exegesis rests upon Ehrhardt's
interpretation of verse 29, and is totally unacceptable. According
to the connection with verse 27, the judgment takes place not
only in the depth of man's heart, but in the reality of life.[29]
The judgment-motif is concretized with great earnestness. Like
a thunderstorm judgment breaks loose upon the divided community which does not discern the body and which for that
reason is guilty of the body and blood of Christ.

The Lord's Supper is full of comfort and solace, but only
for the believer. The judgment of I Corinthians 11 stands as
a warning against all unworthiness with respect to the sacred
food, not to frighten us away from a bold use of the Lord's
Supper, but to warn us against the unbelief and the dividedness
of the Church in which the meaning of Christ's one Supper
is not understood.

Clearly, then, the difference between the Reformed interpretation of the Lord's Supper and that of the *manducatio
indignorum* does not consist in the fact that the one does, and
the other does not, take into account the earnestness of the signs
of the Lord's Supper. Rather, both sides confess the urgent
seriousness of the judgment-motif. The Reformed did not infer
a *manducatio indignorum,* however, because of their conviction
that the substantial presence of Christ's body and blood did
not form the basis for the guilt of the unworthy. They knew
that the profound sacramental connection between sign and
reality was a personal connection, and so in view of the presence of Christ in the Lord's Supper through the Holy Spirit,
they saw in the Supper that was unworthily received, a confrontation that resulted in guilt.

Sometimes objections have been raised against the manner
in which the form for the Lord's Supper refers to Paul's word
of warning in I Corinthians 11. It has been pointed out that
the unworthiness of the divided community in Corinth was
of a special nature. But even though we fully acknowledge this
special character of unworthy eating and drinking (namely, the
breaking-up of the communion), it cannot be denied that this

28. *Ibid.*
29. See A. Kuyper, *E Voto,* III, 155.

was just one form of unworthiness, and that others can also appear in the course of history. It is certainly not accidental that the form of the Lord's Supper follows the citation from I Corinthians 11 with an enumeration of offensive sins such as discord, hatred, and envy toward one's neighbor. These are other ways of making concrete what became concrete in Corinth in a special manner: the nondiscernment of the body of the Lord.

That is why the judgment-motif is sounded in the form for the Lord's Supper. This is not the core of the doctrine of the Lord's Supper, which is instituted for believers. But it is the dark border of the celebration of the Lord's Supper, as we can also observe in the administration of baptism. In the relation between faith and sacrament, the concern does not lie with a stable and unthreatened relation, but with the concrete dynamics of the life of the Church in calling, admonition, and comforting. The judgment-motif in the doctrine of the Lord's Supper is not an independent motif, but the motif that urges us to that communion in which sign and the reality signified are connected with each other. The shadow of judgment upon the unworthy is the shadow that causes us to flee toward the sunshine through which life is re-established in communion with Christ, and wherein the outlook on the unthreatened and undisturbed salvation is kept open.

There is good reason to reflect at this point on the character of unworthiness, for there is a curious duality in the use of this word. We read in the form for the Lord's Supper in the section on the judgment that God is willing to accept and keep us as worthy partakers at the table of his Son Jesus Christ. Here, reference is made to a "worthiness" which is not at all contradictory to the correct approach to the Lord's Supper. It is therefore necessary to distinguish sharply so that the unworthiness to which the judgment corresponds may clearly be recognized. This is all the more so since in the practice of the Lord's Supper the feeling of unworthiness forms an impediment to the confident use of this sacrament.

The striking aspect of the form for the Lord's Supper lies in the term "worthy partakers." Who these persons are is clearly indicated in the preceding passage on true self-examination. They are those who confess their sins in self-abhorrence, humiliation, faith in God's promises, and gratefulness of heart. This is the "worthiness" that belongs with the Lord's Supper. It is not at all meritorious in nature, but is in complete harmony with what is signified and sealed in the Lord's Supper. It is a worthiness that coincides with a confession of "unworthiness" and with trust in the salvation of God. That is why it is a misunderstanding when the Church, thinking of Paul's "in an unworthy manner" in I Corinthians 11, does not come to the Lord's table because of its feeling of unworthiness. The "unworthy" refers to a faulty appreciation of the value, the meaning, the involvement of the Lord's Supper. We do not come to the Lord's Supper to testify there to our "worthiness," but with the acknowledgment that we seek our life in Jesus Christ and that without him we lie in the midst of death.

The worthiness in question is never something that precedes the correct celebration of the Lord's Supper as a meritorious constituent, but exists only in the receiving of the sacred food, in a manner that corresponds to the nature of this food. We are reminded in this connection of the man who comes to Christ with the words: "Lord, trouble not thyself; for I am not worthy that thou shouldest come under my roof; wherefore neither thought I myself worthy to come unto thee" (Luke 7:6-7). It is striking that the elders of the Jews urge help for his dying slave with the argument that he is worthy of it: "He is worthy that thou shouldest do this for him; for he loveth our nation, and himself built us our synagogue" (7:4-5). They speak of his worthiness, he himself only of his unworthiness. And Christ says of this man: "I say unto you, I have not found so great faith, no, not in Israel" (7:9).

Reflection on the Lord's Supper and on unworthiness must therefore always take into account the critical function which the Lord's Supper has with respect to the unworthy, and also of the comfort of this gift of the Supper, that in the way of faith and repentance no sin can hinder us "from being received of God in grace and from being made worthy partakers of this heavenly food and drink."[30]

The worthiness demanded by the Lord's Supper consists, then, in acknowledging one's unworthiness and in knowing that the Supper has been instituted for the "unworthy" who proclaim in the Lord's Supper the death of Christ, not their righteous-

30. Form for the Lord's Supper.

ness.[31] The "unworthiness" can keep us from the Lord's table only if it reveals itself in a disregard of guilt and forgiveness. There is, then, the crisis of unworthiness against which Christ's Church is warned in the light of his coming.[32]

One can thus speak of a *manducatio indignorum* within the confession of the Lord's Supper, but then only as the eating of those "unworthy" who approach the table in faith and confession of sins. There cannot be another *manducatio indignorum,* because this would be contrary to the nature of the Lord's Supper. This denial does not imply a disregard of the earnestness of approaching the table of the Lord. Every celebration of the Lord's Supper stands in the light of this earnestness, which does not endanger the joy of the Supper, but which indicates that joy. The relation between the Lord's Supper and "unworthiness" is not a theoretical problem, but is incorporated in the preaching of the salvation which urges us to true faith. Here, too, the warning is valid: "He who standeth take heed lest he fall" (I Cor. 10:12). The relation that was so violently debated between Roman Catholics, Lutherans, and Reformed receives full actuality in the continuous call to discern the body of the Lord, and so to practice communion with him, the communion of the remembrance and the proclaiming of his death in his holy presence.

31. Compare the manner in which the N. T. speaks of "being worthy," which implies meritoriousness only to the superficial reader. See II Thess. 1:5, where Paul is grateful for the increasing faith, love, and perseverance of the Thessalonians. Also in Acts 5:41, we see a connection with suffering. Cf. Phil. 1:29, where Paul speaks of the grace which is given to suffer for Christ.
32. G. Bornkamm, "Das Anathema in der urchristlichen Abendmahlslehre," *TLZ*, 1950, pp. 227-230, wherein he draws a connection between the anathema passage in I Cor. 16:22 and the Lord's Supper.

CHAPTER THIRTEEN

THE LORD'S SUPPER: A SACRIFICE?

I N REFLECTIONS on the significance of the Lord's Supper throughout the history of the Christian Church, we automatically come into contact with the controversies about the Roman Catholic doctrine of the Supper as offering, with the sacrifice of the mass, which has such great significance for Roman Catholic public worship and forms the core of it. The conflict was fierce already in the sixteenth century, and continues still in connection with the fact that Rome not only defines the eucharist as *sacramentum* but also as *sacrificium*. The Lutherans and Reformed rejected this notion of a sacrifice by appealing to the uniqueness and sufficiency of the only sacrifice of Jesus Christ on the cross. The sharpness of this conflict is clearly revealed in the well-known and much-discussed expression of the Heidelberg Catechism, which defines the mass as "at bottom . . . nothing else than a denial of the one sacrifice and passion of Jesus Christ, and an accursed idolatry" (Q. 80) .

The contrast has nowhere been so sharp as here, concerning the testament of the crucified Christ. The sharp judgment of the Catechism is completely in accordance with the Lutheran criticism, which was not in the first place directed against transubstantiation but against the mass as offering. But Rome maintains the *mirabile sacrificium* as the mystery of all mysteries, and sees in the Reformed denial of the mass a serious failure to appreciate the testament of Christ. How is it possible that such a controversy originated about the cross of Christ and the significance of it for all times?

Our mention of the cross of Christ at this point follows immediately from the fact that in all of the controversy, the crux of the matter turns out to be the significance of the cross. The struggle was concentrated upon the relation between cross-offering and mass-offering. The Reformers did not mean, of

course, that Rome denied the blessed significance of Christ's
sacrifice, but that this sacrifice was put in the shadow through
the doctrine of the mass-offering. They appealed continually to
the "once only" of Christ's offering at the cross, which the
Epistle to the Hebrews emphasized so strongly. It was especially pointed out that precisely the contrast between the
"often" of the Old Testament offerings and the "once only"
of Christ's offering (cf. Heb. 7:27) formed a decisive argument against the concept of a repetition of the offering of Christ
on the cross. We find this argument not only in Calvin (*Inst.*,
IV, XVIII, 3), but already in the Confessio Augustana of 1530,[1]
and we find it confessionally defined in the Heidelberg Catechism when it is said that according to the Roman Catholic
doctrine, Christ is daily offered by the priests (Q. 80).

The question arises whether the general and unanimous
polemics of the Reformation against the "repetition" of Christ's
offering does justice to the Roman Catholic doctrine of the
eucharist as offering. Can the struggle indeed be decided on
the basis of the unmistakable evidence of the "once only"? The
answer on the Roman Catholic side is an emphatic No. This
criticism, they say, misses the most profound meaning of the
mass, which is not simply a "repetition" of the offering at the
cross.[2] For the repetition in question is something altogether
unique, much more mystical than "*l'histoire se répète*," and something different from the Old Testament offerings. Rome wants
to accept the mass-offering without devaluating the "once only"
of Hebrews. The repetition of the mass does not imply the insufficiency of the repeated occurrence. In order to indicate the
mystery of the relation between cross-offering and mass-offering,
the word *repraesentatio* is preferably used, which at the same
time safeguards the continuity of the Roman Catholic development of doctrine, since this word was already used in the de-

---

1. Art. XXIV (Müller, *Bekenntnisschriften*, p. 52). See also the apologia by
   Melanchthon (*ibid.*, pp. 252ff.). See on Luther: E. Bizer, "Römisch-
   Katholische Messe und evangelisches Abendmahl," in *Ecclesia semper
   reformanda: EvT*, special issue for E. Wolf, 1952, pp. 17-40.
2. Cf. E. Bizer, *op. cit.*, p. 19; cf. H. Asmussen, *Warum noch lutherische
   Kirche? Ein Gespräch mit dem augsburgischen Bekenntnis*, 1949, and the
   discussion of the texts from Hebrews by J. van 't Westeinde, *De moderne
   theologie over het misoffer*, 1953, pp. 21-33.

cisions of Trent.[3] This word serves to indicate that the mass-offering is not a simple repetition, but a *repraesentatio,* a placing in the presence of the mass-offering.[4]

It is not very easy to say what is meant by this *repraesentatio.* It is nevertheless necessary to try, since the question could arise whether this interpretation of the mass-offering provides a rapprochement between Rome and the Reformation, the more so since now the side of the Reformation also sometimes uses the word *repraesentatio.*[5]

It is thus important to ask whether the concept of *repraesentatio* introduces motifs which take the wind out of the sails of the Reformation's appeal to the "once only" of Hebrews. When Casel begins to speak of the mass, he first discusses the sacred mystery-act as it is found beyond and apart from the Christian religion.[6] As he sees it, it is "an act, a dramatic performance, in which a community of deeply religious people symbolically represent an act or an occurrence which belongs to a higher, sacred sphere; they represent it not only as actors who take on a strange role but who keep their own personality; they play as actors who seriously represent a fact, even though this fact remains more or less hidden under their symbolic play."[7] It is more than a simple symbol, for under the veil of that symbol the most veritable reality is present. What occurs in the history of religions in such sacred acts, finds its complete fulfilment in the act of the sacred mass.[8] An event is presented in the mass, namely, the redemptive work of Christ. The saving act is not just recalled, but becomes a new reality. "For the deep-searching eye of the religious

3. Christ left to his church a "sacrificium, quo cruentum illud semel in cruce peragendum repraesentaretur eiusque memoria in finem usque saeculi permaneret" (Denz. 938).

4. G. van der Leeuw, *Sacramentstheologie,* p. 245: "an increasing number of Catholic theologians now replace that repetition with representation in some form or other."

5. Van der Leeuw wants to take this concept quite seriously. To be sure, he deduces from it that with representation as oneness of essence in the manner of the mystery the theory of transubstantiation becomes superfluous and powerless (*ibid.,* p. 263); but he thinks the mystery doctrine of Maria-Laach, in which the concept of representation plays such an important role, to be "the most important theological trend in the last 150 years" (*ibid.,* p. 239).

6. O. Casel, *Heilige Bronnen,* 1946, pp. 39ff.; cf. Polman, *Onze Ned. Geloofs-belijdenis,* IV, 164ff., 217ff.

7. Casel, *op. cit.,* p. 47.

8. *Ibid.,* p. 50; cf. p. 59.

man there is no contradiction in the fact that the Lord, who has suffered once for all time and who sits at the right hand of God, suffers death in the *mysterium* anew in a symbolic-real manner, and arises to incorporate the Church into his own life" (p. 53). This "worship of the mysteries" (p. 54) has been instituted by Christ himself.

Casel does not hesitate to speak of repetition (p. 55). To be sure, the mass is based on a historical occurrence (p. 75), namely, the cross and resurrection; but "what Christ then suffered and did, is suffered and done in a mystical-real manner by Christians with him."[9] This happens under the veil of the symbol, but that does not in the least minimize the reality. Christ's redemptive act becomes a new reality in the cult. His work is, so to speak, corporealized in the mass. Therein lies the essence of the doctrine of the mystery, that the divine redemptive act becomes a reality ever again. It is not just a matter of remembrance and recalling.[10] These take place in the mind of man, but in the mass we are confronted with an act in which the redemptive event becomes present. It is not a new historical act, but the same act that now— in the mass — is made present among us *in mysterio*.

This doctrine of the mystery is still debated, especially the question whether the fruits of Christ's "first" offering are present in the mass, or whether his redemptive act is itself present. Casel thinks that this latter, ancient doctrine of the Church has been neglected too much and that thus the real mystery in the sacrament has been lost from sight. The so-called "intentional presence"[11] of Christ's work has been emphasized too much, that is to say, the revealing of the fruits of his work, through which the actual presence of Christ's redemptive act in the mass was lost. Only if one accepts the representation of Christ's redemptive work in the mass, can one do full justice to the mystery-full grace of the sacrament. Casel does not mean that the whole historical occurrence of Christ's suffering and dying — with the characters that were thereby present — is repeated in the mass. He is concerned with the core of Christ's redemptive act, in which

---

9. *Ibid.* See especially O. Casel, *Das christliche Kultmysterium*, 1948, pp. 29ff., and his *Vom wahren Menschenbild*, 1953, pp. 58ff.
10. Monden, *Het misoffer als mysterie*, p. 11.
11. Cf. T. Filthaut, *Die Kontroverse über die Mysterienlehre*, 1947, p. 30.

the accidental historical moments are not incorporated. It is this act that is presented now in the mass.[12]

We shall not discuss the differences that have come to light at this point between Casel and Söhngen, because, although Söhngen opposes Casel, he nevertheless agrees that the death of Christ as a redemptive act is represented in the present.[13] The difference between the two involves the manner of this representation.[14] Much more important than these differences is the fact that both parties accept the limits drawn by Trent.

Regardless of all the varying interpretations of the relation between cross-offering and mass-offering, these Roman Catholic thinkers continue to accept the mass-offering as a real offering. There are no critical reservations regarding the definitions of Trent. And it was precisely this central thought, which is so essential for the doctrine of the mass-offering, that was opposed by the Reformation. With respect to the doctrine of Casel, one can therefore say that it has not brought a principal change into the controversy about the mass. Rather, his doctrine of representation, involving not just the fruits of Christ's redemptive act but that redemptive act itself, reveals the depth of the controversy all the more clearly. It is evident that the criticism of the Reformation does not rest entirely upon an antiquated problem whose relevance is lost in the light of the newer interpretations.

The Council of Trent already made it clear that the mass-offering is a true offering.[15] It is not merely an offering of praise and thanksgiving, nor a mere remembrance of the offering at the cross, but a reconciling offering.[16] It is immediately added that this offering does not at all devaluate the offering at the cross.[17] Already at Trent the relation between cross-offering and mass-offering was discussed, and the Council opposed all attacks against the mass-offering on the basis of the sufficiency of the cross-offering. In order to resist this general attack of the Ref-

12. For Monden's presentation of O. Casel's view, see *Het misoffer als mysterie*, p. 11.
13. For Söhngen, see *Der Wesensaufbau des Mysteriums*, 1938, and *Symbol und Wirklichkeit im Kultmysterium*, 1937.
14. Söhngen also wants to speak of "presence of the mystery," but he does not think of the historical act of the suffering of Christ, or of the historical fact as such (*Wesensaufbau*, p. 75).
15. Denz. 948.
16. Denz. 950.
17. Denz. 951.

ormation, Trent reminded its hearers of the "once only" of Hebrews, and declared that Christ in the night of his betrayal left a *sacrificium* to represent the offering he once brought, and to make the remembrance of that offering valid until the end of the age.

Long before the theory of the "presence of the mystery" began to develop this point in a special way, the question had to arise how this *repraesentatio* should be understood, and what actually happens here. How can the cross-offering and the mass-offering be the same offering, the only difference being in the manner of offering?[18] Unless the mystery can only be approached in completely irrational surrender, one wonders how offerings that take place at different times can be the same. Has the difference in time no influence at all, and does the indication of "one and the same offering" reach beyond all categories of time? Trent itself has not given any clear answer to this question,[19] although it is clear that Trent's decision has been normative for future Roman Catholic views.[20]

In the encyclical *Mediator Dei* (1947) reference is made to Trent, also to the words "one and the same offering."[21] It is a real offering in which Christ, the High Priest, "does the same as what he once did at the cross, by recommending himself to the eternal Father as an agreeable offering."[22]

Christ wanted to leave a visible offering for his people, "as nature requires this of man,"[23] and therefore "the offering, once only presented on the cross, had to be represented; the remembrance of it had to continue until the end of the world."[24] If the offering at the cross was a bloody offering, death has now no longer any power over Christ in his glorified state, and the pouring of his blood is no longer possible.[25] But this does not at all

18. Trent, Sess. XXII, 2 (Denz. 940).
19. Schmaus, *Kath. Dogmatik*, IV, 1 (1952), p. 296.
20. It is unnecessary and impossible to repeat the various solutions brought forward in the meantime. See especially J. van 't Westeinde, *De moderne theologie over het misoffer*, 1953, in which the newest theories are discussed.
21. *Ecclesia docens*, 61.
22. "vera ac propria sacrificatio, qua quidem per incruentam immolationem summus Sacerdos id agit, quod iam in Cruce fecit, semetipsum aeterno Patri hostiam offerens acceptissimam" (*Mediator Dei*, p. 60).
23. "sicut hominum natura exigit" (*ibid.*, p. 59).
24. "repraesentaretur" (p. 59).
25. "effusio sanguinis haud passibilis est" (p. 62).

detract from the offering, for the offering of the Redeemer becomes visible through the outward signs, the symbols of his death.
Christ himself is present through transubstantiation, and the
eucharistic signs symbolize the bloody separation of his body
and blood.[26] "The representation of the remembrance of his
death is thus repeated in every offering of the altar, for by means
of the separated signs it is signified and revealed that Christ is
in the state of a victim."[27] Here mention is made of repetition,
which is implied in the representation unto the remembrance
of his death.[28] Elsewhere the encyclical mentions "renewal," when
it says that the offering of the Redeemer is continually represented and "only the difference in the manner of offering is
renewed."[29] When the polemics of the Reformation speaks therefore of repetition, of offering anew, such speaking finds a clear
and unmistakable point of contact in our time.[30]

But we must still reflect on the nature of this repetition or
renewal as it is meant by Rome, for the Roman Catholics also
speak of the identity between cross-offering and mass-offering.
The mystery of the eucharistic offering would supposedly lie in
precisely that. The mass-offering is not a "natural" offering, like
the one at the cross, which is then repeated "anew" with the same
circumstances in the same historical structure. Nor is it another
offering, standing alongside the cross-offering to complement it by
repetition, as if the historical cross-offering were insufficient. The
mystery of the cross-offering excludes such a repetition, such a
reduplication, once for all. "His death-offering is an event that
occurs only once in history; it cannot be repeated."[31] In the
cross-offering we encounter something altogether different from
the Old Testament offerings, which did not bring about any real
reconciliation and which therefore could be repeated as indicating the future reconciliation. The cross-offering is "the reconciliation with God, valid for all times, and brought about by the

26. "eucharisticae autem species, sub quibus adest, cruentam corporis et
    sanguinis separationem figurant" (p. 62).
27. "in statu victimae" (p. 62).
28. "memorialis demonstratio eius mortis" and "iteratur" (p. 62).
29. Denz. 940.
30. Cf. *Mediator Dei*, p. 75. Cf. also G. Vann, "The Holy Communion in the
    Roman Catholic Church," in *The Holy Communion: A Symposium*, p.
    45: "We are not concerned with a repetition — the mass would indeed
    be an incomplete repetition of Calvary, supposed that repetition was
    possible."
31. Schmaus, *op. cit.*, p. 293.

Son of God who became man. As a result of its completeness, it does not require or tolerate any repetition."[32] That is why the mass-offering can be called dependent upon the cross-offering. "It does not stand by itself; it depends completely on the cross-offering."[33] The relation between cross-offering and mass-offering is not something that has been added later, but "the relation stamps its essence,"[34] so that the "once only" remains unaffected.[35]

From all this, the question arises what the real significance can be of this "identity" of cross-offering and mass-offering, and of the mass-offering as real offering.

If we desire a pure answer to this question we cannot be satisfied with the definition of the mass as repetition, but must also — in order to understand that repetition — pay attention to an extremely important aspect of the eucharistic offering, namely, that of the *applicatio*.[36]

The question arises with respect to the mass of how the cross-offering of Christ can be a blessing in other times. Somehow the blessed offering at the cross — to be really fruitful and effective — must be made "present" among us, and thus the mass is seen as "the represented cross-offering."[37] "The offering of Calvary is not past. It was much too precious to disappear in the gray mists of the past. No, it still stands among us every morning."[38] The application of salvation in the reality of the present is at stake here. Trent had already decided that the mass-offering "represents the cross, applies its power, and perpetuates its remembrance."[39] It is not the intention of the Church to push the cross into the background for the benefit of the mass; on the contrary, the concern in the mass lies with the cross. The Roman Catholic doctrinal decisions show that Rome did not want to lose sight of this involvement. Scriptural testimony makes its strong influence felt in spite of all problematics relating to repetition. Rome expresses the point by saying that the cross-offering becomes per-

32. *Ibid.*
33. *Ibid.*, p. 305. Cf. A. Janssens, *De Heilige Eucharistie*, 1929, p. 135.
34. Schmaus, *loc. cit.*
35. Thomas Aquinas already discussed the problem of repetition (*S.T.*, III, Q. 83, Art. 1).
36. E. Bizer points out that Trent's discussion also shows how central was this *applicatio* (*EvT*, 1952, pp. 29ff.).
37. Schmaus, *op. cit.*, p. 353. Cf. p. 362: representation in the present.
38. K. Steur, *Levende tekens van God*, 1946, p. 93.
39. Cf. Denz. 938.

manent in the mass-offering. The cross-offering acquires its applying power in the mass-offering's *repraesentatio* and *renovatio*. In the eucharistic offering, Christ offers himself to the Father;[40] and the characteristic of the mass-offering lies in the fact that he does this through the Church and especially through the service of the priesthood.[41]

The mass-offering is in the full sense an offering of Christ, but the Church functions herein as a tool in his hand. It is put in operation in the offering of Christ, and thus the Church itself brings the offering.[42] The eucharist is an offering of the Church. To be sure, it has been declared that the application is only a matter of the working of the mass-offering itself (p. 364), but it is understandable that Schmaus says that it is difficult to square this with the "identity of the cross-offering and the mass-offering" (p. 365). Through the thought of the application of the mass as real offering, Rome is automatically confronted with the question about the relation between Christ and the Church in reconciliation. For the Church is involved in the offering of Christ and participates in the "self-surrender of Christ to the Father, in his death on the cross, in the sign of the eucharistic sacramental offering, the sign which is full of reality" (p. 294).

This conclusion is unexpected in the light of the accentuated "once only" and of the universal power of the reconciling cross. One would rather expect that all application would be exclusively oriented toward this reconciling power and that it therefore would not in itself be reconciling in nature. In that case, one could speak of the eucharist as thanksgiving, but not of the reconciling power of the eucharistic offering after the offering at the cross. But Rome confesses a reconciling offering here whereby the Church participates in Christ's self-offering.[43]

The Church takes an active role in the mass-offering when the cross-offering is represented and renewed in a sacramental form. We deal here with the focal point of the controversy. This is not revealed in a formal protest against "repetition," but in a material rejection of this repetition, which is contradictory to the decisive "once only" in Hebrews, and which also reveals its profoundest meaning in the active participation of the Church in

---

40. Schmaus, *op. cit.*, p. 362.
41. "sacerdotum ministerio" (Denz. 940).
42. Schmaus, *op. cit.*, p. 362.
43. Cf. Anscar Vonier, *Het sacrament van het kruisoffer*, 1948, ch. 20.

the offering of Christ. In this renewal, which itself is reconciling in character, Christ is offered by the priests.[44] This offering brings about reconciliation,[45] that is, the mass-offering brings it about[46] that we, if we approach God in repentance, obtain mercy and grace.

Trent cites Hebrews 4:16 here, but in Hebrews the concern is with the exclusive "once-for-all" offer of the High Priest alone. What Hebrews says of him is applied by Trent to the eucharistic offering, which is an offering by the Church. Rome confesses a curious, instrumental conjunction in the reconciliation which forms the essential element of the Roman Catholic problematics of repetition and renewal. Nowhere in the Roman Catholic doctrine — except perhaps in Mariology — is a shadow cast so clearly over the sufficient work of Christ as in this doctrine of the eucharistic offering. The polemics that opposes Rome on the basis of the "once only," rejecting the theory of renewing and repeating, hits the heart of the controversy decisively. At the same time this controversy must be seen in the light of the mode of this repetition, which unmistakably turns out to be the mode of synergism. The *renovatio* functions in a completely synergistic connection, and thus is no foreign element in the whole of the Roman Catholic doctrine of salvation but a striking illustration of it.[47] It is well known that Rome speaks of the mystery precisely in connection with the eucharist.[48] This mystery is revealed in the reality of the reconciliation through the worship of the Church in the offering. That happens in the eucharistic offering as the "remembrance" full of reality (p. 299). What is represented merges into the sign itself (p. 300). The cross-offering in this symbol-drama is sacramentally present in a mysterious manner. That is why one can say with Casel that not just Christ himself is present in the mass-offering, but his offering itself (p. 301). Through the service of the human *participatio,* the cross-offering shines out in the mass-offering and is revealed in it. Not only the fruits of the cross-offering become revealed here, but the offering itself, the *passio Christi,* who himself is present in this mysterious conjunction: the service of the priests. The cross-offering itself is present, albeit without enemies and without the

44. Denz. 949.
45. "vere propitiatorium."
46. "per ipsumque fieri."
47. Cf. K. Barth, *K.D.,* IV, 1 (1953), p. 858.
48. It is an offering *in mysterio* (Schmaus, *op. cit.,* p. 295).

pouring of blood, a mystery that is beyond all our experience and understanding (p. 301). The rays of the cross-offering are caught up in the eucharistic mystery. The offering of Christ is entrusted to the Church and thus "it becomes its offering" (p. 308). The mystery of the eucharistic offering must be correctly understood. It is not just an incomprehensible repetition, mysterious in all times, as if time stops and the eternal reality of the cross-offering destroys every moment of history as the exclusive act of Christ. No, the Church belongs to the essence of this mystery (p. 310).

In that connection, the mass is a true and real offering. That is precisely why the cross-offering is represented, "so that the Church could enter into its occurrence" (p. 310). The eucharistic offering — even though it is brought by the priests[49] — is an offering by the whole Church.[50]

If there remains any doubt as to the real significance of the eucharistic offering, this doubt is removed by the important encyclical regarding liturgy in 1947: *Mediator Dei*. If anywhere, then here the core of the problematics about the mass becomes clear. This is all the more important because the Reformation has repeatedly been reproached for its preoccupation with the problematics before and after Trent, while it is emphasized that Trent deliberately spoke antithetically, though not one-sidedly. In this encyclical we find the exact reason for Reformed problematics in former and later times. That reason lies in the repetition because of the application, or with the application in the repetition, of the cross-offering. The merits of the cross-offering are called infinite,[51] but "this redemption does not have its full effect immediately; thereto is it necessary that Christ, after having redeemed the world with the rich price of himself, actually takes possession of the souls."[52] After the cross-offering, something yet had to happen through which redemption and salvation come about and are accepted by God.[53] It is for that reason necessary

49. Cf. Denz. 430, 949.
50. Cf. *Mediator Dei*, p. 69.
51. *Op. cit.*, p. 65.
52. *Ibid.*: "Haec tamen emptio non statim plenum assequitur effectum suum; oportet siquidem Christus, postquam amplissimo hoc sui ipsius pretio mundum redemerit, in veram reapse animorum hominum possessionem veniat."
53. "opere efficiatur Deoque habeatur accepta" (*ibid.*).

"that man individually come into vital contact with the cross-offering and that thus the merits of it are applied to him."[54]

The relation between cross-offering and application are here clearly placed in the framework of "possibility" and "realization."[55] The creating of the "possibility" is a decisive *conditio sine qua non* for salvation, but is not decisive for salvation itself. Between the possibility and the realization lies the decisive act of the Church: the washing away of unrighteousness. This vision of the application definitely lies in the background of the doctrine of the mass-offering. After the actuality of the cross-offering, something else has to happen which has its own structure and its own merits. "In order to bring it about that sinners are individually cleansed in the blood of the Lamb, the co-operation of the believers is necessary. For although Christ, generally speaking, has reconciled mankind with the Father through his death, he desired that all — especially through the sacraments and the offering of the eucharist — would approach his cross and be brought to him to obtain the fruits of salvation, gained at the cross."[56] The crux of the matter is therefore what follows after the cross. Salvation is made possible through this reconciliation, and then reconciliation is actually realized through the eucharistic offering. Then, man's sins are "actually" washed away. We see, then, that *applicatio* has a very typical co-operative function in the eucharistic offering.

The application also had a place in the Reformation, but in an altogether different manner. This application was not something required to realize the power of reconciliation, but the work of the Holy Spirit in which he orients our faith toward the exclusive reconciling power of Christ's cross-offering. Faith in this sense is an acknowledgment, not a co-operation. It is not a second factor through which reconciliation actually comes about, but an acknowledgment that salvation comes only from Christ and that his blood cleanses from all sins. One can say that the manner in which one interprets the application determines one's whole doctrine of salvation. Already in the encyclical *Mystici Corporis Christi* of 1943, the Pope had declared that Christ at the cross

54. "opus est prorsus ut singillatim homines vitali modo Crucis Sacrificium attingant, ideoque quae ex eo eduntur merita iisdem impertiantur" (*ibid.*).
55. Cf. Barth's criticism of Aquinas, *K.D.*, IV, 1, p. 313.
56. *Mediator Dei*, p. 65.

gave the treasure of redemption to the Church without its co-operation, but that he demands the co-operation of his bride in the distribution of that treasure, and that he even desires "that her working in a certain sense form the origin of it."[57]

Not only are the members of the mystical body in need of Christ as their Head, but Christ — it may be surprising[58] — is also in need of his members. The Pope speaks here of an "immense mystery that can never be considered sufficiently."[59] *Tremendum mysterium* ... that is the co-operation through which the application is revealed in the eucharistic offering, which has a true, real, and reconciling character. The offering occurs in the eucharist, where Christ "hides himself under the veil of the eucharist."[60] The mystery takes place in the Now of all times. The priests take the place of the Redeemer and of the wholly mystical body and of the individual believers, and thus the believers themselves, with the priests, "consecrate through his hands the unspotted Lamb to the eternal Father."[61]

In this *tremendum mysterium,* the redemptive power of the cross-offering fades through reduplication, repetition, and renewal, and because the shadow of "possibility" falls over the true New Testament *mysterion.* These two things are connected firmly in the Roman Catholic doctrinal system: this repetition as realization, and the function of the Church in the offering of Christ.

The doctrine of the mass-offering is therefore now clear and apparent. The cross-offering is the offering of the New Covenant; it does not stand isolated on the hill of Golgotha. It is an offering that is represented throughout history. Jesus Christ wants to offer "himself in us and with us to the Father for the salvation of the world."[62] This is not a matter of the believer's surrender of himself as a sacrifice acceptable to God — with an appeal to God's mercy (Rom. 12:1) — but of the reconciling offering. To be sure, the general causality of redemption lies with the cross-offering; but this causality is connected with another causality,

---

57. *Mystici Corporis Christi,* p. 49.
58. "quamvis mirandum prorsus videatur" (*ibid.,* p. 48).
59. "Tremendum sane mysterium ac satis numquam meditatum."
60. "velisque Eucharistiae delitescit" (*ibid.,* p. 61). Cf. p. 79: "the Lord, hidden under the eucharistic veils."
61. *Ibid.,* p. 79.
62. Romualdus, *De betekenis van de H. Eucharistie,* 1951, p. 147.

that of the eucharist. It is a causality — *ex opere operato* — of the reconciling realization.[63]

The Reformation has ardently protested against this doctrine of the eucharistic offering. It was its power, not its weakness, that it did this with an appeal to the "once only" of Hebrews. The Reformers were not merely concerned with a formal number problem, but with the efficacy of Christ's saving work. Theirs was not a fruitless and romantic protest against repetition as such. The "so often" of the celebration of the Lord's Supper in I Corinthians 11 belongs to the practice of the Church. But the Reformation does not allow any repetition of the reconciling offering of Christ. It also undoubtedly saw the significance of the repeating mass as a problem of application. The testimonies of the Reformation are so numerous that we cannot begin to mention them. But it becomes clear that people saw the real problem quite clearly already in the sixteenth century, when we consider that Calvin defines the mass as "a work by which the priest who offers up Christ, and the others who participate in the oblation, merit God's favor, or it is an expiatory victim, by which they reconcile God to themselves" (*Inst.,* IV, XVIII, 1). Calvin attacks this in harsh words as a scorning of Christ, which "buries and oppresses his cross, consigns his death to oblivion, takes away the benefit which came to us from it, and weakens and destroys the Sacrament" *(ibid.).* Calvin knows that the priest, according to Rome, does not offer independently and that he is only a helper of Christ's eternal priesthood (IV, XVIII, 2); but that does not prevent him from seeing in this co-operation a violation of the cross. He points to the offering of Christ, of which the power and efficacy continue to work without end (IV, XVIII, 3). The "once only" therefore has material significance for Calvin. He combines again and again the "once only" with the power that is eternal (IV, XVIII, 3). He knows that the significance of the cross-offering is not openly denied, but he sees the repetition as implying the insufficiency and weakness of the cross-offering (IV, XVIII, 3).

Calvin's concern lies with the clear truth of Scripture. He knows the Roman Catholic argument that it is one and the same offering; but he does not let himself be confused, for if the offering has once been fulfilled, there is only one possibility, namely,

---

63. Cf. Aquinas, *S.T.,* III, Q. XLIX, Art. 1. Cf. Janssens, *De Heilige Eucharistie,* p. 135.

that the fruit of his offering is communicated to us through the preaching of the gospel and the administration of the Lord's Supper (IV, XVIII, 3). Calvin also speaks of application *(applicatio)*, but it is an application because we participate in it to enjoy it and because we receive it with true faith (IV, XVIII, 3). The remembrance of the Lord's death is not kept, but obliterated (IV, XVIII, 5) when we speak of repetition, no matter how much we surround this repetition with reservations and no matter what motivations direct them.

Hebrews itself says that if the "often" would be somehow connected with Christ's offering, he would have had to suffer often since the foundation of the world (Heb. 9:26; cf. *Inst.,* IV, XVIII, 5). "Though they cry out a hundred times to the contrary that this sacrifice is without blood, I shall deny that sacrifices change their nature at man's whim." That is why Calvin opposes the "new redemption" and the "new forgiveness" in the mass. He isolates sharply the problem of causality and possibility as the basic motif of the eucharistic offering (IV, XVIII, 6), and against this doctrine he poses with great emphasis the evidence of Scripture.

The Roman Catholic defense, seen in this light, can be called weak. Janssens denies that the mass-offering brings about new satisfaction and reconciliation.[64] "The mass-offering only applies the fruits of the offering on the cross to the remission of sins, which are destroyed on Calvary" (p. 155). It supposedly is a matter of application, of distribution and appropriation (p. 157), of making available. But this is nothing but a vicious circle, for Janssens still maintains the truly reconciling character of the mass, where an offering is brought for the sin, punishments, and other needs of believers and also for those who have died and are not yet free from punishment for their sins.[65]

The remission of sins occurs in the application.[66] This raises the question about the power of the eucharistic offering. Because it is an offering by the Church, it is clear that the infinite power of the eucharistic sacrament "does not become effective in every respect,"[67] because the mass has only a finite capacity and the measure of the efficacy of the mass-offering depends on the faith

---

64. Janssens, *op. cit.,* p. 154.
65. *Ibid.,* p. 158; cf. Trent (Denz. 940).
66. *Ibid.,* p. 160.
67. Schmaus, *op. cit.,* p. 363.

of the believers, of the Church which as Christ's tool brings the offering.

It cannot be otherwise, for the mass-offering is the offering of Christ, handed over to the Church.[68] This problem is nothing but the further side of synergism. The *eadem hostia* breaks down in the practice of the Church. The shadows fall over the purifying blood. He who violates the "once only" of Scripture, endangers the blessing contained in the sufficient offering. And this blessing is especially endangered when the "once only" fades because of the co-operation of the Church for the realization of salvation, which is incorporated as an essential moment in the true and reconciling offering.

This background indicates clearly that the eucharistic offering is a matter of a new mystery *hic et nunc,* of a mystery that contains much more than that the sacrament augments the Word to point to what once happened. It is a mystery that is raised to independence, no matter how much ecclesiastical doctrine and theology accentuate the dependence of the mass upon the cross. The mystery-character of the *sacramentum sacramentorum* appears also in the fact that the word of promise does not remain in the center, for the words of consecration may be spoken softly.[69] The sacrament as mystery begins to supersede the Word, although it derives its origin from that Word and is the effective, divine confirmation of that Word. The sacrament as *sacrificium* substitutes for the indicating Word of the "mystery" of the new offering, which exerts an effect upon God and therein constitutes reconciliation. That is why there can be no misunderstanding. The controversy about the mass-offering is a struggle about the power of the reconciliation of the cross.

It has been pointed out that the controversy about the relation between cross-offering and mass-offering involves the relation between time and eternity. When Van der Leeuw[70] says that the new representation idea has the value of making transubstantiation superfluous, he is not altogether wrong, for in his sense of simultaneity one can suppose that the temporal event at the cross is "eternalized," and hence Christ can be present

68. Janssens, *op. cit.,* p. 161. Cf. Bellarminus: "Valor sacrificii missae finitus est," in Ohler, *Symbolik,* p. 593.
69. "S.q.d. ecclesiae Romanae ritum, quo submissa voce pars canonis et verba consecrationis proferentur, damnandum esse . . . A. S." (Denz. 956). Cf. Bizer, *op. cit.,* p. 29.
70. Van der Leeuw, *Sacramentstheologie,* pp. 72, 244.

physically without the act of consecration. But I do not think that Van der Leeuw touched the core of the problem with this observation. The core of the problem is this, that according to Rome Christ's sacrifice, in order to be effective, must be represented among us, and that involves the sacrificial character of the mass. In connection with that, Rome poses transubstantiation as the reality that makes this simultaneity of the sacrifice possible. After all, Rome is not primarily interested in a philosophical view of time and eternity, as appears also from the fact that Roman Catholics can bring all sorts of objections against Casel. Rome is interested here only in the reality of the sacrifice in the Now of the life of the Church.

It is noteworthy in this connection that Van der Leeuw comes — in the light of his theory of representation (without transubstantiation) — to the sacrificial character of the Lord's Supper. To be sure, he acknowledges that in the New Testament the term "sacrifice" is not directly applied to the sacrament of the Lord's Supper, but according to Van der Leeuw, the description in Ephesians 5:2 of the relation of Christ's sacrifice to our life gives us the right to conclude that the Lord's Supper is a sacrifice.[71] The Supper is a participation in and at the sacrifice of the Lord and must therefore be a sacrifice, some sort of sacrificial act. Van der Leeuw then asks about the nature of the sacrifice. It cannot be that we offer Christ to God as sacrifice; rather, the Lord's Supper is *eucharistia,* thanksgiving sacrifice (p. 295), of which he then says: "We sacrifice Christ, because and in so far as he lives in us in a sacramental manner" (p. 297). And he adds the criticism that this real sacrificial act in the sacrament is lacking in most of the interpretations of the Reformation. It remains unclear, however, that the polemics of the Reformation was directed precisely against the sacrificial character of the mass, which belongs to its essence even according to the latest declarations of the Pope, namely, participation in the reconciling sacrifice.[72] Whoever incorporates this participation in his view

---

71. *Ibid.,* p. 293.
72. For the importance of the question about the relation between eucharist and offering, we point also to Anglican theology, wherein this question is discussed with vigor. For a general review, see L. B. Smedes, *The Incarnation: Trends in Modern Anglican Thought,* 1953, pp. 107-134. Here, too, it is clear that the idea of the *participatio* in the offering of Christ is inextricably bound with the whole problem of the *corpus Christi.* It is intriguing to see how all the questions that are discussed

of the Lord's Supper, has not done justice to the decisive power
of the sacrifice at the cross, and no concept of simultaneity —
neither the mysterious, nor the eschatological — is able to change
that.

He who wants to continue speaking of repetition or renewal
or representation against the background of the sufficient sacrifice of Christ, in order thus to expand the sacrifice of Christ over
the breadth of history, has thereby chosen for another interpretation of the sufficiency of Christ's sacrifice than that of the Reformation.[73] It can also be asked whether the doctrine of the
repeatedly new sacrifice has not originated precisely from the
failure to appreciate the supertemporal significance of Christ's
cross and reconciliation, in which God was reconciling the world
with himself. This supertemporal has nothing to do with the
idealistic emptying of history, but points to the significance which
this historical act of reconciliation — *sub Pontio Pilato* — has
for all times. Because of this confession of faith, the Reformation
has thought the struggle against the mass necessary. That it has
done so with a continuous appeal to Hebrews' "once only," is
only to the good, for that reveals clearly that it is impermissible
to deduce a renewal of this sacrifice on the basis of a desire to
"bridge" the times. In this struggle, the essential point at issue
is again — as with baptism — the nature of the New Testament
mysterion. When people began to connect the New Testament
in this manner with the *sacramentum* of the Church as infusion
of supernatural grace, the important point was, how one could
continue to see the New Testament *mysterion* in its exclusive
and sufficient efficacy. In the history of the eucharist and especially in the doctrine of the sacrificial mass it became evident that
this way was closed, because in this doctrine the *mysterion* had to

---

in Roman Catholic theology come also to the fore here, for instance, the
relation between cross and mass-offering, the meaning of anamnesis,
participation in the offering, eucharist and incarnation, the function of
the human nature of Christ. For the scope of this problematic, we refer
to some statements by Thornton, who speaks of the eucharist as "the
mystically re-enacted drama of the redemption, which embodied in
history the Son's response of love, which we proclaim" (L. S. Thornton,
The Common Life in the Body of Christ, 1950, p. 345). "We are the
extension of his sacrificial organism; we are the camp of Israel surrounding the tabernacle" (*ibid.*, p. 344).

73. Cf. Van der Leeuw's criticism of Cullmann, in *Sacramentstheologie*.

be duplicated in that act in which the Church itself participates in the self-sacrifice of Christ to the Father.

That is why the controversy about "once only" involves more than a nuance with respect to the application of salvation, but indicates a different insight into the significance of the cross. The attempt to connect the New Testament "once only" with the reconciling character of the mass reveals, through the multiplicity of sacrificial theories, the impossibility of bringing about this synthesis. All considerations regarding representation or repetition, the renewal of the eternity of Christ's sacrificial act, reveal the weakness of the concept of the reconciling application which is necessarily linked with the structure of Roman Catholic ecclesiastical doctrine. One should not say that the struggle has become obsolete, that it can no longer be fought with the motifs and the appeals to Scripture used in the days of Luther and Calvin. Rather, it is surprising time and again that the new theories prove all the more that the Reformation has recognized the essence of the sacrificial mass for what it is. For while there may be many different descriptions of the sacrificial character of the mass, there is one respect in which no difference can be indicated. It is the idea of reconciliation in the mass which forms the focal point of each new interpretation of the relation between cross-offering and mass-offering.

When the Reformation confessed that the Lord's Supper was full of involvement with the New Testament *mysterion,* it intended to speak of a radically different involvement than the one ascribed to the mass-offering. This controversy will remain as long as the decisive power of the "once only" does not penetrate the definitive Roman Catholic concept of application.[74] If that ever did happen, it would structurally be as important as a penetration of the Roman Catholic Mariology or the Roman Catholic doctrine of the merit of good works. Ultimately, all these doctrines involve one and the same fundamental problem. Against this central interpretation of the work of Christ, which, I think, is revealed with special clarity in the encyclical *Mediator Dei* and thus fully justifies the implicit criticism of the Reformation, the interpretation of the Lord's Supper on the part of the Reformation stands in sharp contrast. The Reformation is aware that there is a danger of devaluating the Lord's Supper as a

74. Regarding the appeal to the "once only" in Hebrews, see my *De strijd om het R.K. dogma,* 1940, pp. 255ff., and *The Work of Christ,* pp. 81ff.

gift of Christ when one rejects sharply the mass-offering, for the act of Christ and his presence may be obscured by the emphasis on remembrance. But these dangers may never lead to a weakening of the significance of the controversy with Rome. For in this controversy the point at issue is the mystery of the application of Christ's work through the Holy Spirit, as an application which does not endanger the sovereignty of salvation, but which makes man rest in that salvation.

CHAPTER FOURTEEN

THE LORD'S SUPPER: A COMMON TABLE?

IT REMAINS one of the most pathetic features of the history of the Lord's Supper that there has been so much controversy about a sacrament that is so eminently the sacrament of communion. Anyone who does not intuitively know that this sacrament is an act wherein is revealed the communion of believers with Christ and with each other, must have become very estranged from the richness of the Supper. It is impossible to understand the Lord's Supper apart from this communion, which is related to the communion of saints, of which we confess "that believers, all and every one, as members of Christ, are partakers of Him and of all His treasures and gifts; [and] that every one must know himself bound to employ his gifts . . . for the advantage and salvation of other members."[1] As there is only one baptism, one faith, and one Lord, so there is also one Supper, because it is the Supper of Christ himself, and because believers do not gather together in a self-chosen liturgy, but sit "at his table." That is why, with respect to the Lord's Supper, one will always automatically think of the Church as "a holy congregation of true Christian believers, all expecting their salvation in Jesus Christ, being washed by His blood, sanctified and sealed by the Holy Spirit."[2]

The one Supper and the one *ecclesia Christi* — that does not lead us to a vague, unreachable, and romantic ecumenicity. We speak here, rather, of one of the most fundamental and simple givens of the New Testament. There cannot possibly be an individualistic enjoyment of the gift of the Lord's Supper, for this is communion with Christ, who is the Lord of his one *ecclesia* and who blesses it with his holy presence.

The form for the Lord's Supper speaks emphatically of this

1. Heidelberg Catechism, Q. 55.
2. Conf., Art. 27.

communion. When mention is made of true communion with
Christ, it is added that we are united through the Holy Spirit in
a bond of brotherly love, as the apostle says: "Seeing that we, who
are many, are one bread, one body; for we all partake of the
one bread." This mutual communion is not detached from communion with Christ. Rather, it is necessarily connected with it.
This is not a matter of a humane and self-evident communion,
based on our own flesh and blood, but it finds its basis in the
act of Christ's mercy which precedes all celebration of the Lord's
Supper and all communion of believers.

The Church of Jesus Christ has always understood something
of these connections, which may not and cannot be sundered
without violating the mystery of the Lord's Supper.[3]

The question now arises as to the grounds which could possibly be advanced for excluding someone from the Supper communion. To be sure, in the celebration of the Supper we do see
limits indicated, and the form for the Lord's Supper also speaks
of this; but these words are directed as a warning against those
who by their confession and behavior do not reveal themselves
as "worthy" partakers at the table of the Lord,[4] and who act as
unbelieving and ungodly persons.[5] The keys of the Kingdom
are employed here to exclude those who are not displeased with
themselves for their sins and who therefore kindle God's wrath
against the whole congregation because they approach the Lord's
table unworthily.[6] This is not the drawing of a boundary line
other than God's; in the sacred food, the meaning of the Lord's
Supper is proclaimed anew: medicine for the sick, and life for
those who lie in the midst of death.

Christ does not come in the Supper to call the righteous, but
to bless and encourage sinners with his reconciling salvation.
The healthy do not need this medicine. Therein lies the boundary line around the celebration of the Lord's Supper. It is a line
drawn in the light of the significance of the Supper itself.

But separate communions may not always be explained by this
line, for the lines of division do not simply coincide with that of

---

3. Augustine, Luther and Calvin — not to mention more — have strongly
   seen and emphasized the oneness in the Lord's Supper and the unity of
   believers. Cf. Augustine, *Tract.* 26 on John 13, and Calvin, *Inst.*, IV,
   XVII, 38.
4. Form for the Lord's Supper.
5. H.C., Q. 82.
6. *Ibid.;* cf. Q. 81.

"unworthiness." When the Lord's Supper is involved, the boundaries do not precisely correspond with the decision regarding salvation and perdition. It is the firm impression of everyone who observes the practice of separate communions that this practice of the Church does not belong in the area of the words about the wrath of God which is kindled against the whole congregation. That is why we now stand before a problem that cannot easily be solved in the light of the New Testament. This problem stands before us clearly when we hear Asmussen emphatically say: "For the denial to the Lord's Supper, only the unworthiness of him who desires to participate can be a biblical reason. There is no other reason for refusing a person from approaching the Lord's table."[7] Asmussen thinks that this way is abandoned whenever other criteria are employed for admission to the table. He sees the Churches using the correct standard in their own ecclesiastical life, but at the boundaries of the divided Church they begin to ask whether someone is (e.g.) Lutheran or Reformed. Thus the question about "unworthiness" does not, or at least does not directly, receive any consideration. Asmussen thinks this to be a "false decision,"[8] because the decision no longer depends upon "worthiness" or "unworthiness" but upon adherence or non-adherence to a specific confessional doctrine.

The confessional Churches began with the assumption that they were the true Church of Christ, but they ended by acknowledging other Churches as other "forms" of the one Church of Christ.[9] Asmussen thinks it to be a grave matter that the Protestant Churches no longer dare to say that the other Churches are not Churches of Christ, but àt the same time they accept separate communions within the "multiformity."[10]

It cannot be denied that Asmussen has posed here a profound and serious problem, at least if one has any awareness at all of the relation between the Lord's Supper and communion, between the one bread and the *corpus Christi* in the New Testament. It is the problem of a boundary line that is drawn around the sacred bread which in practice does not coincide with the line of unworthiness. To be sure, we have become somewhat accustomed

7. H. Asmussen, "Abendmahlsgemeinschaft?" in *Abendmahlsgemeinschaft?,* 1937, p. 6.
8. *Ibid.,* p. 7.
9. *Ibid.,* p. 17.
10. *Ibid.,* p. 19.

to this division, and we can appreciate with a certain equanimity the celebration of the Lord's Supper in other Churches; but that does not eliminate the seriousness of the questions that become revealed in this problem.

It is understandable that in a time when a divided world was confronted with numerous appalling problems threatening its unity, people began again to look to the Church, and that the Church itself began to think once again about its visible unity.[11] It was asked what the real reason could be for this dissension, and what possibility there was for a single communion of the Lord's Supper.

This is not simply an impractical form of longing, or a special trait of those believers who feel very much the distress of dissension, but a matter that calls for dogmatic reflection and cannot be detached from it. If the Supper were merely a custom based on human institution, one could reconcile himself to the almost unconquerable dissension which becomes revealed in all aspects of life. But when the one table is concerned, the table of the Lord himself, it is not possible to speak the last word in reconciliation or to appeal to custom.

Precisely in connection with the Lord's Supper, many have spoken of a tragic aspect of Christ's Church, because its focal point was the testament of this Lord which he left in the night of his betrayal: the remembrance and proclaiming of his death. In the midst of poverty and dissension, people looked for a demonstration of the richness and the unity of the body of Christ, of the sacramental glory of the Lord's Supper as "*vinculum unitatis et caritatis.*"

The Lord's Supper was sometimes seen as the only possible means to reunite the Churches as the one body of Christ. But there was also a different opinion, namely, that this way would lead to an invalid and impossible compromise, to an impermissible anticipation without a truly comforting outlook on the *Una Sancta*. The question arose why it was possible to proclaim the death of Christ together in the Supper while the Church remained divided. Was it possible and responsible to detach the unity of the Church of Christ from the celebration

11. Cf. H. van der Linde, "De niet-theologische factoren in de eenheid en de gescheidenheid der kerk," in *Drie oecumenische studien*, 1953; H. v.d. Linde, "Perspectieven van een oecumenisch kerkbegrip," in *Jubileumbundel voor Prof. Kreling*, 1953, pp. 13-48.

of the Lord's Supper in such a manner that one could have communion in the Lord's Supper, but no communion in the Church? Especially Rome and the representatives of the Eastern Church emphasized this connection between Church and Supper. Congar, too, emphasized the Church as "a single communion" and pointed out that in the Church as the body of Christ there cannot be an *intercommunio*, but a true *communio* showing the true unity of the Church. "There is a profound reason for the identity of name between the eucharistic communion and the church communion." To the question whether communal celebration of the Lord's Supper could not lead to reunification of the Church, Congar answers that that would be so "if the sacrament were a means *outside the church*, which one could use in order to enter or build her, as one takes a key to enter a house and stones to build one. But not one of the constitutive elements of the church is exterior to her: not faith, nor the Bible, nor tradition, nor the sacraments."[12]

Congar believes that the aim cannot be to bring about the unity of the Church, for the Church is already one: the one true *catholica*. If we should be united in the visible unity of the Church, "then we could celebrate and communicate together. Until then intercommunion is, alas, impossible."[13]

A similar position is taken by George Florowsky, Orthodox patriarch, who maintains that the refusal to participate in the communal table cannot be explained as exaggerated confessionalism or lack of ecumenical awareness. He urges, further, that an open communion "would compromise the whole endeavour" of the ecumenical movement.[14] "It would be falsely to pretend that Christendom has already been reunited."[15] The reproach of "confessional loyalty" refers to his belief that the Orthodox Church is the only true Church. That is why he takes so seriously the objections against intercommunion. One can accept it only if he relativizes his convictions. A Roman Catholic would not be admitted to open communion since others think his interpretation of the mass to be in error. One should not speak, says Florowsky, of somebody's "obstinate resistance" to

12. Y. M. J. Congar, "Amica Contestatio," in *Intercommunion*, ed. D. Baillie and J. Marsh, 1952, p. 150.
13. *Ibid.*, p. 151.
14. G. Florowsky, "Confessional Loyalty in the Ecumenical Movement," *ibid.*, pp. 196-205.
15. *Ibid.*, p. 204.

participating in this, for it would be true of such a Catholic that "his participation would be a nonsensical betrayal on his side and a concealed insincerity on the other."[16]

In the background of these considerations of Congar and Florowsky there is evidently the notion of the one indivisible and undivided Church of Christ, namely, the Roman Catholic Church or the Eastern Church. In this light intercommunion is impossible and nothing can be accomplished by it for the unity of the Church, for it involves a vicious circle to seek what is already reality. Intercommunion is impossible because the Church is one.

There are those who do not agree with this presupposition, that there is one true visible Church concretely realized in East or West, and yet feel that it would be paradoxical to unite at the communion table while continuing to live in ecclesiastical separation. Furthermore, reference is then made to the complexity of such a communion service when so many interpretations of the Lord's Supper exist in the various churches.[17] It may be true that the Lord's Supper is not primarily a matter of theoretical unity, but of a true communion with the Lord of the community. Nevertheless, the act of communion at the Lord's Supper cannot be a purely unthinking enjoyment of the gifts of Christ, for the believer must commune with his Lord in conscious faith, in song and prayer, and in the receiving of the signs. Since the Supper is a proclamation of Christ's death, it cannot be regarded as a ceremony that simply transcends all reflection on the relation between signs and the reality that they signify.

These important matters all confront us when we reflect on the New Testament teaching about the Lord's Supper of Christ's Church, on the one communion, the one table, the one bread. No one can wholly avoid this problematical aspect of the communion of the Lord's Supper, for we are faced with the question that is asked in the midst of the dissension of the Church: *communio* and *intercommunio*.

The questions posed by Congar and Florowsky have their point of connection in the New Testament, for they concern the Lord's Supper and the communion of saints. Especially Paul

16. *Ibid.*, p. 200.
17. Cf. for the various interpretations of the Lord's Supper: D. Cairns *et al.*, *The Holy Communion: A Symposium*, 1947.

has spoken to this point. Although Paul was not confronted with the "phenomenon" of a divided Church as we know it, he saw nevertheless that the Lord's Supper is violated by social relations that conflict with the teachings of the gospel. He asks the congregation in Corinth: "or despise ye the church of God?" (I Cor. 11:22). Evidently, the communion in the one bread is not an individual "religious" matter, having no relation to the other believers. On the contrary: because communion in the Lord's Supper is communion with Christ, it is full of consequences for the Church. These consequences arise out of the reality signified and sealed in the Supper. The communion of saints belongs essentially to the Lord's Supper.[18]

This teaching is made clear by the passage which had its clear echo in the history of the Christian Church and which for many became a word of longing in the midst of dissension: "Seeing that we, who are many, are one bread, one body; for we all partake of the one bread" (I Cor. 10:17).

It will not do to say that this unity belongs only within a specific congregation. It involves the one *ecclesia* of the New Testament, the people of God which is the people of the Messiah at the end of time, and which lives in the anticipation of Christ's return. Nor is it a matter of a voluntary communion of like-minded people who together follow established rites, but rather of the one body of Christ in which believers partake of the bread and therein of his reconciling suffering and dying. How is it possible that dissension can enter this communion of the body of Christ, erecting barriers that remain standing after so many centuries (cf. I Cor. 12:27)?

One of the most notable attempts to answer these questions proceeds by way of confessional relativizing, in which the attempt is made to overcome differences through an act, namely, the act of communion in the Lord's Supper. This solution seems to be clear and simple. That which cannot yet be obtained in the organic reunion of the Churches, is here realized — albeit temporarily — in a particular act.

It is clear, however, that this does not solve the problem of dissension and separation at the communion table. As a matter of fact, the complexity of this way became evident, and people became aware that the ecumenical urge of the Churches

18. Cf. A. Schlatter, *Paulus der Bote Jesu*, p. 297.

often led to deeper reflection on one's own confessions and hence accentuated the importance of the differences.[19]

It is therefore a real "question for discussion" that was posed in the World Council of Churches: "would the tragic and sinful disunity of the church become less tragic and sinful, if the various churches could have full intercommunion with each other? Or would that merely be an unrealistic glossing over of the disunity?"[20]

This question is important, for communion in the Lord's Supper is always a matter of communion with Christ. How could Churches still be divided if they partake of the one bread, and how can they remain divided once they have been truly united in this communion? Can one return to dissension, and can a communion of the Lord's Supper ever be seen as a joyful interruption of the dissension of the Church?

The report also asks whether intercommunion can precede reunion, but it could also be asked whether this intercommunion must not necessarily lead to union. For are not all problems solved here, and if they are not, where could they ever be solved? Therein lies the problem of the communion of the Lord's Supper if the solution is made by simplifying confessional differences. It is impossible, having taken this route, to return later to the way of confessional dissension. That which is no longer important for the communion of the Lord's Supper, cannot be important anywhere in the life of the Church.

If one wants to follow this route anyway, confessional differences must forever be abandoned and refuge must be taken in a mystical Supper communion where these differences can never form a threatening background. One would thus come to a "communion of the Lord's table" whereby it would be impossible to exclude Rome — even though it has connected the celebration of the Lord's Supper with the mass-offering — for after relativizing confessional differences one could not ex-

---

19. Cf., e.g., H. Berkhof, *De hervatting van een confessioneel gesprek*, 1938, pp. 114ff., esp. p. 122.
20. Cf. in this report: "The ecumenical movement, by deepening the sense of the church and bringing members of widely different churches together in Christian fellowship, has driven many Christians to seek a deeper understanding of the distinctive positions of their own churches. Thus paradoxically the growth of the ecumenical consciousness had led to a widespread revival of confessional or denominational consciousness" (*Intercommunion*, p. 10).

clude someone by appealing to a specific interpretation of the Lord's Supper. But Rome *is* often excluded, leaving as the only remaining problem the matter of "pulpit communion."[21] Doctrinal differences no longer threaten the communion of the Lord's Supper.[22] They come to lie in the "theological" plane, while in the Church it is a matter of "real communion" and not "of fine and detailed definitions at the limit of reason."[23] We must see the true communion behind the definitions.

It is clear that this simple way is impracticable. The very exclusion of Rome shows that the whole problem remains unsolved, for it is precisely Rome that teaches that believers are united with Christ in a special manner in mass and communion. In connection with that, the Churches of the Reformation did not interpret the controversy about the communion of the Lord's Supper as an unimportant side issue, but as a matter that touches directly upon the reality of this communion. That is why the Reformers struggled with, and why Luther opposed the Calvinistic doctrine of the Lord's Supper, and why Luther and Calvin both rejected the Zwinglian doctrine, holding that Zwingli did not do justice to the meaning of the Lord's Supper.

Those who ignore the meaning of the Lord's Supper when discussing the communion of saints in that Supper, bypass the problem proper. For the celebration of the Lord's Supper is a response of the believer to an act of Christ in the sacrament; in this act the believer proclaims the death of the Lord in an act of remembrance, until he comes. Those who relativize their own confession in the communion of the Lord's Supper in order to eliminate dissension in Christ's Church are thereby admitting that their confession was only a matter of opinion, perhaps of theological opinion, and that this confession had little or nothing to do with what the early Church meant by its confession.

In longing for the visible unity of the Church, one must listen seriously to what Asmussen has to say: "The contemporary state of distress of the Church produces the temptation to seek a common Lord's Supper at any price."[24] To be sure, the "plurality" of the Lord's Supper is a disquieting matter because of

21. E. Deter, "Abendmahl und Einheit der Kirche," *EvT*, 1948-49, p. 575.
22. *Ibid.*, p. 573.
23. *Ibid.*, p. 574.
24. H. Asmussen, *Abendmahlsgemeinschaft?*, p. 25.

its contradiction with the one bread and the one body of Christ, but precisely because of this serious situation, one will not be able to solve the problem by superficializing the confession of the Church, unless one wants to abandon the Lord's Supper to absolute irrationality. One may think that he has thus preserved the Church, or at least its prospects for unity, but at the same time he has lost the Lord's Supper, which has been given to us through the sacred institution and which therefore asks for faith and can be received in the communion of the Church only if that faith is present.

If the Church were only a society of like-minded people, it would be possible to work out a single Lord's Supper from among the many arbitrary rites of this church, which could be relativized at any time. But if the Church is really the body of Christ and if we still understand something of the reality of which the New Testament speaks with respect to that body, we will not be able to solve the problem of a common Lord's Supper by way of relativizing the confession of the Church regarding the present Lord and his holy gift.

It is not surprising that questions pertaining to a common Lord's Supper have come up repeatedly, and that there has been so much contention about them, especially in the Lutheran Church in Germany after the union of 1817, when the way of relativizing was followed. All this reveals an awareness in the Church that the Lord's Supper knows no plurality and that the New Testament contains no warrant for plurality, but makes that plurality impossible. Nor can one take refuge in the one "invisible Church" to quiet one's conscience, for the Lord's Supper is precisely one of the characteristics of Christ's Church on earth,[25] and in that Supper the proclamation as an act of remembrance belongs to the essence.

That is also why it is impossible to justify the abandonment of confessional thinking by an appeal to love. It is possible that behind much dissension lovelessness is hidden, and that among the nontheological factors operative in church division lovelessness plays a role; nevertheless, the problem of the Lord's Supper can never be solved by a love that is detached from the body of Christ, the message of the Supper, and from its content. To flee from confessional differences in the name of love is to re-

25. Conf., Art. 29.

treat to a love undefined, and to portray as loveless all those who desire earnestly to commune truly with the present Lord and to receive his gifts. That is why Asmussen writes that "the communion of the Lord's Supper is violated if a love separated from faith is made the basis for the communion of the Lord's Supper."[26] For this love can never be detached from the concrete love which is related to the reconciliation of Christ, and which finds the foundation for the following of Christ in that love, the following to which the Lord's Supper calls us.

Confessional relativizing is not the only route that has been proposed to solve the tension between the dividedness of the Supper and the unity of the Lord's Supper as taught in the New Testament. We think of the proposal made lately to re-interpret the Lord's Supper purely as a "love feast." The back-ground of this solution is found in the fact that from all sides objections were raised against intercommunion and that there-fore it was necessary to ask whether it is not possible to find "not a solution, but an easing of our tensions along an en-tirely different line."[27] The intention is to come to a love feast: "the simple Christian meal of love and fellowship, which is known to have been practiced among the early Christians."[28] Every thought of the Lord's Supper is hereby excluded, for the purpose of this love feast is to evoke a feeling of the unity of the Church in visible form at the time when intercommunion is not yet possible. Could such a love feast not be a first step to unite the divided Churches "in a common act of worship and fellowship"?[29] To be sure, intercommunion and the ulti-mate unity of the Church is the real goal; but this goal is still far away, and is it not possible to find in the love feast an answer for the time being to the problem of dissension in the Church? The participants are given to understand that this love feast is not the Lord's Supper. The bread is broken, but it is not the "sacred" bread; it is a normal meal without sac-ramental aspects. The symbolism of unity then consists of the commonly eaten bread, so we can understand why the liturgy of

26. Asmussen, *loc. cit.*
27. Cf. "Intercommunion: A Possible First Step," *The Ecumenical Review,* 1949, pp. 443-45.
28. *Ibid.,* p. 444.
29. G. I. F. Thomson, "The Revival of the Agape: A Possible Ecumenical Way of Worship," *Intercommunion,* pp. 388-396.

this meal should employ the well-known prayer from Didache IX, which points to the unity of the Church.

It is clear that this proposal encounters great difficulties when measured by the New Testament. It is true that the New Testament speaks of such feasts, and Paul did not object to them except when social distinctions violated the principle of agape (cf. I Cor. 11:17ff.; Jude 12; II Pet. 2:13). But the attempt to overcome divisions in the Church through such love feasts reveals the extent of the dividedness. One should not underestimate the significance of the communion of saints apart from the Lord's Supper. It is expressed in the many facets of ecclesiastical life. But there has been a historical development from the love feast to the Lord's Supper. The issue here is not just a matter of communion in the love feast, but of a Supper on which this mutual love is based. That is why the love feast of the ancient Christian Church, insofar as it had not degenerated, cannot be revived now, after the institution of the Lord's Supper, in order to gain some communion after all. What the English churchmen called "the first step" is basically nothing but a declaration regarding the problem of dividedness which gives the impression that through this communion of the love feast something had already been gained for the communion of the Lord's Supper. They isolated this love, and therefore it could not function for a solution of the problem of the Lord's Supper. Furthermore, by giving the impression that the love feast is a substitute for the Lord's Supper because of the manner in which the breaking of the bread is made the most essential constituent, this proposal understandably created confusion. That is why this solution can only be seen as a new accentuation of the problem, not as a way out of it. It cannot be a solution, not because love is not central in the Church of Christ, but because the love feast can never, not even for the time being, replace the Lord's Supper.

It is no accident that many current discussions of the common Supper now urge that the problems are insoluble as long as the Church is divided in such a complex way. These problems cannot be blamed upon personal stubbornness or narrow churchism,[30] but are closely linked with the nature of the Lord's

---

30. That, of course, does not mean that these dangers can never threaten the Church's reflection on the communion of the Lord's Supper. It is also

Supper. Many are now aware that the Lord's Supper is not just an act of personal faith, but a ceremony involving the presence of Christ and therein of Christ's act in his Church. That explains why the problem of a common Lord's Supper is treated with great care. There is a general attempt not to decide the issues simply by posing an intercommunion which depends upon the relativizing of confessional differences.[31] Intercommunion is once more being discussed in a theological situation where people desire more than ever to emphasize the presence of Christ in the Lord's Supper, and it is understandable that this emphasis should make its impact on the relativizers.[32]

It cannot be denied that the different confessions regarding the nature and the benefits of the Lord's Supper exert a decisive influence on the possibility of a common Lord's Supper, and for a very good reason. When Maan says that the sacrament is primarily a matter of the act of God and that our doctrinal formulations are never adequate to describe the content of the divine act, he cannot escape the important question about the relation between this divine acting and the response of believers. It appears, then, that an emphasis on what is "primary" cannot help us to arrive at a satisfactory solution either.[33]

Not only the Roman Catholic and Eastern solutions emphasize strongly the problem of Supper and communion, but also the different Protestant Churches (because of new reflections on the Church as body of Christ) are finding themselves in serious crisis on the question of a common Lord's Supper. This fact is ultimately linked with the confession of the Lord's Supper. Think of a confession in which the Supper is seen in the Zwinglian sense, as an activity of believers in remembrance, in contrast with the Roman Catholic interpretation of the com-

---

possible, however, that one becomes accustomed to separation at the Lord's Supper, even though this separation does not at all coincide with the limit of absolute unworthiness.

31. Cf. the criticism by P. J. Maan of the unification-attempts in Germany in 1817 (Union) and in 1830 at the occasion of the commemoration of the Confessio Augustana. P. J. Maan, "Problemen rondom de intercommunie," in *VT*, 1949, p. 72.

32. Cf. A. C. Outler on this problem, "which is insoluble in its present terms": *Ecumenical Review*, 1952, p. 310; and J. Derby, "A Thorn in the Flesh," *ibid.*, pp. 316ff.

33. P. J. Maan, "Problemen rondom de intercommunie," *VT*, p. 791; he himself says that he does not want to flee from the question of truth.

munion and the mass, or of the differences between the Lutheran and Reformed interpretations of the presence of Christ in the Lord's Supper. It would be a very sad picture indeed if Heiler's words of some twenty years ago were correct: "Practical intercommunion hardly harbors any problems for today's Protestant Churches, because they no longer possess a sacramental dogma."[34]

Those who think about the relation between Supper and communion in the light of the essence of the Lord's Supper, cannot fail to take into account the differences that exist with respect to the reality of the Lord's Supper, wherein the act of God and the acts of believers are necessarily linked with each other according to the meaning of the Supper and for faith, for that conjunction belongs to the essence of the sacrament as it is instituted by Christ. To take a concrete example, there is a world of difference between the Roman Catholic and Reformed views of the Supper, which no synthesis could possibly reconcile. The mutual protest of the Reformed confession in Question 80 of the Heidelberg Catechism and of the Council of Trent is only one reflection of this deep divergency. The same can be said regarding many modern interpretations of the sacrament[35] in which the Supper is made into a form of religious experiencing of communion and peace with God, with no reference to reconciliation through the blood of Jesus Christ. Those who plead here for a common Lord's Supper on the basis of love and an "overarching" communion are really pleading for a further emptying of the Lord's Supper of Jesus Christ.

The relation between the Lutheran and Reformed Churches in earlier and later times is altogether different. In countries where the Lutheran Churches are quantitatively in the minority, this problem of diversity in the Lord's Supper is no longer an urgent problem of conscience. That does not mean, however, that the problem no longer exists. The differences between the Lutherans and the Reformed did not touch immediately upon the reconciliation through blood, nor upon the question whether the Lord's Supper is an offering, nor upon the issue of spiritu-

---

34. Cf. the acknowledgment of Heiler, *Im Ringen um die Kirche*, 1931, p. 317.
35. Cf., e.g., N. C. Meyer, "Naar een avondmaalsliturgie," *Theologie en Practijk*, II, 1939, pp. 298ff.; Immink, "Ontwerp van een avondmaalsliturgie door de kring Eredienst," *Theol. en Practijk*, III, 1940, p. 296.

alizing the Lord's Supper. Behind the Reformed and Lutheran confessions the *sola fide* and the *sola gratia* are still spoken, and the outlook on Christ's reconciling suffering is kept open. That is why the conflict between these two Churches about the Supper will remain one of the most regrettable in the history of the Reformation. The sharpness of the conflict is fully revealed when a Lutheran denies the bare mention of intercommunion with the Reformed, since the Reformed do not accept the Lutheran interpretation of the presence of Christ's body and blood.[36] Attempts have been made in our time to show that the differences are more "theological" than "religious," and that it might be possible to come to a deeper common understanding of the gift of the Lord's Supper and of the nature of Christ's presence. Only if the common motif is acknowledged, namely, that of the comfort and proximity of the real Christ in the time preceding his return, and the will to be guided by the Word of God and the wisdom of the Holy Spirit, also in the questions concerning Christ's words about his body and blood — only then will it be possible not to abandon all hope that in the history of the Church (which is not ultimately determined by the psychology of determinism) a communion can be re-established that is meaningfully preluded in the power of the *sola fide* and the *sola gratia*.

The situation is still different when we think of the confession of the Lord's Supper in the various Reformed denominations.[37] There is often no essential difference regarding the meaning of the Lord's Supper. The actual situation, therefore, is that separate Suppers exist not because of the limit of "unworthiness," but because of other reasons that prevent an ecclesiastical living-together. With respect to the Lord's Supper, we do not have a case here of the No versus the Yes, nor the absolute warning at the entrance to the table of the Lord. The separation does not rest in a radical divergency concerning salvation but in the ecclesiastical separation itself. In practice there is therefore a mutual recognition of each other's Supper, in the sense of acknowledging that in the other Reformed denominations there is also communion with Christ

36. Cf., e.g., F. W. Hopf, "Zur Frage nach der Abendmahlsgemeinschaft," in *Vom Sakrament des Alters*, 1941, p. 238.
37. Cf. especially the article by D. Nauta, "Gemeenschappelijk kerkdiensten," *Het Ouderlingenblad*, Dec. 1953.

and the partaking of the one bread in the Lord's Supper. A communion is confessed, but this communion is not proclaimed and confirmed around the *"vinculum unitatis"* par excellence.

There are in the various Reformed Churches factors that make for dissension, but which have no direct bearing on the Lord's Supper. That, however, is precisely why, with the acknowledgment of a "spiritual" communion and brotherhood, the problem of the Lord's Supper does not lose its urgency, that is to say, so long as we think in the light of the relation between the body of Christ and the breaking of the bread. Precisely when the differences do not have direct bearing on the confession of the Lord's Supper, one can say that there must be all the more urgency to look at the separating factors with great earnestness in the light of the coming Lord, so that his return may not become for us a time to flee from the responsibility that lies contained in the prayer of the Redeemer: "that they may all be one; even as thou, Father, art in me, and I in thee, that they also may be in us: that the world may believe that thou didst send me" (John 17:21).

The problem of a common Lord's Supper cannot be solved by a simple reference to the *ecclesia pressa*. That has sometimes been done in the expectation that separation could be done away with only through the need of the Church in times of persecution. Nobody can say what the pressure of the times may bring, when everything might be at stake, and the "sign" of Christ's body and blood receives more meaning than ever in the struggle of the Church. It may be that the dark sign of the Antichrist will make it more understood that the New Testament teaching about the Lord's Supper is primarily a matter of worthiness and unworthiness, of the sickly and the healthy, of the radicality of being for Christ or against him, of being together with him or of being dispersed. But speculation about the future of the *ecclesia pressa* may never weaken the responsibility of the Church now, when it is divided about the nature of the *praesentia Christi,* or about other questions regarding the history and the practice of the Church.

If there is one thing clear, it is this, that the remembrance of the death of Christ will ring out into the world only if the boundary between Supper and many other "signs" will coincide with the boundary between worthiness and unworthiness. Not until then will it be possible to proclaim the death of the Lord — also in the Supper — in the Church which is his body.

So long as this unity of the Church and the urgent word about unworthiness do not go together *in concreto* in the warning and the calling of the Church, the distress of the Church will remain, not least in connection with the meal of the Covenant. That does not mean that somehow one must begin a sacramental fasting in order to prove his repentance and remorse about dissension in the Church. While we acknowledge the division and at the same time its "impossibility," as becomes revealed in the one bread of the New Testament, the call to remembrance yet remains undiminished.

With that, we have returned to the theme that involves the whole history of the Church: the remembrance, which is immediately based on the institution of the Lord's Supper. This remembrance is so significant for the Church of Christ because it is directly connected with the proclaiming of Christ's death. In this remembrance lies the real and most urgent motif for the Lord's Supper, which will become all the more significant in the measure that the significance of Christ's suffering and dying in the world receives its due attention. This remembrance receives its most urgent actuality not from the *ecclesia pressa;* rather, it has always been felt most strongly when decisions are made of unprecedented import. We would recall here those strange words of the New Testament about the judgment upon the Church at Corinth, where in the distress of sickness and death it became clear to Paul that either the Lord's Supper is taken completely seriously, or else it is neglected with a failure to appreciate that the wheat has died and thus produced fruit. That neglect can be revealed in many ways, in the nondiscerning of the body of the Lord and in the neglect of one's brother, in the things that attract attention and in those that do not because they remain hidden in the depth of man's heart. But it will all be one neglect, which cannot exist over against the voice that calls: "until Christ comes."

Where this neglect is overcome through the power of the Holy Spirit, and where the body of the Lord is discerned and the neighbor discovered at the table around the one bread, the communion of the Lord's Supper, deep joy will become evident in the daily struggle of life. People will then again be able to understand anew that picture of the first Christian Church of which we read that the unity was preserved between "the home" and "the temple," when joy and unity were revealed and they in turn led to the song of praise (Acts 2:46f.). The tension is overcome here, the contrast between oasis and desert; and the Church receives — through the presence of its Lord — a view of the mystery of its calling in the world.

"The Lord added to them day by day those that were saved" (Acts 2:47).

> Elect from every nation,
> Yet one o'er all the earth;
> Her charter of salvation,
> One Lord, one faith, one birth;
> One holy Name she blesses,
> Partakes one holy food,
> And to one hope she presses,
> With every grace endued.

INDEX OF PRINCIPAL SUBJECTS

INDEX OF PERSONS

INDEX OF SCRIPTURES

DATE DUE

NOV 0 7			
NOV 1 7			